Training and Alternatives

Edited by
Denis Gleeson

Open University Press
Milton Keynes • Philadelphia

Open University Press
Celtic Court
22 Ballmoor
Buckingham MK18 1XW

and
1900 Frost Road, Suite 101
Bristol, PA 19007, USA

First Published 1990

Copyright © The Editor and Contributors 1990

All rights reserved. No part of this publication may be
reproduced, stored in a retrieval system or transmitted in
any form or by any means, without written permission from the
publisher.

British Library Cataloguing in Publication Data

Training and its alternatives.
 1. Great Britain. School leavers. Vocational preparation
 I. Gleeson, Denis
 373,14'25

 ISBN 0-335-09332-9
 ISBN 0-335-09331-0 (pbk)

Library of Congress Cataloging-in-Publication Data

Training and its alternatives/edited by Denis Gleeson.
   p.   cm.
   ISBN 0-335-09332-9   ISBN 0-335-09331-0 (pbk)
  1. Vocational education--Great Britain. 2. Occupational training--
 Great Britain. 3. Youth--Employment--Great Britain. I. Gleeson, Denis.
 LC1047.G7T73 1990
 374'.013'0941--dc20   89-39081
                                                                      CIP

Typeset by Burns & Smith Ltd., Derby
Printed in Great Britain by Bookcraft Limited

Contents

List of contributors vii
General introduction ix

Section 1 Origins, context and alternatives to youth training
Introduction 1

1 An alternative road? Problems and possibilities of the Crowther Concept 4
   Gary McCulloch
2 The failure of training in Britain: analysis and prescription 18
   David Finegold and David Soskice
3 The context of the Youth Training Scheme: an analysis of its strategy and development 58
   David Raffe
4 Youth labour market processes, outcomes and policies 76
   Ken Roberts, Sally Dench and Deborah Richardson
5 Some alternatives in youth training: franchise and corporatist models 91
   Joan Chandler and Claire Wallace

Section 2 Alternatives in secondary and further education: a case study approach
Introduction 111

6 Beyond the 1944–88 educational interregnum: the case of Sands Community College 113
   Máirtín Mac an Ghaill
7 Student responses to the curriculum: towards an alternative practice 124
   James Avis
8 Gender reproduction and further education: the case of domestic apprenticeships 138
   Beverley Skeggs

9	Industry and education: changing the meaning of work-experience *Chris Shilling*	157
10	Making YTS responsive to its clients *Anthony Rosie*	171

Section 3 **Beyond vocationalism**
Introduction 185

11	Skills training and its alternatives *Denis Gleeson*	187
12	Knowledge, practice and the construction of skill *Rob Moore*	200
13	Beyond vocationalism: a new perspective on the relationship between work and education *Ken Spours and Michael Young*	213

Postscript 225
Some abbreviations 228
Author index 231
Subject index 236

List of contributors

James Avis	Lecturer in charge of full-time GCSE studies in the Department of General Studies, Wulfrun College of Further Education, Wolverhampton
Joan Chandler	Research fellow, Department of Social and Political Studies, South West Polytechnic, Plymouth
Sally Dench	Research associate, Department of Sociology, University of Liverpool
David Finegold	Research officer, Centre for Education and Industry, University of Warwick
Denis Gleeson	Director of Centre for Social Research in Education, University of Keele
Máirtín Mac an Ghaill	Head of sociology in a state school
Gary McCulloch	Senior lecturer in education, The University of Auckland, New Zealand
Rob Moore	Lecturer in sociology, Homerton College, Cambridge
David Raffe	Director of Centre for Educational Sociology, University of Edinburgh
Deborah Richardson	Researcher in the department of sociology, University of Liverpool
Ken Roberts	Head of department of sociology, University of Liverpool
Anthony Rosie	Senior lecturer in the department of secondary education, The College of St Paul and St Mary, Cheltenham
Chris Shilling	Lecturer in social policy University of Southampton

Beverley Skeggs	Lecturer in education, Department of Education, University of York
David Soskice	The Mynors Fellow in economics, University College, Oxford
Ken Spours	Development officer, Post-16 Education Centre, Institute of Education, University of London
Claire Wallace	Senior lecturer in the Department of Social and Political Studies, South West Polytechnic, Plymouth
Michael Young	Coordinator, Post-16 Education Centre, Institute of Education, University of London

General introduction

Innovation and change have been almost continuous features of education over the past hundred and fifty years, with perhaps the most notable period of reform following on the 1944 Education Act. Yet, despite the effects of the 1944 Act and ensuing struggles to establish comprehensive education in the 1950s, the speed at which change has occurred in the past decade is unprecedented. In the period extending from the Conservative government's New Training Initiative (1981) through to the Education Reform Act (1988) much has happened to traditional patterns of schooling and, in particular, vocational education and training.

Prior to the so called Great Education Debate (1976–79) vocational education and training attracted little political or public interest. Indeed, prevailing conceptions of vocational realism in schools and society at the time associated it with craft studies, 'night school' and apprenticeship. Yet, if in the 1960s and 1970s vocational education and training could be described as marginal to mainstream educational development, that situation dramatically altered in the 1980s. Since the rising youth unemployment of the 1970s, school and further education have been through an extended period when the very ground rules of liberal education have radically changed. The spearhead of this change has been the dramatic collapse of the youth labour market, which has significantly affected traditional conceptions of the relationship between school and work. This collapse has meant that for many young people schools are no longer seen as the main transition or transmission points into work or adult life. Almost simultaneously, a politically inspired debate about the purposes and practices of schooling and further education has taken place. At one level this debate has been fuelled by long standing criticism of the apparent failure of schools and further education to ensure a proper correspondence between the vocational needs of young people and those of the economy. At another, unemployment and a dramatic change in pupil destinations have prompted greater awareness of the plight of school leavers, many of whom traditionally entered dead end jobs and received next to no further education or training.

Following on the various crises which beset schooling in the late 1970s and early

1980s, a wide range of curricular initiatives and reforms have emerged. Such reforms are, however, premised on political strategies designed to reshape school, FE and LEA budgets, to make them responsive to national curricular and central government requirements. Indeed, a major rallying cry of Conservative government education reform in the 1980s is that the only way to ensure a better motivated, educated and trained workforce is via a national system of vocational education and training which makes more efficient use of existing resources. Paradoxically, this is backed by the call to resolve duplication, fragmentation and repetition in the system, seen to be generated by overlapping provision, qualifications and the credential inflation generated by the expansionist phase of 1960s' development. Thus, following in the wake of the NTI (1981) and the rise of the MSC, YTS (1981), TVEI (1983), CPVE (1985) and related prevocational initiatives, a number of important measures have paved the way for the Education Reform Act (1988), which has since ensured central government greater direct access to the content, policy and delivery of education and training at the local level. In a relatively short space of time the legislative impact of White Papers such as *A New Training Initiative* (MSC 1981), *Training for Jobs* (DES 1984), *Better Schools* (DES 1985) and *Working Together* (DES 1986), has radically transformed mainstream education. Moreover, new ESG, INSET and assessment arrangements, including the setting up of bodies such as the NCC, NCVQ and TECs, have ensured that the bootstraps of the new national system of education and training are now firmly in place.

Yet, as Dale (1985) and others have noted, the new vocationalism is paradoxical and does not go unresisted; it reflects the simultaneous emergence of two potentially conflicting developments (Gleeson 1987). On the one hand, it reflects strong central control of a kind which has permitted the detailed intervention of government and employer influence right down to the classroom level (Harland 1987). On the other, YTS, TVEI and LMS support local policy initiatives which, in many cases, can be highly experimental and creative. In practice, however, the rather fashionable concepts of 'ownership' and 'delivery' associated with such changes are not something teachers, students and parents readily identify with. A crucial feature of education training reform is that it is not to do with *them*. Rather, it is to do with radically altering traditional arrangements of school, further education and work, in favour of more vocationally oriented and employer-led considerations. This is most apparent in current preoccupations with work-related, work-relevant and work-specific tasks in the curriculum, many of which eschew broader social, historical, political and moral forms of understanding. Perhaps, not surprisingly, there are those who view the new vocationalism as narrowing the options available to young people, reflecting the government's desire to create a more compliant workforce. For others, however, the nature of such vocational realism is long overdue, at last providing a relevant curriculum for that 40 per cent of school leavers for whom school has been a major disappointment.

It is perhaps too convenient to caricature educational change in either of these terms. Yet the speed at which innovation has taken place, with a plethora of new policy, legislation and programmes arriving in quick succession, would surely seem to confirm this view. Moreover, feelings of innovation shock expressed by experienced professionals, seasoned observers, parents and students would again seem to indicate that the system is fundamentally in change. However, an alternative view suggests that, despite the apparent trend toward centralism and control, there is, in practice, little sign of any coherent national system of education and training emerging. Indeed, if anything, one effect of the passage of legislation from New Training Initiative (1981) to the Education Reform Act (1988) has been to destabilize systematic educational development in favour of disparate initiatives – YTS, TVEI, CPVE, BTEC, CTCs, assisted places, opting out and privatization – which reduce effective coordination policy and curricular balance across the 14–19 age range. In addition, far from reducing duplication and repetition in the system, government policy has increased competition and overlap between various intermediary *bodies* (e.g. NCC, NCVQ, TECs), various *courses* (e.g. BTEC, CPVE, YTS) and various *sectors* (e.g. CTCs, grant-aided schools, comprehensives, FE, tertiary and sixth-form colleges). In curricular terms such haphazard development defies concepts of society, system or citizenship, making it all the more difficult to establish a coherent comprehensive pattern of education and training *for all*. Instead, educational provision now operates on the basis of *delivering* agreed national objectives, generated via consumer demand, market forces, sponsorship and enterprise. In this respect, education for citizenship has little to do with nurturing the complex relationship between individual and society, and everything to do with *sponsoring* individuals acting in support of their own sectionalized interests. This is particularly noticeable in the ways government has targeted its various educational projects to specific audiences, notably the assisted places scheme, CTCs, new grant-aided schools and, elsewhere, has conscripted the less fortunate into youth (YTS) and adult (ET) training programmes backed by changes in social security legislation.

If, by now, such criticisms have a familiar ring to them, it is equally important to recognize that in the 1980s the conditions to which such reforms relate have altered. While in the 1980s 'crisis' reforms were essentially geared toward a collapsed youth labour market, and a surplus of youth and adult labour, that situation has now reversed. In the 1990s a shortage of adult skilled workers, and a fall in the number of available school leavers, is likely to affect the ways in which employers relate to schools and colleges, as well as recruit and train young workers. Yet, ironically, many of the crisis measures and reforms of the 1980s which the system has since inherited are no longer applicable to the changing political and economic climate of the 1990s. The fragmentation, proliferation and duplication of provision referred to so far, linked with the failure to establish a coherent pattern of post-16 tertiary education, is unlikely, for example, to sustain the new knowledge, skill and qualification requirements of young people and employers in the years to come. The danger is that the disparate range of curricular and institutional reforms set in motion in the 1980s is more likely to reinforce traditional differences between academic, technical and general knowledge, a factor which was recognized as a blockage to social, political and economic progress in the 1950s and which has been a major source of conflict in education and society ever since.

In identifying this 'innovation without change' scenario *Training and its Alternatives* anticipates the likely alternative programmes necessary to build a more equable, efficient and balanced system of education and training across the 14–19 age range. In so doing, a central theme of the book, made more or less explicit by all the authors, is that new responses, initiatives and reforms are required if educational standards and skill levels are to be raised throughout the workforce.

Thus, in drawing on a variety of perspectives – economic, historical, sociological and comparative, including various case studies – this book seeks to go beyond the narrow confines of the new vocationalism in identifying major alternative *curricular*, *institutional* and *policy* issues necessary to meet the needs of the 1990s.

If in the past decade schooling and further education have experienced unprecedented innovation and change, this book maintains that there has been little sign of any real or lasting educational reform. A principal argument is that vocational education and training for the majority of school leavers remains patchy and meets the needs of neither individual nor society. Indeed, one effect of government policy in the period from the New Training Initiative (1981) through to the Education Reform Act (1988) has been to fragment secondary and further education provision, in favour of a wide range of disparate institutional and curricular initiatives and in response to market forces. Such anarchic development has, ironically, not only reduced effective national coordination and systematic educational reform, but it has also reduced the effectiveness of education in responding to the changing social, economic, demographic and labour market trends of the 1990s. Skill shortages, changing work practices and new labour market conditions, are all likely to have a major impact on school, college and work relations in the years to come.

In order to focus more effectively on these key issues the book is divided into three main interrelated sections. The first, 'Origins, Context and Alternatives to Youth Training', looks at the essential social, economic and historical aspects of youth training, identifying how past and present trends figure significantly in the search for alternative education and training strategies. The focus here is on policy issues, with particular reference to the changing contexts of youth training, labour markets, work, government and industrial intervention. The second section, 'Alternatives in Secondary and Further Education', deals more specifically, via case studies, with the ways in which such changing contexts find their expression at the neglected area of the school and college level. A principal argument here is that institutional and curricular alternatives do not simply follow on from developments in policy, technology, work, labour markets and so forth, but constitute an integral feature of the change process itself. Again, this theme is taken further in the final section, 'Beyond Vocationalism', which considers the alternatives to skills training and the more effective integration of academic, technical and vocational education in the relationship between school, college and work.

The chapters in this book are concerned with a wide range of perspectives on vocational education and training across the 14-19 age range. A more important aim, however, is to provide discussion which goes beyond analysis and critique of the new vocationalism, exploring alternative possibilities for change. In various ways all the authors in this volume are committed to identifying the alternative curricular, institutional and policy strategies necessary to implement real and lasting reform. While a book such as this cannot claim to have covered every facet of the debate, it has sought to break new ground in two ways: first, in providing a comprehensive review of education and training reform to date and, second, in identifying key social, economic, demographic and labour market factors likely to influence education innovation and change in the future. It is for such reasons that the chapters in this volume draw on a range of historical, sociological, economic and comparative perspectives, including case studies of education practice,

General introduction

designed to provide the reader with both theoretical and practical insight into the issues involved.

In identifying some of the key factors involved, *Training and its Alternatives* has not sought to produce simplistic solutions of the kind which the Conservative government's new vocationalism promised as answers to the problems which beset schooling in the 1970s and 1980s. Rather, it seeks to go beyond the narrow confines of vocationalism, anticipating the likely alternative curricular, institutional and policy issues necessary to initiate comprehensive reforms across secondary and further education. In so doing, the book challenges the prevailing view that market forces are the most effective means of determining educational policy. While it is not the intention of this book to exaggerate the possibilities of change, the evidence and arguments provided here provide insight into where alternative possibilities lie.

References

Dale, R. (ed.) (1985). *Education, Training and Employment: Towards a 'New Vocationalism'?*, Oxford, Pergamon.
Department of Education and Science (DES) (1984). *Training for Jobs*, White Paper, London, HMSO.
DES (1985). *Better Schools*, White Paper, London, HMSO.
DES (1986). *Working Together: Education and Training*, White Paper, London, HMSO.
Gleeson, D. (ed.) (1987). *TVEI and Secondary Education: A Critical Approach*, Milton Keynes, Open University Press.
Harland, J. (1987). 'The TVEI experience: issues of control, response and the professional role of teachers', in D. Gleeson (ed.), *TVEI and Secondary Education: A Critical Appraisal*, Milton Keynes, Open University Press.
Manpower Services Commission (MSC) (1981). *A New Training Initiative: An Agenda for Action*, London, MSC.

Section 1

Origins, context and alternatives to youth training

Introduction

The purpose of this section is to draw together complementary and contrasting perspectives on historical, economic, comparative and developmental aspects of vocational education and training in post-war Britain. McCulloch's contribution (Chapter 1) sets the scene of both the book and the section by exploring some of the uses that can be made of the historical dimension when constructing alternatives to contemporary policies, and also some of the problems such an historical approach will involve. It does so by examining the Crowther Report, *15–18* (1959) in its historical context. In particular, the Crowther concept of the 'alternative road', put forward in Chapter 35 of that report, provides a vivid contrast to the assumptions and proposals of the training policies of the 1980s. It exemplified the tradition of liberal vocationalism from which recent initiatives have, to some extent, departed. But it also suffered from several difficulties that were never resolved. According to McCulloch, these need to be addressed rather than minimized if further use is to be made of Crowther's broad approach. The Crowther Report also suggests the importance of seeking to establish a positive rationale, a cohesive ideology, for the 'practical' in education, a position which McCulloch translates into the more immediate and contemporary context of present day training reform.

Following on this, Finegold and Soskice (Chapter 2) argue that Britain's traditional failure to train young people results in a 'low skill equilibrium' in which the relevant actors (i.e. companies, employees, unions, educators, administrators and politicians) have been trapped. Given the behaviour and expectations of the other actors, attempts at change by any one group are likely to fail. The authors argue that British companies have tended to produce standardized goods and services requiring low skills from many employees. Over time, this has generated a chain reaction: young people have not seen the acquisition of high level skills as critical for employment; schools and colleges have thus had only limited success in persuading young people to stay on; companies which have tried to move up market have been thwarted by skill shortages; and attempts to develop long-term internal training strategies have been undermined by the short-term profit requirements of the financial sector and the cost cutting bias of much of British management. The authors argue that neither weak employer organizations, reflecting the fragmented nature of British industry, nor unions, often divided between skilled and semi-skilled workers, have had the power to impose change on employers or force change on to the government. Finegold and Soskice maintain that government itself has also been ham-strung by this institutional equilibrium. Only in the last decade has inaction been broken by the Thatcher administration; but its action has not been coordinated, i.e. it has not sought to change all institutions simultaneously in the right direction. On the contrary, the government's free market strategy has led it to remove what small pressures ITBs exerted on employers to train, while it changed only the education and post-16 training systems – and then only in a limited way via YTS because of its deflationary public expenditure strategy. Thus the UK remains in a low skill equilibrium. According to the authors, effective change needs to be coordinated; it needs to change the product markets businesses are in; to give incentives to business to develop internal training infrastructures; and to ensure that skill acquisition is seen to lead to employment; and be prepared to devote resources to quality training.

Yet, as Raffe (Chapter 3) points out, YTS owes its existence to the political opportunities created by youth unemployment and it retains unemployment-related as well as training-related objectives. His chapter explores the tension between these two sets of objectives. Part of the problem, as Raffe sees it, arises because YTS attempts to innovate from the bottom up, thereby risking entrapment in a vicious circle of low status training and employment. The current strategy of YTS assumes that the employment prospects of YTS trainees depends primarily on the content and quality of YTS training. It is Raffe's view that YTS is *internally differentiated* and that recruitment and selection in the labour market (as well as effective dissemination of YTS and its training philosophy) depend primarily on the context rather than simply on the content of the scheme. According to the author, the only likely way of breaking the vicious circle is via one of two strategies: either through providing specific skills, credibly certified, which are in demand in the local labour market or through giving trainees privileged access to the employment network through which employers recruit, and thereby enhancing the 'context' of YTS.

Taking up this point, Roberts, Dench and Richardson's contribution (Chapter 4) emphasizes neglected aspects of the education, training and labour market processes. Their chapter uses evidence drawn from surveys of employers and 17–18 year olds in three parts of Britain with contrasting economic histories and current labour market conditions to identify the underlying trends that have restructured school leavers' prospects since the 1960s. It is argued that school leavers' problems have been exacerbated by, but have not been entirely due to, economic recessions and demographic trends. Rather, it is maintained that long-term shifts of employment from manufacturing to services, from lower level to higher level occupations, and between different parts of the country, have created mismatch problems in all areas. The authors explain how and why government, educational and training initiatives during the 1980s tend to have been absorbed into, instead of correcting, the prevailing imbalances. They then outline alternative policies for restoring equilibrium to Britain's youth labour markets.

The comparative implications of this perspective are, in various ways, taken up in the concluding chapter of this section by Chandler and Wallace (Chapter 5). Their paper compares British and West German systems of youth training in terms of two contrasting models: the *franchise* and the *corporatist* models. The franchise model is characterized by the subcontraction of training to agencies on a privatized market model, encouraging an ideology of competition and entrepreneurship. The corporatist model is characterized by national coordination and legal sanctions with the cooperation of unions, employers and the education system. Ironically, these are both examples of private initiative and state intervention – but within different historical and political settings take different forms. Having compared the two systems, the authors go on to consider what a national training system would require, including such topics as a youth incomes policy and equal opportunities strategies. They conclude with the argument that an improved quality of training, comparable with European systems, will become even more important with the merging of the European labour markets in 1992, if British workers are not to be disadvantaged.

Gary McCulloch 1

An alternative road? Problems and possibilities of the Crowther Concept

The publication of the Crowther Report, *15–18*, in December 1959 was greeted warmly and in some cases with extravagant acclaim.[1] Several recommendations in the report attracted strong support, particularly the raising of the school leaving age from 15 to 16, and the provision of compulsory part-time education for all young persons of 16 and 17 who were not engaged in full-time education. Perhaps the most important section of the report, certainly in the opinion of Crowther himself, was Chapter 35, entitled 'The alternative road'. The present chapter will reassess Crowther's concept of 'rehabilitating the practical', and consider the extent to which it suggests alternatives to the training policies of the 1980s.

Problems and possibilities

The lack of historical sensitivity in recent training policies needs to be challenged and redressed, not least because it threatens to reduce or distort the effect of the reforms themselves. Margaret Mathieson and Gerald Bernbaum also argue that the current drive for reform should be placed 'in a context which treats the current prescriptions and recommendations as themselves problematic, and as being at risk precisely because the level of analysis from which they begin is inadequate'.[2] Awareness of the historical context of these policies should help policy makers at least to avoid 're-inventing the wheel' and at best to understand the complexities and problems involved in curriculum reform. It may also allow greater understanding of alternatives to the approaches and prescriptions that currently dominate the policy agenda.

At the same time, if we are to make greater use of the historical dimension in informing, improving and challenging current policy orthodoxies, we should also be aware of the problems and special requirements of such an approach. It has to avoid the temptation to 'raid' the past in a selective way that will have deliberate consequences in the present. As Ivor Goodson points out, some sociological work tends to misuse historical evidence for particular purposes: 'When historical evidence is presented it is provided as a snapshot from the past to prove a contemporary point'.[3] This is, of course, a tendency to which politicians are also prone: history can be used as an ideological crutch to support current policies and be used as a weapon against their opponents, critics and victims. A detailed historical account will, by contrast, bring out the complexity of the past and will often warn against simple solutions to problems. Past and present initiatives need to be related to each other in a way that highlights continuity and change, similarities and differences, short-term conjunctures and longer-term structures. It is important to explain 'alternatives' within the framework of the historical circumstances and contexts in which they arose, were contested and declined.[4]

The 'Crowther concept' is of continuing significance in relation to current schemes because it suggests an alternative approach both to the 'grammar school curriculum' that has been so resilient in English secondary education in the twentieth century, and to the 'new vocationalism' of the 1980s.[5] It exemplifies what Silver and Brennan have described as a 'liberal vocationalism'.[6] Silver, in particular, has shown how debates on the character of and relationship between the 'liberal' and the 'vocational' persisted well into the twentieth century.[7] The 'alternative road' of the Crowther Report represented an important attempt to redefine this relationship, and yet its implications have tended to be either neglected or distorted.

The Crowther concept was an outcome of the problems and possibilities of the post-war era. A rapid increase in national demand for scientists and technologists had helped to stimulate an expansion of provision at various stages of education. It was evident that the universities on their own would not be able to expand sufficiently to cater for this anticipated manpower demand, especially for applied scientists and technologists. Support for an extension of higher technological education therefore began to grow.[8] The proposals of the Percy Report, which had suggested new avenues of expansion in higher technological education as early as 1945, were acted upon in the 1950s.[9]

At the same time, attention was increasingly directed towards the problems of secondary education. An expansion in higher education facilities would be of little value if increased numbers of able recruits were not forthcoming from the schools. The secondary schools, and especially the established grammar schools, were expected to provide these potential recruits. The grammar schools were hampered in responding to these new and urgent requirements by a 'serious shortage in the supply of science teachers'.[10] However, the 'vocal and insistent' demand for attention to be given to the training of scientists and technologists was recognized by the science teaching associations, based in the grammar schools, and by such interest groups as the Incorporated Association of Head Masters (IAHM). F.L. Allan of the IAHM noted that increased economic productivity would require larger numbers of highly skilled technologists: 'This brings us back to the output from the universities, and the universities in turn depend on their intake from the schools. The Sixth Forms in the Public Schools and Grammar Schools are therefore the key to the whole position.'[11] The Science Masters' Association (SMA) sought to respond by emphasizing the social value of science as it had long been taught in most grammar and public schools – liberal in approach, cultural in scope and rigorous in its intellectual and academic demands. Both the SMA and the IAHM argued strongly that science in the grammar schools should continue to provide a solid grounding in scientific principles rather than any specifically vocational preparation. This established approach, it was claimed, would produce many more high quality recruits for science and technology than would any attempt to introduce specialized training at the school level. As A.G. Russell, the president of the IAHM, declared in 1956, 'We do not aim to turn out "specialists" – we try to build the foundations on which a large number of "specialisms" can ultimately be erected'.[12] Thus, it was argued, a secure understanding of general scientific principles was the essential prerequisite for training in technology and engineering just as much as for scientific research. The SMA did acknowledge that there was 'a need to stimulate or maintain pupils' interest in engineering while they are at school', but insisted that this should happen only after a solid foundation of scientific principles had been laid:

> Proposals have been made to include in the school curriculum some studies which are labelled 'Engineering' and include some practice or technology which is not normally touched upon until a later stage in technical education. The view taken here is that such studies are inappropriate if they lead to a reduction of science studies in order to find room for some elementary technology.

It conceded that 'It might be that science teachers, through lack of information and a natural shortage of personal experience, do not quote engineering applications when, perhaps, they might with advantage', but it concluded, somewhat optimistically, that this matter could 'be safely left to the judgement of the science teachers'.[13]

On the other hand, it was widely recognized that this approach was not suitable for all pupils, and that other avenues needed to be explored in order to meet the perceived national demand for scientific and technological manpower. The minister of education, Sir David Eccles, was not convinced that a higher proportion of children should be allocated to grammar schools.[14] At the same time it seemed clear that many pupils who might benefit from further educational provision were leaving school at the minimum leaving age of 15, and the question of how to cater for this 'wasted talent' became a major issue.[15] Secondary technical schools had been established in the 1940s to provide a less academic approach than grammar schools, but hoping for an equal quality of intake from those 'selecting the sphere of industry or commerce as their particular link with the adult world'.[16] However, by the 1950s only a few hundred of these schools had been established and they were beset with difficulties of selection, assessment and rationale. The public, many LEAs, most educational pressure groups, and political and industrial concerns all but ignored the efforts of the secondary technical schools to come to terms with these problems and fulfil their potential.[17] Another problem was how to integrate the many and varied institutions of further education with the rest of educational provision in order to provide greater numbers of qualified technologists and technicians.

Eccles himself was particularly concerned to improve and extend the system of further education in England and Wales. He hoped that by widening the interests and the appeal of technical colleges, while also increasing their numbers, they might be better placed to satisfy the growing demand for technological manpower. In 1955 he appointed a national council to be headed by Lord Hives, the chairman of Rolls-Royce, for making awards to successful technological students in technical colleges. The purpose of this was to encourage the creation of 'a broad road to the top of the technical tree alternative to the normal university route'.[18] In February 1956, a four-year programme of investment for technical colleges of £85 million was announced in the White Paper *Technical Education*. This document stressed the danger of the English system of technical education being left behind by those in the United States, the Soviet Union and Western Europe.[19] It also declared that technical education should be flexible and versatile rather than 'narrowly vocational'. It was evidently hoped that broader and more liberal courses would attract more recruits from secondary education.[20]

The White Paper also emphasized that the phases of secondary and of further education should be much better integrated than they then were. Further expansion of the technical colleges, it pointed out, depended upon 'strengthening the base of the pyramid of technical education by improving the education in the schools and raising the numbers of school-leavers who are able and willing to take successfully the courses offered at technical colleges'.[21] The creation of the Hives awards, and the publication of the *Technical Education* White Paper, seem to have represented part of an attempt to identify a 'practical route' in education comparable in stature to the 'academic route' provided by the grammar schools and universities but appealing to a different type of pupil. These initiatives were also designed to encourage intellectual and liberal qualities in the pupils using the 'practical route'. Yet it was still not clear how this 'practical route' should be developed and sustained, nor how to forge a distinctive and coherent rationale for all types of 'practical' education. It was surely no coincidence that only a few weeks after the publication of the White Paper, Eccles invited the Central Advisory Council for Education to investigate the education of boys and girls of between 15 and 18 years of age.

The Crowther Committee

The Advisory Council began its inquiry into this subject in March 1956, chaired by Geoffrey Crowther, the deputy chairman of the *Economist* Newspaper Ltd. Born in Leeds, Crowther had been educated at Leeds Grammar School and then at Oundle, and then Cambridge; perhaps not surprisingly, he had a reputation as a 'pragmatist' in educational matters. Despite his double first in economics at Cambridge, he was not an academic economist, preferring to concentrate on his business and publishing interests. This predilection inspired one commentator to observe that 'In business as in economics as in education Crowther prefers the practice to the theory'.[22] The report produced by Crowther in 1959 gave added weight to this view.

The committee itself was composed of seven representatives from the universities, two from the local authorities, two from technical colleges, seven from schools (maintained and independent), one from the field of teacher training, two from trade unions, two from employers and three from elsewhere.[23] It was immediately divided into three fact finding groups, on tripartite lines, concerned with the 'channels and avenues of flow through the schools via further education to different levels of employment'.[24] Group A was to concentrate on the problems of sixth-form pupils and Group C on the less able pupils in secondary modern schools who were currently failing to find a place in sixth forms or in further education. Group B was intended to work out a coherent relationship between the various commercial, technical and industrial courses in many different types of institutions that were then on offer, in order that the committee as a whole might then be able to define and recommend a viable 'practical route' within the English educational system.

This was no easy task. It was admitted that this group 'offered the greatest difficulty of demarcation, and in certain fields might require a negative definition, i.e. boys and girls not clearly falling into A or C'.[25] In practice, Group B aimed to cater for 'those boys and girls whose careers demand some formal education beyond the age of 15 but whose probable "ceiling" is below professional status'.[26] It wrestled with the problem of identifying a 'practical route' for such pupils, and formulating a clear rationale for this route. Influential members of this 'technical group' on the Crowther Committee included Dr H. Frazer, head of Gateway Boys' School in Leicester, Dr P.F.R. Venables, principal of the college of advanced technology in Birmingham, and Mr George Bosworth, chief technical personnel administrator at the English Electric Company.

The difficulties involved in 'strengthening the base of the pyramid of technical education' engaged much of the attention of the technical group. Technical schools were seen as providing, at least potentially, a useful avenue for secondary school pupils to proceed into further education. Crowther himself equated 'the curriculum of secondary technical education' with 'the education in the schools of those who are proceeding to Technical Colleges'. In his view, the question of 'the future of the Secondary Technical School' was closely related to the wider issue of 'what can be done to swell the volume and improve the quality of entrants to the Technical Colleges'.[27] However, members were unsure as to exactly how the education offered in secondary technical schools differed from that in grammar schools. Dr Frazer circulated a lengthy note on the background and purposes of technical schools, arguing that grammar schools had generally resisted the introduction of technical subjects into the curriculum, and that such subjects could therefore only be encouraged through the establishment and further development of secondary technical schools.[28] Even so, the rationale of these schools, especially with regard to their relationship with further education, remained elusive. The assessor of the committee, David Ayerst, suggested that a 'unifying theme' for this area of discussion was still missing. He noted that the idea of 'a technical age and mechanically-interested boys and girls' had been 'prominent in all our discussions', but that it failed to provide a precise or coherent basis for secondary technical education.[29] It proved to be Crowther himself who suggested a fruitful approach to this problem. He argued that rather than looking for ways in which technical education might be based upon and oriented towards employment and industrial needs, the committee should formulate an explicitly *educational* rationale for the 'practical route'. He proposed, indeed, that

> the whole of this area should be gradually transformed from being primarily designed to meet industry's needs (with some education thown in) to being primarily designed to continue the education of a large slice of the nation's boys and girls (without destroying the usefulness to industry of the present system).[30]

This emphasis upon educational as opposed to vocational and industrial needs was vividly reflected in the final report and was most helpful in constructing a general account of the 'alternative road'.

The outcome of the Crowther Committee's discussions on the 'practical route' was contained in part 6 of the report, entitled 'Technical Challenge and Educational Response'. This explored the 'varied collection of plans for vocational training' that constituted further education, and proposed that it should be transformed into 'a coherent national system of practical education'.[31] It calculated that only one in eight young people of between 16 and 18 were continuing in full-time education, and recommended that this proportion should be increased to 50 per cent within twenty years. It also contended that those young people who left school at 15 but continued in some form of further education – about one-quarter of the age group – should be encouraged to remain at school to prepare for entry into a technical college. This would entail the creation of 'a greater degree of integration' between the schools and further education than was currently the case. It would also involve the development of a clear rationale for technical education that was able to embrace activities in both schools and technical colleges.

Chapter 35 of the report comprised the final chapter of Part 6 and attempted to outline the nature and implications of the 'practical approach' in education. It stressed that not all pupils were attracted to or motivated by 'the academic tradition which inspires and is embodied in our grammar schools and universities'.[32] There were, in fact, 'two kinds of minds', which should be educated in different ways.[33] The first kind of mind was the academic type, 'which is readily attuned to abstract thinking and can comprehend the meaning of a generalisation'.[34] These were best catered for by grammar school education. However, '... there are other minds which cannot grasp the general except by way of the particular, which cannot understand what is meant by the rule until they have observed the examples'.[35] Such minds, which 'move more easily from the practice to the theory', or which 'reason better in non-verbal ways', were 'not necessarily inferior', and more provision should be made for them.[36] In the past, the only alternatives for most boys and girls at the age of 15 or 16 had been 'the full-time academic route, for which they may not be suitable and which may not attract them', and 'the part-time route, which, for all its merits, had the disadvantages of requiring a prior entry into the labour market, of being rather narrowly vocational, of being very arduous, and of not being available at all to many boys and most girls'.

The report argued that a major task of English education was 'to construct a new system of education for the years between 15 or 16 and 18 which would neither suffer from these defects of the part-time route nor be academic in the old conventional sense'.[37] This new system would involve 'practical' education, but it would not be narrowly technical or vocational. It would be intended to provide 'the widest range of instruction for young people who will be proceeding into a wide variety of different employments'. Above all, however, 'If the country is to benefit fully from the intelligence of all its able boys and girls, it will be necessary to rehabilitate the word "practical" in educational circles – it is often used in a pejorative sense – and to define it more clearly'.[38] This alternative approach might be fostered in the schools, Crowther suggested, by encouraging the secondary technical schools, some of which had already been able to develop 'a practical education making progressively exacting intellectual demands'.[39] But the report acknowledged that such education, marked as it was by a 'broad scientific curiosity', rather than by 'narrow vocational interest',[40] was only in its 'early stages of development' and so it recommended that further inquiry should be made into the problems associated with the general notion of the 'alternative road'.[41]

Views of the alternative road

The conception of the 'alternative road' that the Crowther Committee had developed and recommended was very different from the traditional academic approach of the grammar schools. It was broad and 'liberal' in its account of practical education, and sought an educational rather than a vocational rationale for its growth. In its analysis of 'different types of minds' the report leaned heavily upon the prescriptions of the Norwood Report of 1943.[42] Lawrence Stenhouse, in a stimulating early essay, noted that Crowther's 'alternative road' was still not 'open to traffic', and that when it was opened it would still be 'narrow and selective'. For the lower streams in the secondary modern schools, Stenhouse pungently observed, 'there is no choice of road to confuse us: we are still trying to make these pupils roadworthy'.[43] Crowther's acceptance of tripartite divisions in education is an important point that must not be overlooked when we come to assess the report's continuing significance. For the moment, let us examine the influence of the Crowther Report's advocacy of the 'alternative road'.

Crowther himself was disappointed at the lack of practical response to this section of his report. The House of Commons debated the report on 21 March 1960 and Eccles, on behalf of the government, was warm in his praise.[44] Nevertheless, in a careful speech, he did not commit the government to carrying out its proposals. This was probably in part because of the financial implications of its recommendations. The annual cost of education in England and Wales had already grown from £280 million to £700 million in the previous ten years and the Crowther Report estimated that the cost of its own proposals would be another £200 to £250 million a year. The government had already committed itself to a large expansion of the technical colleges and was probably already anticipating the further expansion of the university system. Also, Eccles himself was somewhat ambivalent about the secondary technical schools as separate institutions, and probably felt that their future as an element in the 'alternative road' was limited. Particularly in view of the fact that a general election had only recently taken place, the government may well have decided to wait before making a firm decision on educational priorities and planning.

The *TES* was quick to condemn the mixture of 'vague assurances and pious hopes' offered by Eccles in the House of Commons debate, concluding:

> The Government have looked at the Crowther Report and have decided to do nothing about it. ... When the history of our present education comes to be written it will surely be seen that with chances unseized and opportunities lost Monday was its sorriest day.[45]

Crowther was less scathing, but also expected little:

> It is at least very gratifying to know that the Minister accepts the report in principle – though I have lived long enough to be a little sceptical about what

it means when a Government accepts a report in principle and leaves it to future circumstances to decide when and how it will be put into practice.[46]

He did allow himself to express his 'keen disappointment' at the lack of interest in the sections devoted to technical education: 'here is the biggest gap in English education, and by the same token the most exciting opportunity, and nobody is interested'.[47] Even so, over the following decade the notion of the 'alternative road' that the Crowther Report had put forward did have an important effect upon efforts to 'rehabilitate the practical', especially at the school level.

It led indirectly to the creation of the Schools Council project in technology which was launched in 1967. The Association of Heads of Secondary Technical Schools (AHSTS) seized upon the idea of the 'alternative road' to explain the approach adopted by such schools and to plead for their retention as independent institutions. In particular, Edward Semper, the head of Doncaster Technical High School for Boys and a leading figure in the association, sensed a vital opportunity to clarify this approach and press for further publicity. Semper responded promptly to the Crowther Report's suggestion that a further inquiry should be made into the meaning and implications of the 'practical approach'.[48] At the annual conference of the AHSTS held in Doncaster in 1961, the technical school heads called unanimously for the minister of education to appoint another committee specifically on the 'alternative road'.[49] When this appeal went unheeded, Semper organized his own curriculum research project on this theme. A small development committee was set up under the chairmanship of Professor Boris Ford of the University of Sheffield, with Semper acting as secretary. Private foundations showed little interest in financing a national research project in this area, but the joint secretaries of the new Schools Council offered to take over the whole project under their own auspices.[50] The development committee handed over the project, which ultimately evolved into Project Technology.

The leaders of the Schools Council project were keenly aware of their debt to the Crowther concept of the 'alternative road'. Donald Porter, a craft inspector who was a key figure in the creation of the project, was strongly influenced by this general notion. Porter wrote a curriculum bulletin entitled *A School Approach To Technology*, which was published by the Schools Council, in an attempt to build upon the ideas that Crowther had put forward.[51] He noted that since the secondary technical schools had by now all but disappeared because of the introduction of new schemes of reorganization on comprehensive lines, 'if the "alternative road" is to survive ... it must be found a place at the appropriate stage in all secondary schools'.[52] The organizer of the project, Geoffrey Harrison, also acknowledged the influence of the Crowther concept. He later remarked that

> The Alternative Road of the Crowther Report suggests the best approach, for many students, might be from application to fundamentals rather than vice versa. This order also coincides with what is frequently the order of thought of the engineer who may find himself using accepted techniques which are known to work, without fully understanding the fundamental scientific principles behind them. Indeed it is often necessary to use these techniques in order, ultimately, to understand the fundamentals.[53]

Some other attempts to encourage applied science and technology in schools were also influenced by this view that topics could be approached by tackling particular applications in order to understand the general principles behind them. The Duke of Edinburgh, a patron of applied science and technology in schools, urged teachers to 'Work from the motor car to the physical laws and from soap to the chemical laws'.[54]

Other would-be reformers did not go so far as this, but agreed that an alternative to the traditional grammar school science tradition needed to be found. For example, Gerd Sommerhoff of Sevenoaks School in Kent argued that 'traditional school science' dealt only with 'the analytical function of science', and he established a 'technical activities centre' within the school to encourage an intellectual and practical appreciation of the applications of science.[55] Meanwhile G.C. Sneed, head of applied science at Ealing Grammar School, developed an applied science course that also attracted considerable attention. He claimed that his school was 'the only grammar school in the country which has created a special course whose aim is to try and persuade able boys in the science-sixth to take engineering degrees at the university', in itself an indictment of the large majority of grammar schools at this time. The course at Ealing included the study of fluid flow, heat engines, strength of materials and electronics, and made it possible not only to 'teach the mathematical principles', but also to 'allow boys to carry out useful practical work'.[56]

The Duke of Edinburgh, Semper and Harrison were effectively advocates of a 'strong' or 'hard-line' version of the 'alternative road' in insisting that school science teaching need not begin with theoretical principles, but could usefully proceed from particular applications. Such reformers as Sneed and Sommerhoff, meanwhile, favoured a 'weak' or 'soft-line' version of the 'alternative road' because they continued to stress intellectual rigour as a basis for 'useful practical work'. There was some tension between these 'strong' and 'weak' versions of the 'alternative road', and the distinction remains an important one. A more recent echo of the debate was provided by a discussion between Frank McKim of Marlborough College and Tom Dodd of the Association of Advisers in Design and Technical Studies. McKim argued that 'there should be at least a component of technology or applied science in what we school teachers teach and what is examined'. In reply, Dodd questioned McKim's 'basic assumption' that 'the main route to technological understanding for many pupils is through science', and suggested instead that there might be 'a route the other way round, through technology to an understanding of science and a scientific body of knowledge'.[57] While the most intrepid, like Dodd, were prepared to risk the hazards of the high road, others, equally committed to change, preferred to take the low road. Yet in an important sense they all ended up where they had started, in individual schools with exceptional teachers and circumstances that were not readily replicated elsewhere.

It seems likely, indeed, that if the notion of the 'alternative road' influenced these various initiatives of the 1960s, the persistent ambiguities and problems associated with the notion help to explain the disappointing impact of the initiatives. The practical implications of the 'alternative road' in curriculum terms were never fully worked out. The Crowther Committee itself acknowledged that further enquiry was needed into the 'practical' approach in education. Very few secondary technical schools lived up to the ideals of the Crowther Report. Semper admitted not only that 'we have scarcely begun to develop a practical approach to education in our schools', but also that the 'alternative road' would 'remain a pipe dream' unless prompt action were taken 'to stimulate enquiry and foster research into the many problems associated with it'.[58] The development committee that Semper established failed to clarify the implications of the 'alternative road', and was divided on important points of emphasis and opinion. For instance, George Bosworth was alienated by Semper's increasing preoccupation with 'creativity' and 'problem-solving'. According to Bosworth, such topics were an 'intellectual cul-de-sac', and he complained that creativity was rather 'airy-fairy' and 'impossible to communicate'.[59] The Schools Council project in technology was plagued by such differences, and indeed was strongly criticized even by Semper and the Duke of Edinburgh. Harrison later acknowledged that the Schools Council project had been beset with pressures from all directions, and that the word 'technology' retained an 'awkward ambiguity' even in the 1980s.[60] The Action Group and the Schools' Science and Technology Committee, which were created partly out of dissatisfaction with the outlook of the Schools Council project, themselves failed to formulate a coherent and effective vision of the 'alternative road'. The Standing Conference on Schools' Science and Technology, founded in 1971, continued to be surrounded by differing interpretations and tensions on the nature of the 'practical approach' in education.[61]

Thus the 'practical' still needed elucidation in specific curriculum terms, no less than 'rehabilitation'. The notion of the 'alternative road' in a sense helped to evade this problem of definition. It was a broad, all embracing conception that permitted varying emphases and interpretations, and 'strong' and 'weak' versions of its central theme, and this meant that it could be invoked to support differing and even conflicting approaches to the introduction of applied science and technology in schools. It was a slogan that provided not one 'practical' approach in education, but legitimation for a number of 'practical' approaches in education. Its supporters had in common a dissatisfaction with traditional grammar school education, and a desire to 'rehabilitate the practical' within secondary education; but they were as divided as ever when it came to positive proposals for action.

It is also apparent that one vital aspect of the Crowther concept was often neglected in the initiatives of the 1960s. The AHSTS, the Schools Council project and the various other attempts to 'rehabilitate the practical' were preoccupied with finding new methods and approaches to topics, and thus encouraging their introduction in the school curriculum. This meant that they put much less emphasis upon the idea of the 'practical route' from schools to further education, which was just as important an element in the Crowther concept as was the idea of the 'practical approach'. It is true that several such reformers sought to foster a closer relationship between education and industry. George Bosworth felt that the creation of an 'alternative road' in education would entail the establishment of a 'matching section' between education and employment, 'designed to ensure the efficient conversion of the university graduate into an effective industrial technologist, and which will attract a higher proportion of the ablest graduates into industry'.[62] Semper's development committee and the Schools Council technology project both attracted support and representation from industrial concerns. However, there was a strong tendency to seek respectability by appealing to grammar schools, acquiring academic examinations and aspiring to university entry. Initiatives to follow up the Crowther concept became increasingly divorced from further education and even from the new polytechnics. Some advocates of the 'alternative road' at the school level feared that close association with technical colleges might damage their cause. Indeed, one study concluded that one of the reasons for the low esteem in which technology was held among sixth formers was that 'Technology is too easily associated in students' minds with the technical college route'.[63] In order to avoid 'second class status', and to 'break down the popular misconception that an engineer is someone in a boiler suit with greasy hands',[64] Crowther's 'practical route' was studiously avoided. Rehabilitation involved respectability, which meant laundering all connotations of the practical curriculum that related to work and industry.

An alternative road?

The Technical and Vocational Education Initiative (TVEI) was established at the end of 1982 specifically to resolve the problems that the secondary technical schools had faced, in the interests of industry and enterprise. In 1986, plans were announced to develop 'city technology colleges' (CTCs) for pupils from 11 to 18 years of age, in collaboration with local industries. The Crowther concept of the 'alternative road' is still of potential relevance and value for these and other new initiatives. In some ways, the situation has changed little since 1959. Crowther argued that it was necessary 'to rehabilitate the word "practical" in educational circles', and this is still needed. He aimed to encourage the transformation of 'a varied collection of plans for vocational training into a coherent system of practical education'; today the collection of plans for vocational training is more varied than ever. The Crowther Report also suggested that 'a practical education making progressively exacting intellectual demands', marked by 'broad scientific curiosity' rather than 'narrow vocational interest', should be developed and elucidated, and this has still not been accomplished. Indeed, greater attention to the principles outlined in the Crowther Report might provide a useful corrective to the 'new vocationalism', especially of current youth training schemes. The 'alternative road' was proposed as an alternative 'to both the merely theoretical and the rather narrowly technical'.[65] Its educational rationale would retain much appeal among educators suspicious of narrow vocational criteria. Its symbolic value as a link with the past might also be useful.

Yet if we are to make use of the Crowther concept in the new schemes of the late 1980s and 1990s, we should also be aware of its unresolved difficulties. First, it seems necessary to decide whether to opt for separate technical schools – a 'practical route' – or for 'absorption' of existing secondary schools within which to develop an 'alternative road'. Failure to make such a choice may well renew confusion, rivalry and conflicts over resources. At the same time it seems crucial to revise Crowther's original notion to replace its tripartite connotations of 'three types of mind' with recognition of the 'rehabilitation of the practical' for *all* pupils. Equally, it remains unfinished business to clarify the nature of the Crowther concept in curriculum terms, with regard to everyday practices and relationships within the schools.

Thus it is easy to argue that the Crowther concept, formulated in 1959, retains some value in our own day, and that its potential has been badly neglected. But even if we were to claim that the idea is now outmoded and useless, the Crowther Report holds a further lesson that seems of relevance for more recent initiatives. The report attempted to establish a potent and positive rationale, a cohesive ideology, for the 'practical' in education. It came too late to save the secondary technical schools, and it did not wholly succeed in defining such a rationale. And yet it still remains true that any initiative of this kind needs a strong ideological basis if it is to achieve any lasting success. Political convenience and popularity are too ephemeral to sustain any such project for long. Awareness of the historical dimension makes it less easy to pretend that there are no alternatives to, or problems involved in, the policies of the present. The Crowther concept helps to place current training policies in a broader context to remind us of problems and possibilities both in the past and in the present.

Acknowledgement

The author and editor are grateful to Professor David Layton for permission to use material from the author's paper 'Views of the alternative road: the Crowther concept', in David Layton (ed.), *The Alternative Road: The Rehabilitation of the Practical* (1984), Leeds, University of Leeds. The paper has been substantially revised and modified for the purpose of this book.

Notes

1. 'Generally welcome: reactions to Crowther report', *TES*, 18 December 1959.
2. Margaret Mathieson and Gerald Bernbaum, 'The British disease: a British tradition?' in *British Journal of Educational Studies*, Vol 26, No 2, 1988, p. 127.
3. Ivor Goodson, 'Subjects for study', in Ivor Goodson (ed.), *Social Histories Of The Secondary Curriculum*, London, Falmer, 1985, p. 344.
4. See Gary McCulloch, *The Secondary Technical School: A Usable Past?* London, Falmer, 1989, for further discussion of the relationship between 'history' and 'policy'.
5. Useful discussions of the 'new vocationalism' include Roger Dale (ed.), *Education, Training and Employment: Towards a New Vocationalism?*, Oxford, Pergamon, 1985; Richard Pring, 'Curriculum for ages 14-18: "the new vocationalism"?', in *Melbourne Studies in Education 1986*, pp. 93-115; Stuart Maclure, 'The educational consequences of Mr Norman Tebbit', *Oxford Review of Education*, vol 8, No 2, 1982, pp. 103-20; and Maurice Holt (ed.), *Skills and Vocationalism: The Easy Answer*, Milton Keynes, Open University Press, 1987.
6. Harold Silver and John Brennan, *A Liberal Vocationalism*, London, Methuen, 1988.
7. Harold Silver, 'The liberal and the vocational', in his *Education as History*, London, Methuen, 1983, pp. 153-72.
8. Advisory Council on Scientific Policy (ACSP), 3rd Annual Report, Cmd 7992, 1950, pp. 6-7.
9. Ministry of Education, *Higher Technological Education*, Percy Report, London, HMSO, 1945.
10. ACSP, 3rd Annual Report, p.6.
11. F.L. Allan to Sir G. Allen, 23 October 1957, British Association for the Advancement of Science papers.
12. A.G. Russell, 'The aims of the schools and how they are achieved', in Federation of British Industries, *Report of the Conference on Industry and the Public and Grammar Schools*, London, FBI, 1956, p. 14.
13. SMA memorandum, 'Further notes on the stimulation of engineering interest in schools', for SMA general committee, 7 June 1958, SMA papers.

14 David Eccles, Foreword to Ministry of Education, *Early Leaving: A Report of the Central Advisory Council for Education (England)*, London, HMSO, 1954.
15 *Ibid.*, p. 11.
16 Ministry of Education, *The New Secondary Education*, pamphlet No 9, London, HMSO, 1947, p. 23.
17 McCulloch, *The Secondary Technical School*.
18 Sir David Eccles to Dr Willis Jackson, 11 October 1955, Jackson papers, Imperial College, London, file F1.
19 Ministry of Education, *Technical Education*, 1956, p. 4.
20 Silver, 'The liberal and the vocational'.
21 Ministry of Education, *Technical Education*, p. 4.
22 'Observer Profile' on Geoffrey Crowther in *The Observer*, 13 December 1959.
23 Central Advisory Council for Education (England), 85th meeting, 22 March 1956, minute 3, Raybould papers, Museum of Education, University of Leeds.
24 CAC for Education, 86th meeting, 23-24 April 1956, minute 15, Raybould papers.
25 *Ibid*.
26 David Ayerst, 'Suggested approach to the Council's work for 1956', 12 April 1956, Raybould papers.
27 Geoffrey Crowther, 'Issues for consideration: note by the chairman', May 1957, Raybould papers.
28 H. Frazer 'Note on the secondary technical school', 8 May 1957, Raybould papers.
29 David Ayerst, issues paper, 'Unsolved problems in part 3', n.d., Raybould papers.
30 'Note on Mr Ayerst's paper by the Chairman', addendum to above paper.
31 Ministry of Education, *15-18: A Report of the Central Advisory Council for Education (England)*, Crowther Report, 1959, p. 370.
32 *Ibid.*, p. 391.
33 *Ibid.*, p. 394.
34 *Ibid.*, p. 394.
35 *Ibid.*, p. 394.
36 *Ibid.*, p. 468.
37 *Ibid.*, p. 394.
38 *Ibid.*, p. 391.
39 *Ibid.*, p. 397.
40 *Ibid.*, p. 393.
41 *Ibid.*, p. 398.
42 Board of Education, *Curriculum and Examinations in Secondary Schools*, London, Heinemann, 1943. See also Gary McCulloch, 'The Norwood Report and the secondary school curriculum', *History of Education Review*, Vol 17, No 2, 1988, pp. 30-45.
43 Lawrence Stenhouse, 'General education in the light of the Crowther report', lecture, 1960, in his *Authority, Education and Emancipation*, 1983, p. 10.
44 *Hansard*, House of Commons debates, 21 March 1960, col. 40.
45 'Dodging the issue', Leading article, *TES*, 25 March 1960.
46 'First reply to critics', *TES*, 25 March 1960.
47 'Parliament debates Crowther', *Technology*, April 1960.
48 AHSTS northern region, meeting, 4 February 1960, AHSTS papers, University of Leeds.
49 Report of AHSTS annual conference, 8-10 June 1961, AHSTS papers.
50 Edward Semper, Circular to members of the development committee, 4 February 1965, Semper papers. Also Schools Council memorandum, 'Engineering Science in Schools — Schools Council Conference: May 6, 1965', AEC papers, file A31(c), University of Leeds.
51 Schools Council curriculum bulletin No 2, *A School Approach to Technology*, London, Schools Council, 1967.
52 *Ibid.*, p. 13.

53 G.B. Harrison, 'Technological interpretations of design education in Britain', in A.R. Pemberton and S.J. Eggleston (eds), *International Perspectives of Design Education*, Keele, University of Keele, 1973, p. 99.
54 'Challenge of engineering: from particular to general', *TES*, 2 April 1965.
55 Gerd Sommerhoff, 'The Technical Activities Centre' in L.C. Taylor et al., *Experiments in Education at Sevenoaks*, Sevenoaks, Kent, 1965, pp. 57-72.
56 G.C. Sneed to Prof. P. Blackett, 6 December 1965, Blackett papers, file J.96, c/o Royal Society.
57 Standing Conference on Schools' Science and Technology, report on autumn conference, 29 October 1980.
58 Edward Semper, 'The need for a report on the Alternative Road', in *Technical Education*, Vol 2, No 7, 1960, pp. 19-20.
59 2nd meeting of development committee, 7 June 1963, Semper papers; and George Bosworth, interview with the author, 28 October 1982.
60 G.B. Harrison, 'The role of technology in science education', in C.P. McFadden (ed.), *World Trends in Science Education*, 1980, pp. 18-26.
61 For further details of these tensions and conflicts, see Gary McCulloch, Edgar Jenkins and David Layton, *Technological Revolution? The Politics of School Science and Technology in England and Wales since 1945*, London, Falmer, 1985.
62 Working Group on Engineering Training and the Requirements of Industry, 1st report, *Education and Training: Requirements for the Electrical and Mechanical Manufacturing Industries* (Bosworth Report), London, HMSO, 1966, p. 16.
63 J. Heywood, J. Pollitt and V. Nash, 'The schools and technology', *Lancaster Studies in Higher Education*, 1 April 1966, p. 187.
64 G.B.R. Feilden to Sir Harold Hartley, 16 September 1963, Hartley papers, Box 211, Churchill College, Cambridge.
65 Report of 1st meeting of development committee, 18 January 1963, Semper papers.

David Finegold and David Soskice 2

The failure of training in Britain: analysis and prescription

Introduction

In the last decade, education and training (ET) reform has become a major issue in many of the world's industrial powers. One theme which runs throughout these reform initiatives is the need to adapt ET systems to the changing economic environment. These changes include: the increasing integration of world markets, the shift in mass manufacturing towards newly developed nations and the rapid development of new technologies, most notably information technologies. Education and training are seen to play a crucial role in restoring or maintaining international competitiveness, both on the macro-level, by easing the transition of the workforce into new industries, and at the micro-level, where firms producing high quality, specialized goods and services require a well qualified workforce capable of rapid adjustment to changes in the work process and continual product innovation (Fonda and Hayes 1988).

This chapter will highlight the need for policy makers and academics to take account of the two-way nature of the relationship between ET and the economy. We will argue that Britain's failure to educate and train its workforce to the same levels as its international competitors has been both a product and a cause of the nation's poor relative economic performance: a product, because the ET system evolved to meet the needs of the world's first industrialized economy, whose large, mass production manufacturing sector required only a small number of skilled workers and university graduates; and a cause, because the absence of a well educated and trained workforce has made it difficult for industry to respond to new economic conditions.

The best way to visualize this argument is to see Britain as trapped in a low skills equilibrium, in which the majority of enterprises staffed by poorly trained managers and workers produce low quality goods and services.[1] The term 'equilibrium' is used to connote a self-reinforcing network of societal and state institutions which interact to stifle the demand for improvements in skill levels. This set of political–economic institutions will be shown to include the organization of industry, firms and the work process, the industrial relations system, financial markets, the state and political structure, as well as the operation of the ET system. A change in any one of these factors without corresponding shifts in the other institutional variables may result in only small, long-term shifts in the equilibrium position. For example, a company which decides to recruit better educated workers and then invest more funds in training them will not realize the full potential of that investment if it does not make parallel changes in style and quality of management, work design, promotion structures and the way it implements new technologies.[2] The same logic applies on a national scale to a state which invests in improving its ET system, while ignoring the surrounding industrial structure.

The argument is organized as follows: the second section uses international statistical comparisons to show that Britain's ET system turns out less qualified individuals than its major competitors and that this relative ET failure has contributed to Britain's poor economic record. The third section explores the historical reasons for Britain's ET problem and analyses the institutional constraints which have prevented the state from reforming ET. Section four then argues that the economic crisis of the 1970s and early 1980s and the centralization of ET power undertaken by the Thatcher administration have increased the possibility of restructuring ET, but that the Conservative Government's ET reforms, both the major changes already implemented and the changes likely to result from the 1988 Education Reform Act, will not significantly improve Britain's relative ET and economic performance. The fifth section proposes an alternative set of ET and related policies which could help Britain to break out of the low skills equilibrium.

International comparisons

Britain's failure to train

Comparative education and training statistics are even less reliable than cross-national studies in economics: there are few generally agreed statistical categories, wide variations in the quality of ET provision and qualifications and a notable lack of data on training within companies. Despite these caveats, there is a consensus in the growing body of comparative ET research that Britain provides significantly poorer ET for its workforce than its major international competitors. Our focus will be on differences in ET provision for the majority of the population, concentrating in particular on the normal ET routes for skilled and semi-skilled workers. This need not be technical courses, but may – as in Japan or the US – constitute a long course of general education followed by company-based training.

The baseline comparison for ET effectiveness begins with how students in different countries perform during compulsory schooling. Prais and Wagner (1983) compared mathematics test results of West German and English secondary schools and found that the level of attainment of the lower half of German pupils was higher than the average level of attainment in England, while Lynn (1988, p. 6) reviewed 13 year olds' scores on international mathematics achievement tests from the early 1980s and found that 'approximately 79 per cent of Japanese children obtained a higher score than the average English child'. The results are equally disturbing in the sciences, where English 14 year olds scored lower than their peers in all 17 countries in a recent study (Postlethwaite 1988).

This education shortfall is compounded by the fact that England is the only one of the world's major industrial nations in which a majority of students leave full-time education or training at the age of 16. The contrast is particularly striking with the US, Canada, Sweden and Japan, where more than 85 per cent of 16 year olds remain in full-time education. In Germany, Austria and Switzerland, similar proportions are either in full-time education or in highly structured three- or four-year apprenticeships. Britain has done little to improve its relative position. It was, for example, the only member of the OECD to experience a decline in the participation rate of the 16–19 age group in the latter half of the 1970s (OECD 1985, p. 17). Although staying on rates have improved in the 1980s – due to falling rolls and falling job prospects – Britain's relative position in the OECD rankings has not.

The combination of poor performance during the compulsory schooling years and a high percentage of students leaving school at 16 has meant that the average English worker enters employment with a relatively low level of qualifications.

Table 2.1 Percentages of population with a degree or qualification

	First degree graduates (3- and 4-year, full time) (%)	Workers with recognized qualifications (%)
West Germany (1980)	8	66
Japan (1980)	17	60
USA (1980)	19	78
UK (1981)	7	33

Source: NEDO/MSC (1984)

Workers' lack of initial qualifications is not compensated for by increased employer-based training: on the contrary, British firms offer a lower quality and quantity of training than their counterparts on the Continent. A joint NEDO/MSC study (1984, p.90) found that employers in Germany were spending approximately three times more on training than their British rivals, while Steedman's analysis (1986) of comparable construction firms in France and Britain revealed that French workers' training was more extensive and less firm-specific. Overall, British firms were estimated to be devoting 0.15 per cent of turnover to training compared, in the early 1980s, with a 1–2 per cent in Japan, France and West Germany (Anderson 1987, p. 69). And, as we will show in the fourth section, neither individuals nor the government have compensated for employers' lack of investment in adult training.

Why train? The link between ET and economic performance

Britain's relative failure to educate and train its workforce has contributed to its poor economic growth record in the post-war period. While it is difficult to demonstrate this relationship empirically, given the numerous other factors which affect labour productivity, no one is likely to dispute the claim that ET provision can improve economic performance in extreme cases: i.e. a certified engineer will be more productive working with a complex piece of industrial machinery than an unskilled employee. Our concern, however, is whether marginal differences in the quality and quantity of ET are related to performance. We will divide the evidence on this relationship in two parts: first, that the short-term expansion of British industry has been hindered by the failure of the ET system to produce sufficient quantities of skilled labour; and second, that the ability of the British economy and individual firms to adapt to longer-term shifts in international competition has been impeded by the dearth of qualified manpower.

A survey of the literature reveals that skill shortages in key sectors such as engineering and information technology have been a recurring problem for UK industry, even during times of high unemployment. The Donovan Commission (1968; p. 92) maintained that 'lack of skilled labour has constantly applied a brake to our economic expansion since the war'; a decade later, a NEDO study (1978, p. 2) found that 68 per cent of mechanical engineering companies reported that output was restricted by an absence of qualified workers. The problem remains acute, as the MSC's first *Skills Monitoring Report* (May 1986, p. 1) stated: 'Shortages of professional engineers have continued to grow and there are indications that such shortages will remain for some time, particularly of engineers with electronics and other IT skills'.

The shortages are not confined to manufacturing. Public sector professions, e.g. teaching, nursing and social work, which rely heavily on recruiting from the limited group of young people with at least five O-levels, are facing a skilled (wo)manpower crisis as the number of school leavers declines by 25 per cent between 1985 and 1995. In the case of maths and science teachers, the shortages tend to be self-perpetuating, as the absence of qualified specialists makes it harder to attract the next generation of students into these fields (Gow 1988b, p. 4; Keep 1987, p. 12).

The main argument of this paper, however, is that the evidence of skill shortages both understates and oversimplifies the consequences Britain's ET failure has on its economic performance. Skill shortages reflect the unsatisfied demand for trained individuals within the limits of existing industrial organization, but they say nothing about the negative effect poor ET may have on how efficiently enterprises organize work or their ability to restructure. Indeed, there is a growing recognition among industry leaders and the major accounting firms that their traditional method of calculating firms' costs, particularly labour costs, fails to quantify the less tangible benefits of training, such as better product quality and increased customer satisfaction (*Business Week* 1988, p. 49).

There are, however, a number of recent studies which show the strong positive correlation between industry productivity and skill levels. Daly (1984, pp. 41–2) compared several US and UK manufacturing industries and found that a shift of 1 per cent of the labour force from the unskilled to the skilled category raised productivity by about 2 per cent, concluding that British firms suffered because 'they lacked a large intermediate group with either educational or vocational qualifications'. The specific ways in which training can harm firm performance were spelled out in a comparison of West German and British manufacturing plants (Worswick 1985, p. 91):

Because of their relative deficiency in shop-floor skills, equivalent British plants had to carry more overhead labour in the form of quality controllers, production planners; ... the comparative shortage of maintenance skills in British plants might be associated with longer equipment downtime and hence lower capital productivity.

Likewise, employee productivity levels in the French construction industry were found to be one-third higher than in Britain and the main explanation was the greater breadth and quality of French training provision (Steedman 1986).

While these studies have all centred on relatively comparable companies producing similar goods and services, a high level of ET is also a crucial element in enabling firms to reorganize the work process in pursuit of new product markets (what Reich has called 'flexible-system' production strategies (Reich 1983, pp. 135–6); Walton and Susman 1987). 'Flexible-system' companies are geared to respond rapidly to change, with non-hierarchical management structures, few job demarcations and an emphasis on teamwork and maintaining product quality. They can be located in new industries, e.g. biotechnology, fibre optics, or market niches within old industries, such as speciality steels and custom machine tools.

A number of recent studies have highlighted the role of training in 'flexible-system' production: in Japanese firms, Shirai (1983, p. 46) found that employees in 'small, relatively independent work groups ... grasped the total production process, thus making them more adaptable when jobs have to be redesigned'. Streeck (1985) took the analysis one step further in his study of the European car industry, arguing that the high quality training programmes of German car manufacturers have acted as a driving force behind product innovation, as firms have developed more sophisticated models to better utilize the talents of their employees. Even in relatively low tech industries, such as kitchen manufacturing, German companies are, according to Steedman and Wagner (1987), able to offer their customers more customized, better quality units than their British competitors because of the greater flexibility of their production process – a flexibility that is contingent on workers having a broad skill base.

Why has Britain failed to train?

Economists' normal diagnosis of the undersupply of training is that it is a public good or free rider problem: firms do not invest in sufficient training because it is cheaper for them to hire already skilled workers than to train their own and risk them being poached by other companies. While the public good explanation may account for the general tendency to underinvest in training, it does not explain the significant variations between countries' levels of training nor does it address the key public policy question: given the market's inability to provide enough skilled workers, why has the British government not taken corrective action? To answer this question we will look first at why political parties were long reluctant to intervene in the ET field and then at the two major obstacles which policy makers faced when they did push for ET change: a state apparatus ill equipped for centrally led reform and a complex web of institutional constraints which kept Britain in a low skills equilibrium.

Political parties

Through most of the post-war period the use of ET to improve economic performance failed to emerge on the political agenda, as a consensus formed among the two major parties on the merits of gradually expanding educational provision and leaving training to industry. Underlying this consensus was an economy producing full employment and sustained growth, which obscured any deficiencies in the ET system. The broad consensus, however, masked significant differences in the reasons for the parties' positions: for Labour, vocational and technical education were seen as incompatible with the drive for comprehensive schooling, while the party's heavy dependence on trade unions for financial and electoral support prevented any attempts to infringe on union's control over training within industry (Hall 1986, p. 85). In the case of the Conservatives, preserving the grammar school track was the main educational priority, while intervening in the training sphere would have violated their belief in the free market (Wiener 1981, p. 110). An exception to the principle of non-intervention came during the Second World War, when the coalition government responded to the manpower crisis by erecting makeshift centres that trained more than 500,000 people. When the War ended, however, these training centres were dismantled.

The state structure

One of the main factors which hindered politicians from taking a more active ET role was the weakness of the central bureaucracy in both the education and training fields. On the training side, it was not until the creation of the Manpower Services Commission (MSC) in 1973 (discussed in the fourth section) that the state developed the capacity for implementing an active labour market policy. The staff of the primary economic policy making body, the Treasury, 'had virtually no familiarity with, or direct concern for, the progress of British industry' (Hall 1986, p. 62) and none of the other departments (environment, trade and industry, employment or education and science) assumed clear responsibility for overseeing training. There was, for example, a dearth of accurate labour market statistics, which made projections of future skill requirements a virtual impossibility (Reid 1980, p. 30). Even if the state had come up with the bureaucratic capability to develop a coherent training policy, it lacked the capacity to implement it. Wilensky and Turner (1987, pp. 62-3) compared the state structure and corporatist bargaining arrangements of eight major industrialized nations and ranked the UK last in its ability to execute manpower policy.

While responsibility over education policy in the central state was more clearly defined, resting with the Department of Education and Science (DES), the historical decentralization of power within the educational world made it impossible for the DES to exercise effective control (Howell 1980; OECD 1975). Those groups responsible for delivering education, local authorities (Jennings 1977) and teachers (Dale 1983a), were able to block reforms they opposed, such as vocationalism. The lack of central control was particularly apparent in the further education sector, an area accorded low priority by the DES until the 1970s (Salter and Tapper 1981).

The main obstacle to ET reform, however, was not the weakness of the central state, which could be remedied given the right external circumstances and sufficient political will, but the interlocking network of societal institutions which will be explored in the following sections, beginning with the structure, or lack of it, for technical and vocational education and entry level training.

The ET system

Technical and work-related subjects have long suffered from second class status in relation to academic courses in the British education system (Wiener 1981). The Norwood Report of 1943 recommended a tripartite system of secondary education, with technical schools to channel the second quarter of the ability range into skilled jobs; but while the grammar schools and secondary moderns flourished, the technical track never accommodated more than 4 per cent of the student population. In the mid-1960s two programmes, the Schools Council's Project Technology and the Association for Science Education's Applied Science and the Schools, attempted to build an 'alternative road' of engineering and practical courses to rival pure sciences in the secondary curriculum (McCulloch *et al.* 1985, pp. 139–55). These pilot experiments were short lived due to conflicts between and within the relevant interest groups, minimal coordination of the initiatives and the absence of clearly defined objectives and strategies for implementing them (*ibid.*, pp. 209–12).

The efforts to boost technical education were marginal to the main educational transformations of the post-war period: the gradual shift from division at 11-plus to comprehensives and the raising of the school leaving age to 15 and eventually 16 in 1972. The education establishment, however, was slow to come up with a relevant curriculum for the more than 85 per cent of each age cohort who were now staying longer in school but could not qualify for a place in higher education. Success for the new comprehensives continued to be defined by students' performance in academic examinations (O- and A-levels), which were designed for only the top 20 per cent of the ability range (Fenwick 1976) and allowed many students to drop subjects, such as mathematics and science, at the age of 14. The academic/ university bias of the secondary system was reinforced by the powerful influence of the public schools, which while catering for less than 6 per cent of students produced 73 per cent of the directors of industrial corporations (Giddens 1979), as well as a majority of Oxbridge graduates, MPs and top education officials; thus, a large percentage of those charged with formulating ET policy, both for government and firms, had no personal experience of state education, much less technical or vocational courses.

The responsibility for vocational and training (VET) fell by default to the further education (FE) sector. The 1944 Education Act attempted to provide a statutory basis for this provision, declaring that county colleges should be set up in each LEA to offer compulsory day-release schemes for 15–18 year olds in employment. The money was never provided to build these colleges, however, with the result that 'a jungle' of different FE institutions, courses and qualifications developed (Locke and Bloomfield 1982). There were three main paths through this 'jungle': the academic sixth form, the technical courses certified by independent bodies, such as City and Guilds, BTEC or the RSA, and 'the new sixth form' or 'young stayers on', who remain in full-time education without committing themselves to an A-level or specific training course (MacFarlane Report 1980). A host of factors curtailed the numbers pursuing the intermediate route: the relatively few careers requiring these qualifications, the lack of maintenance support for FE students and the high status of the academic sixth, which was reinforced by the almost total exclusion of technical students from higher education.

The majority of individuals left education for jobs which offered no formal training. Those who did receive training were almost exclusively in apprenticeships. The shortcomings of many of these old style training programmes, which trained 240,000 school leavers in 1964, were well known: age and gender barriers to entry, qualifications based on time served (up to seven years) rather than a national standard of proficiency and no guarantee of off-the-job training (Page 1967). The equation of apprenticeships with training also had the effect of stifling training for positions below skilled level and for older employees whose skills had become redundant or needed updating.

In the early 1960s the combination of declining industrial competitiveness, a dramatic expansion in the number of school leavers and growing evidence of skill shortages and 'poaching' prompted the government to attempt to reform apprenticeships and other forms of training (Perry 1976). The route the state chose was one of corporatist compromise and minimal intervention, erecting a network of training boards (ITBs) in the major industries staffed by union, employer and government representatives (Industrial Training Act 1964). The ITBs' main means of overcoming the free rider problem was the levy/grant system, which placed a training tax on all the companies within an industry and then distributed the funds to those firms that were training to an acceptable standard, defined by each board (Page 1967).

The boards created a fairer apportionment of training costs and raised awareness of skill shortages; but they failed to raise substantially the overall training level because they did not challenge the short-term perspective of most companies. The state contributed no new funds to training and each board assessed only its industry's training needs, taking as given the existing firm organization, industrial relations system and management practices and thus perpetuating the low skills equilibrium. Despite the Engineering ITB's pioneering work in developing new, more flexible training courses, craft apprenticeships remained the main supply of skilled labour until Mrs Thatcher came to power in 1979.

Industrial/firm structure

Industry type One of the main reasons that British industry has failed to update its training programmes is the concentration of the country's firms in those product markets which have the lowest skill requirements, goods manufactured with continuous, rather than batch or unit production processes (Reich 1983). An analysis of international trade in the 1970s by NEDO found that the UK performed better than average in 'standardized, price-sensitive products' and below average in 'the skill and innovation-intensive products' (Greenhalgh 1988, p. 15). New and Myers's 1986 study of 240 large export-oriented plants confirmed that only a minority of these firms had experimented with the most advanced technologies and that management's future plans were focused on traditional, mass production market segments.

Training has also been adversely affected by the long-term shift in British employment from manufacturing to low skill, low quality services. Manufacturing now accounts for less than one-third of British employment and its share of the labour market has been declining. The largest growth in employment is in the part-time service sector where jobs typically require and offer little or no training. The concentration of British service providers on the low skill end of the labour market was highlighted in a recent study of the tourist industry (Gapper 1988).

While the type of goods or services which a company produces sets limits on the skills required, it does not determine the necessary level of training. Recent international comparisons of firms in similar product markets (i.e. Maurice *et al.* 1986; Streeck 1985) have revealed significant variations in training provision depending on how a company is organized and the way in which this organizational structure shapes the implementation of new technologies. In the retail trade, for instance, 75 per cent of German employees have at least an apprenticeship qualification compared with just 2 per cent in the UK. The brief sections which follow will outline how, in the British case, the many, integrally related components of firms' organizational structures and practices have combined to discourage training.

Recruitment British firms have traditionally provided two routes of entry for young workers: the majority are hired at the end of compulsory schooling, either to begin an apprenticeship or to start a semi- or unskilled job, while a select few are recruited from higher education (HE) for management posts (Crowther Report 1959). (Nursing is one of the rare careers which has sought students leaving further education (FE) at the age of 18.) As a result, there is little incentive for those unlikely to gain admittance to HE to stay on in school or FE. Indeed, Raffe (1984, Chapter 9) found that Scottish males who opted for post-compulsory education actually had a harder time finding work than their peers who left school at 16. Vocational education is perceived as a low status route because it provides little opportunity for career advancement and because managers, who themselves typically enter employment without practical experience or technical training, focus on academic examinations as the best means of assessing the potential of trainees.

Job design and scope After joining a company, employees' training will depend upon the array of tasks they are asked to perform. Tipton's study (1982, p. 33) of the British labour market found that 'the bulk of existing jobs are of a routine, undemanding variety' requiring little or no training. The failure to broaden individuals' jobs and skill base, i.e. through job rotation and work teams, has historically been linked to craft unions' insistence on rigid demarcations between jobs; but there is some evidence that these restrictive practices have diminished in the last decade. The decline in union resistance, however, has been counter-balanced by two negative trends for training: subcontracting out skilled maintenance work (Brady 1984) and using new technologies to deskill work (Streeck 1985). The latter practice is particularly well documented in the automobile industry, where British firms, unlike their Swedish, Japanese and German rivals, have structured new automated factories to minimize the skill content of production jobs, instead of utilizing the new technology to increase flexibility and expand job definitions (Scarbrough 1986). Tipton concludes (p. 27): 'the key to improving the quality of training is the design of work and a much needed spur to the movement for the redesign of work ... may lie in training policies and practice'.

Authority structure In the previous section we used job design to refer to the range of tasks within one level of a firm's job hierarchy (horizontal scope); how that hierarchy is structured – number of levels, location of decision making power, forms of control – will also affect training provision (vertical scope). *A Challenge to Complacency* (Coopers and Lybrand 1985, pp. 4–5) discovered that in a majority of the firms surveyed, line managers, rather than top executives, are generally responsible for training decisions, thereby hindering long-term manpower planning. British firms also lack structures such as German work councils, which enable employees to exercise control over their own training.

Career/wage structure A company's reward system, how wages and promotion are determined, shapes employees' incentives to pursue training. While education levels are crucial in deciding where an employee enters a firm's job structure, the incentives to train are low after workers have taken a job because pay and career advancement are determined by seniority not skill levels (George and Shorey 1985). This disincentive is particularly strong for the growing number of workers trapped in the peripheral sector of the labour market (Mayhew 1986), which is characterized by part-time or temporary work, low wages and little or no chance for promotion.

Management Linking all of the preceding elements of firm organization is the role of management in determining training levels. The poor preparation of British managers, resulting from a dearth of technical HE or management schools and a focus on accounting rather than production, is often cited as a reason for the lack of priority attached to training in Britain (i.e. Davies and Caves 1987). A recent survey of over 2,500 British firms found that less than half made any provision at all for management training (Anderson 1987, p. 68). In those firms which do train, managers tend to treat training as an operating expense to be pared during economic downturns and fail to incorporate manpower planning into the firm's overall competitive strategy. For managers interested in career advancement, the training department is generally seen as a low status option (Coopers and Lybrand 1985, pp. 4–5). And for poorly qualified line managers, training may be perceived as a threat to their authority rather than a means of improving productivity. It is important, however, to distinguish between bad managers, and able ones who are forced into decisions by the institutional structure in which they are operating. We will explore two of the major forces impacting on their decisions, industrial relations and financial markets, in the following sections.

Financial markets

The short-term perspective of most British managers is reinforced by the pressure to maximize immediate profits and shareholder value. The historical separation of financial and industrial capital (Hall 1986, p. 59) has made it harder for British firms to invest in training, with its deferred benefits, than their West German or Japanese competitors, particularly since the City has neglected training in its analysis of companies' performance (Coopers and Lybrand 1985). Without access to large, industry-oriented investment banks, British firms have been forced to finance more investment from retained profits than companies in the largest industrial countries (Mayer 1987).

Industrial relations

Just as the operation of financial markets has discouraged training efforts, so too the structure, traditions, and common practices of British industrial relations have undermined attempts to improve the skills of the workforce. The problem results in part from the inability of the central union and employer organization to combine with government to form a coordinated national training policy and also from the historically evolved structure of individual unions.

Employer organizations The strength of the CBI derives from its virtual monopoly status – its members employ a majority of Britain's workers and there is no competing national federation. But while this membership base has given the CBI a role in national training policy formulation, the CBI lacks the sanctions necessary to ensure that employers implement the agreements which it negotiates with the government. The power lies not in the central federation, nor in industry-wide employers' associations, but in individual firms. The CBI's views on training reflect its lack of control, as Keep (1986, p. 8), a former member of the CBI's education, training and technology directorate, observes: 'The CBI's stance on training policy ... was strongly anti-interventionist and centred on a voluntary, market-based approach. Legislation to compel changes in training policy ... was perceived as constituting an intolerable financial burden on industry.'

This free-market approach, combined with the absence of strong local employer groups, such as the West German chambers of commerce, has left British industry without an effective mechanism for overcoming the 'poaching' problem. Among the worst offenders are the small and medium-sized firms, poorly represented in the CBI, which lack the resources to provide broad-based training.

Trade Unions There are four key, closely connected variables which determine the effectiveness of a central union federation in the training field (Woodall 1985, p. 26). They are: degree of centralization, financial membership and organization resources, degree of youth organization and structure and practice of collective bargaining. Woodall compared the TUC with European central union federations and found it weak along all of these axes. Like the CBI, it could exert a limited influence on government policy, but it lacked the means to enforce centrally negotiated initiatives on its members.

The TUC has had to deal with 'the most complex trade union structure in the world' (Clegg 1972, p. 57), while having little control over its affiliated unions. And whereas the German central union federation, the DGB, claims 12 per cent of its member unions' total receipts, the TUC has received less than 2 per cent and devotes only a small fraction of these resources to training. This inattention to education and training is reflected in unions, lack of involvement in the transition from school to work. Britain's major youth organizations, the National Union of Students and Youthaid, grew outside the formal union structure and have often criticized the labour movement for failing to address the needs of the nation's school leavers, particularly the unemployed. The uncoordinated nature of British collective bargaining, with agreements varying from coverage of whole industries to small portions of a particular factory, and the lack of central input in the negotiations further hinder TUC efforts to improve training provision. The combination of these factors prompted Taylor (1980, p. 91) to observe that 'by the standards of other Western industrialized nations, Britain provides the worst education services of any trade union movement.'

From an historical perspective this is not surprising, on account of the division between craft and general unions. Craft unions had little incentive to push for improvements in training: they would have weakened their bargaining position. And general unions had little incentive because they would have lost newly skilled members to craft unions.

Although we have broken down this analysis into separate sections for conceptual clarity, it is essential to view each element as part of a historically evolved institutional structure which has limited British ET. In the next part we will examine how the economic crisis of the 1970s destabilized this structure, creating the opportunity for the Thatcher Government's ET reforms.

Mrs Thatcher's education and training policies

During the 1970s a confluence of events brought an end to the reluctance of central government to take the lead in ET policy making. The prolonged recession which followed the 1973 oil shock forced the Labour Government to cut public expenditure, necessitating a re-examination of educational priorities. This reassessment came at a time when the education system was drawing mounting criticism in the popular press and provoking the far Right's Black Papers for allegedly falling standards and unchecked teacher progressivism (CCCS 1981). The response of the then Prime Minister, Callaghan, was to launch the Great Debate on education in a now famous speech at Ruskin College, Oxford, in October 1976, where he called on the ET sector to make a greater contribution towards the nation's economic performance (*TES*, 22 October 1976, p. 72).

The increase in bipartisan political support for vocational and technical education was matched by a strengthening of the central state's capacity to formulate ET policy. The Manpower Services Commission (MSC), a tripartite quango funded by the Department of Employment, was established in 1973 to provide the strong central organization needed to coordinate training across industrial sectors which was missing from the industrial training board structure. In practice, however, the ITBs were left to themselves, while the MSC concentrated on the immediate problem of growing youth unemployment. The commission supervised the first substantial injection of government funds into training, beginning with TOPS (Training Opportunities Scheme) and later through YOP (Youth Opportunities Programme). The rapid increase in government spending, the MSC budget rose from £125 million in 1974–75 to £641 million in 1978–79, did little to improve skills; however, since the funds were concentrated on temporary employment, work experience and short-course training measures and the demands for quick action precluded any long-term manpower planning.

Spurred on by its new rival, the MSC, the DES set up the Further Education Unit (FEU) in 1978, which produced a steady stream of reports that helped shift educational opinion in favour of the 'new vocationalism' (i.e. *A Basis for Choice*, 1979). The Department teamed up with the MSC for the first time in 1976 to launch the Unified Vocational Preparation (UVP) scheme for school leavers entering jobs which previously offered no training. Although this initiative never advanced beyond the early pilot phase, it set a precedent for subsequent reform efforts.

The state structure was in place for the new Thatcher Government to transform the ET system. The first half of this section will outline three distinct phases in the Conservatives' ET reform efforts (see Table 2.2), examining how the government has avoided many of the pitfalls which plagued past efforts at change, while the latter portion will argue that these reforms, while leading to significant shifts in control over ET, will not raise Britain's relative ET performance.

Phase I: preparation

It is only in retrospect that the first few years of the Thatcher administration can be seen as an effective continuation of the movement towards greater centralization of ET power. At the time, government economic policy was dominated by the belief that controlling the money supply and public expenditure were the keys to reducing inflation and restoring competitiveness. Education and training accounted for approximately 15 per cent of the budget and thus needed to be cut if spending was to be curtailed. The cuts included across the board reductions in education funding, a drop in state subsidies for apprenticeships and the abolition of 17 of the 24 training boards (one new one was created), despite the opposition of the MSC. The financial rationale for the cuts was underpinned by the then strongly held view of the government that training decisions were better left to market forces.

The net effect of these cuts, coming at the start of a severe recession in which industry was already cutting back on training, was the collapse of the apprenticeship system. The number of engineering craft and technician trainees, for example, declined from 21,000 to 12,000 between 1979 and 1981, while construction apprentice recruitment fell by 53 per cent during the same period (from EITB and CITB in *TUC Annual Report* 1981, pp. 434–5). The destruction of old style apprenticeships, combined with the government's attacks on trade unions' restrictive practices through industrial relations legislation, meant that when the state eventually chose to reform initial training within companies there was only minimal resistance from organized labour and employers.

Phase II: The New Training Initiative

By 1981 the deepening recession and the dramatic rise in youth unemployment which it caused compelled the government to reassess its non-interventionist training stance. While the Conservatives' neo-liberal economic philosophy offered no immediate cure for mass unemployment, it was politically essential to make some effort to combat a problem which the polls consistently showed to be the

Table 2.2 Mrs Thatcher's education and training policies

Phase date	Characteristics	Programmes		
		Education	Youth training	Adult training
I. Preparation 1979–81	Market orientation Weaken resistance Lack overall strategy	Budget cuts	Apprenticeship collapse	Dismantle ITBs
II. NTI 1982–86	Focus on 14–18s Concern with youth unemployment Enterprise economy Increase central control	TVEI: pilot into national programme in 4 years	YOP into 2-year YTS YTS apprentice route	TOPS into new JTS Focus on 18–25 unemployment
III. Expansion 1987–	Education–new priorities Adults – first attempt at coherence	ERA/CTCs TVEI: extension or extinction?	Weaken MSC Compulsory YTS NCVQ finish in 1991	Weaken MSC Employment Training 600,000 places, no new money.

voters' primary concern (Moon and Richardson 1985, p. 61). This electoral need was highlighted in a Downing Street policy unit paper from early 1981:

> We all know that there is no prospect of getting unemployment down to acceptable levels within the next few years. [Consequently] we must show that we have some political imagination, that we are willing to salvage something – albeit second-best – from the sheer waste involved.
>
> (Riddell, 1983, p. 50)

What this 'political imagination' produced was the New Training Initiative (NTI, 1981), whose centrepiece, the Youth Training Scheme (YTS), was billed as the first 'permanent' national training programme for Britain's school leavers. YTS replaced YOP, which had begun as a temporary scheme in 1978 to offer a year's work experience and training to the young unemployed. In just four years, however, YOP had swelled to more than 550,000 places, and as the numbers grew so did the criticism of the programme for its falling job placement rates and poor quality training. YTS attempted to improve YOP's image by upgrading the training content, 'guaranteeing' a year's placement with at least 13 weeks off-the-job training to every minimum age school leaver and most unemployed 17 year olds and more than doubling the programme's annual budget, from £400 to £1,000 million.

Despite these improvements, the scheme got off to a difficult start, with a national surplus of close to 100,000 places, as school leavers proved reluctant to enter the new programme. In response, the MSC implemented a constant stream of YTS reforms: the scheme was lengthened from one to two years, with off-the-job training extended to 20 weeks, all 16 and 17 year-olds, not just the unemployed, were made eligible, some form of qualification was to be made available to each trainee, and monitoring and evaluation were increased by requiring all training providers to attain approved training organization (ATO) status. While the majority of YTS places continue to offer trainees a broad sampling of basic skills ('foundation training') and socialization into a work environment, some industries, such as construction, engineering and hairdressing, have used the scheme to finance the first two years of modernized apprenticeships.

The other major ET reform originating in this period was the Technical and Vocational Education Initiative (TVEI) launched by the Prime Minister in November 1982. TVEI marked the Thatcher administration's first attempt to increase the industrial relevance of what is taught in secondary schools, through the development of new forms of teacher training, curriculum organization and assessment for the 14–18 age group. Under the direction of MSC chairman David (now Lord) Young, the initiative grew extremely rapidly, from 14 local authority pilot projects in 1983 to the start of a nationwide, £1 billion extension just four years later. Lord Young conceived TVEI as a means of fostering Britain's 'enterprise economy', by motivating the vast majority of students who were not progressing to higher education: 'The curriculum in English schools is too academic and leads towards the universities. What I am trying to show is that there is another line of development that is equally respectable and desirable which leads to vocational qualifications ...' (*Education*, 19 November 1982, p. 386).

This line of development was extended into the FE sector in 1985 with the introduction of the Certificate of Pre-Vocational Education (CPVE), a one-year programme of broad, work-related subjects for students who wished to stay on in full-time education, but were not prepared for A-levels or a specific career path.

In 1985 the government set up a working group to review Britain's increasingly diverse array of vocational qualifications. The De Ville Committee's Report (1986) led to the establishment of the National Council for Vocational Qualifications (NCVQ), which has the task of rationalizing all of the country's training qualifications into five levels, ranging from YTS to engineering professionals, with clear paths of progression between stages and national standards of proficiency. The council, which is scheduled to complete its review in 1991, will be defining broad guidelines for training qualifications into which the courses of the independent certification bodies (i.e. RSA, BTEC, City and Guilds) can be slotted.

Taken together these initiatives represent a dramatic reversal in the government's approach to ET. The scope and pace of reform was made possible by the centralization of power in the hands of the MSC, an institution which has proved adept at securing the cooperation required to implement these controversial changes. In the case of YTS, the MSC retained trade union support, despite protests from over one-third of the TUC's membership that the schemes lead to job substitution and poor quality training (*TUC Annual Reports*, 1983–86), because the TUC leadership refused to give up one of its last remaining channels for input into national policy making.

The MSC also became a major power in the educational world because it offered the Conservatives a means of bypassing the cumbersome DES bureaucracy (Dale 1985, p. 50). The commission was able to convince teachers and local authorities, who had in the past resisted central government's efforts to reform the curriculum, to go along with TVEI through the enticement of generous funding during a period of fiscal austerity and the use of techniques normally associated with the private sector, such as competitive bidding and contractual relationships (Harland 1987). Its influence over education increased still further in 1985, when it was given control over 25 per cent of non-advanced further education (NAFE) funding, previously controlled by the LEAs. This change has, in effect, meant that the MSC has the power to review all NAFE provision.

Phase III: expanding the focus

The constantly changing nature of ET policy under Mrs Thatcher makes it hazardous to predict future developments, but early indications are that education and training reform will continue to accelerate in her third term. The combination of a successful economy (low inflation, high growth and falling unemployment) and a solid electoral majority has enabled the Conservatives to turn their focus toward fundamental social reform. As a result, the narrow concentration of ET policy on the 14–18 age group appears to be broadening to include both general education (Education Reform Act (ERA), 1988) and adult training (the White Paper *Training for Employment*, 1988).

The 1987 Conservative election manifesto signalled the emergence of education reform as a major political issue. While ERA is primarily an attempt to raise standards by increasing competition and the accountability of the educational establishment, a number of its provisions will impact on the vocational education and training (VET) area: the National Curriculum, which will ensure that all students take mathematics and science until they reach 16; city technical colleges, which may signal the beginning of an alternative secondary school track, funded directly by the DES with substantial contributions from industry; the removal of the larger colleges of further education (CFEs) and polytechnics from LEA control, freeing them to compete for students and strengthening their ties with employers; and increased industry representation on the new governing body for universities, the UFC (University Funding Council).

At the same time, the government has begun restructuring adult training provision. Over the previous eight years, the MSC concentrated on reducing youth unemployment, while financing a succession of short duration training and work experience programmes for the long-term unemployed: TOPS (Training Opportunities Scheme – short courses normally based in CFEs), JTS, and new JTS (Job Training Scheme) – work placement with minimal off-the-job training for 18–24s), and the CP (Community Programme – state-funded public work projects). In February 1988 the government's White Paper, *Training for Employment*, introduced a plan to combine all of these adult initiatives into a new £1.5 billion programme that was intended to provide 600,000 training places, with initial preference given to the 18 to 24 age group. To attract the long-run unemployed into the scheme the government is using both carrot and stick: a training allowance at least £10 above the benefit level, along with increases in claimant advisors and fraud investigators to ensure that all those receiving benefit are actively pursuing work.

The new scheme will be administered by the Training Agency, the heir to the MSC. The employment secretary surprised both critics and supporters when he announced that the government's most effective quango would come to an end in 1988. The new Training Agency lacks the MSC's employment functions, which have been transferred to the Department of Employment, and its governing board structure has been altered to give industry representatives, some now appointed directly rather than by the CBI, effective control. The changes seem to indicate that the Thatcher government no longer feels the need to consult trade unions and wants to play down the role of the CBI in order to push forward its training reforms.

The government has also started to devote a limited amount of resources to broadening access to ET for those already in employment. The DES is expanding its PICKUP (Professional, Industrial and Commercial Updating Programme), which is now spending £12.5 million a year to help colleges, polytechnics and universities tailor their courses more closely to employers' needs. And in 1987 the MSC provided startup money for the Open College, which along with Open Tech uses open learning techniques to offer individuals and employers the chance to acquire new skills or update old ones.

Problems with Mrs Thatcher's ET policies

While Mrs Thatcher has brought about more radical and rapid changes in the ET system than any British leader in the post-war period, there are a number of reasons to doubt whether her reforms will succeed in closing the skills gap which has grown between Britain and its major competitors. Rather than detail the shortcomings of specific programmes, we will focus on two major flaws in this government's ET policy: the lack of coherence and weakness in the many initiatives designed to change the transition from school to FE or employment (reforms for the 14–18 age group) and the absence of an adult training strategy and sufficient funding to facilitate industrial restructuring.

The transition from school to work Oxford's local education authority has coined a new term: GONOT. GONOT is the name of a committee set up to coordinate GCSE, OES (Oxford Examination Syndicate), NLI (the New Learning Initiative, part of the Low-Attaining Pupils' Programme (LAPP)), OCEA (Oxford Certificate of Educational Achievement, part of the Record of Achievement Initiative) and TVEI, just some of the reforms introduced by the government since 1981 for the 14–18 age group. The need to create abbreviations for abbreviations is symptomatic of the strains which the Conservatives' scatter-shot approach to ET policy has placed on those charged with implementing the reforms. The case of TVEI provides a clear illustration of the difficulties created by this incoherence.

When TVEI was first announced one of its primary objectives was to improve staying on rates. This goal has since been deemphasized, however, because TVEI's 16–18 phase comes into direct conflict with YTS. Students have a dual incentive to opt for the narrower training option: first, because YTS offers an allowance, while TVEI does not, and second, because access to skilled jobs is increasingly limited to YTS apprenticeships. The failure of the MSC to coordinate these programmes is evident at all organizational levels, from the national, where the headquarters are based in different cities, to the local, where the coordinators of the two initiatives rarely, if ever, come into contact.

The success of individual TVEI pilot schemes is also threatened by recent national developments. Local TVEI consortia, for example, have built closer ties between schools and the FE sector to rationalize provision at 16-plus, a crucial need during a period of falling student numbers. But these consortia are in jeopardy due to the ERA's proposals for opting out, open enrolment and the removal of the larger colleges of further education from LEA control, which would foster competition rather than cooperation among institutions. Likewise, TVEI's efforts to bridge traditional subject boundaries and the divide between academic and vocational subjects are in danger of being undermined by the proposed individual subject testing in the National Curriculum and the failure to include academic examinations (GCSE and A-level) in the national *Review of Vocational Qualifications* (De Ville Report 1986, p. 4).

These contradictions stem from divisions within the Conservative Party itself. Dale (1983b) identifies five separate factions (industrial trainers, populists, privatizers, old style Tories and moral educationalists), all exercising an influence on Thatcher's ET policies. Do the Conservatives, for instance, want to spread technical and vocational subjects across the comprehensive curriculum (the TVEI strategy) or resurrect the old tripartite system's technical school track (the city technical college route)? Another conflict has emerged in the examination sphere, where modular forms of assessment pioneered under TVEI and GCSE, which are already improving student motivation and practical skills (HMI 1988), have been stifled by Conservative traditionalists, such as the minister of state at the DES, Angela Rumbold, insisting on preserving the narrow, exclusively academic focus of A-levels and university admissions (Gow 1988a, p. 1). The splits within the party were highlighted in a leaked letter from the Prime Minister's secretary to Kenneth Baker's secretary, indicating Mrs Thatcher's reservations concerning the forms of assessment proposed by the Black Committee to accompany the National Curriculum (Gow and Travis 1988, p. 1).

Emerging from this uncoordinated series of reforms appears to be a three-tiered, post-compulsory ET system (Ranson 1985, p. 63) which will not significantly raise the qualifications of those entering the work-force. At the top, higher education will continue to be confined to an academic elite, as the White Paper *Higher Education – Meeting the Challenge* (1987) projects no additional funds for HE in the next decade, despite growing evidence of graduate shortages; the middle rung of technical and vocational courses in full-time FE seems equally unlikely to expand, given that the government refuses to consider educational maintenance allowances (EMAs) and that the extension funding for TVEI appears inadequate to sustain its early successes (Dale forthcoming); the basic training route, then, will remain some version of YTS,[3] a low cost option which has not succeeded in solving the skills problem (Deakin and Pratten 1987; Jones 1988). As of May 1987, more than half of all YTS providers have failed to meet the quality standards laid down by the MSC (Leadbeater 1987). And though the quality of training may since have improved, organizations are finding it increasingly difficult to attract school leavers on to the scheme, as falling rolls lead to increased competition among employers for 16 year olds to fill low skill jobs (Jackson 1988).

Restructuring/adult training As we have shown the capacity for continuously updating the skills of the workforce is a key factor in the process of industrial restructuring, either at firm or national level. But in the rush to develop new ET initiatives for the 14–18 sector, the Conservatives have neglected the largest potential pool of trainees: adults in employment. The government has not secured sufficient extra resources from any of the three basic sources of funding for post-compulsory ET – the state, individuals or companies – to finance a major improvement in British ET performance.

The largest increase in expenditure came in the state sector; but it is crucial to examine where the money was spent. Although the MSC's budget tripled (to £2.3 billion) during the Conservatives' first two terms, only just over 10 per cent of these funds were spent on adult training, the vast majority on the long-term unemployed. Those courses, like TOPS, which did offer high quality training geared to the local labour market, have been phased out in favour of the much criticized JTS and new JTS, which offer less costly, lower skill training. This emphasis on quantity over quality was continued in the new *Training for Employment* package, which proposes to expand the number of training places still further without allocating any new resources. Mrs Thatcher's efforts to improve training within companies have been largely confined to a public relations exercise designed to increase 'national awareness' of training needs (*Training for Jobs*, White Paper, DES, 1984). Former MSC Chairman Bryan Nicholson made the government's position clear: 'The state is responsible for education until an individual reaches sixteen. From sixteen to eighteen, education and training are the joint responsibility of industry and government. But from eighteen on, training should be up to the individual and his employer' (Press Conference at People and Technology Conference, London, November 1986).

The Conservatives, however, have had little success in convincing the private sector of the need to assume its share of responsibility for training. While the MSC gradually placed a greater portion of YTS funding on employers, the bulk of the cost was still met by the state. In fact, a 1987 study revealed that private training organizations were making a profit off the MSC's training grants. The government may be regretting its decision to do away with the one legislative means of increasing employers' funding for training, as this remark made by Nicholson indicates: 'Those industries who have made little effort to keep the grand promises they made when the majority of ITBS were abolished should not be allowed to shirk forever' (Clement 1986, p. 3).

Mrs Thatcher has made somewhat more progress in her attempts to shift the ET burden on to individuals, who can fund their own ET either through direct payments (course fees, living expenses) or by accepting a lower wage in exchange for training. The state has compelled more school leavers to pay for training by removing 16 and 17 year olds from eligibility for benefits and then setting the trainee allowance at a level well below the old apprenticeship wage. It has also forced individuals staying on in full-time education to make a greater financial contribution to their own maintenance costs through the reduction of student grants, a policy which seems certain to accelerate with the introduction of student loans.

These measures, however, are not matched by policies to encourage adults to invest their time and money towards intermediate or higher level qualifications. This failure can be traced to three sources: lack of opportunity, capital and motivation. The state's assumption of the full costs of higher education (HE), among the most expensive per pupil in the world, has resulted in a strictly limited supply of places. Those individuals who wish to finance courses below HE level suffer both from limited access to capital and a tax system which, unlike most European countries, offers employees no deductions for training costs (DES 1988). But the main reason for workers' reluctance to invest in their own training is that the government has done nothing to alter the basic operation of British firms which, as we saw above, are not structured to reward improvements in skill levels.

This underinvestment in ET raises a question: if it is true that training is critical to economic restructuring and that Mrs Thatcher has failed to improve Britain's poor ET record, why has the UK grown faster than all the major industrial nations, except Japan, over the last eight years? Part of the answer lies in the Conservatives' success in creating a more efficient, low cost production and services economy. A series of supply-side measures, weakening wage councils and employment security legislation, subsidizing the creation of low wage jobs (the Young Workers' Scheme) and attacking trade unions, have improved labour mobility and company profitability. Training programmes, like YTS, have played a pivotal role in this process, providing employers with a cheap means of screening large numbers of low skilled but well socialized young workers (Chapman and Tooze 1987). The liberalization of financial markets, with the resultant pressure on firms to maximize short-term profits, and the explosion of accountancy-based management consultancy (*Business Week*, June 1988) have further reinforced industry's cost cutting approach. The irony is that while Britain is striving to compete more effectively with low cost producers such as South Korea and Singapore, these nations are investing heavily in general education and training to enable their industries to move into flexible, high technology production.

Policies for the future

This section suggests in broad terms what policies could remedy the insufficiencies of our system of education and training. It covers both those in the 16–20 age group and the (far larger) adult labour force. We take the quantitative goal to be the broad level which the Japanese, German and Swedes have achieved, namely where about 90 per cent of young people are in full-time highly structured education and training until 19 or 20. And, less precisely, that major improvements take place in the training of those already in the workforce, both by the employer and externally. Training of managers, in particular of supervisors, is treated in relation to these goals.

What type of education and training? There is broad agreement about the need to raise ET standards and levels, but less about its content. This reflects the failure of the (opposed) ET methodologies of the post-war decades: manpower planning, on the one hand, and human capital theory, on the other. Manpower planning has proved too inflexible in a world in which long-run predictions about occupational needs can seldom be made. And the rate of return calculations underlying human capital approaches to optimal training provision have foundered on the difference between social and market valuations. While both approaches have a role to play when used sensibly, few practitioners would see either as sufficient to determine the quality and quantity of ET.

Reform of education and training is seen in this section as part of the process of 'managing change'. This context argues for three general criteria as determining the content of education and training. First, the uncertainty of occupational needs in the future requires *adaptability*. Many people in the labour force will have to make significant career changes in their working lives, which will require retraining. There is some agreement that successful retraining depends on a high level of general education and also on previous vocational training. Moreover, as much training for new occupations covers skills already acquired in previous ET (e.g. computing skills), a modular approach to training is efficient.

Second, ET needs to equip workers with the skills required for *innovation in products and processes* and the *production of high quality goods and services*. One implication is that participation in higher education will have to steadily increase. And there is a more radical implication, as Hayes and others have stressed: effective innovation and quality production requires participation; that means that workers and managers should acquire not just technical competence, but also the social and managerial skills involved in working together. We may need increasingly to blur the distinction between management ET and worker ET. The implications are various: a high level of general education, sufficiently broad for young people to be both technically competent and educated in the humanities and arts; strong emphasis on projects, working together and interdisciplinary work; vocational education and training which provides management skills as well as technical understanding. More generally, ET should be designed to reduce class barriers not only as a good in itself, but also because of the requirements of innovation and high quality production.

Third, ET must be *recognizable* and *useful*, so that employers want to employ the graduates of the ET system and young people and adults want to undertake ET. There is a potential tension here with the previous paragraph. For the abilities stressed there are at present demanded only by a minority of companies. Vocational education is thus a compromise between the characteristics needed in the longer term and the skills and knowledge which companies can see as immediately useful to them. A second implication of the need for recognition and usefulness is that there be a widely agreed and understood system of certification, based on acceptable assessment.

Much policy discussion, sensibly, concerns potential improvements within the broad context of the existing framework of ET provision within the UK. As a result less thought has been given to the wider transformations which we believe the management of change and the move to a high skills equilibrium imply. The discussion of this section thus takes a longer-term perspective. There are five interdependent parts to these recommendations for reform: ET provision for the 16–20 age group; training by companies; individual access to training; the external infrastructure of ET; and the macro-economic implications of a major ET expansion.

The education and training of 16–20 year olds

The focus of this section is on how incentives, attitudes, institutions and options can be changed so that young people will choose to remain in full-time education and training until the age of 19–20, rather than entering the labour market or YTS at age 16.

For two reasons the next decade offers a window for reform which was not previously open. First, the demographic decline in the 16-plus age cohort will mean a drop of more than a quarter over the next ten years in the numbers of young people aged between 16 and 19. It will therefore be an ideal period for bringing our system into line with that of other advanced countries. For the resource cost, although considerable, of a substantial increase in the ET participation ratio of 16 to 19 year olds will be significantly less than in the past decade.

The second reason was spelt out in the last section. The institutional constraints against change are in two ways significantly weaker now than a decade or two decades ago. Unions at national level, far from seeking to frustrate change, would support it in this area; they would see it as a means of regaining membership, rather than a threat to the bargaining position of existing skilled workers. The education system (teachers, LEAs, educationalists, teachers' unions) no longer sees itself as having the right to determine education policy alone; central government has far stronger control over it than in the past, and this will increase over the next decade as opting out develops; the larger CFEs will no longer be run by LEAs; teachers' unions are moving away from the belief that they can successfully oppose government to the view that they need to cultivate wider alliances, including industry; and educationalists today are far more aware of the role which schools can play in helping children to get employment. In addition political parties are no longer constrained as they were (say) two decades ago in formulating policy in these areas.

What basic requirements are implied for a 16–20 ET system by the discussion in the introduction above? Five should be stressed:

- good general education, covering both technical subjects and the humanities;
- education designed to encourage interaction (project etc.) and reduce social class differences;

- rising percentage over time going into an HE system which makes it easier to switch between vocational and academic routes;
- structured vocational training for those not going on to HE, with acquisition of broad skills, including communications and decision making competences;
- modularization and certification.

Despite the 'window of opportunity', how feasible is the sort of major change envisaged? Aside from the question of financing, formidable problems will need to be resolved:

- Young people have the option at 16 to remain in full-time education. About 55 per cent choose not to. Raising the legal minimum school leaving age to 18 is politically not a possibility, and in any case it is desirable that young people should *choose* to stay on. How are incentives to be structured and attitudes changed to raise the staying-on rate to above 80 per cent?
- Relatively few businesses are currently capable of providing high quality training. And, while employer organizations are becoming more committed to involvement in ET, effective action on their part will require a coordinating capacity which is beyond their present power or resources.
- In comparison to other countries with well developed vocational training systems the UK lacks an effective administrative structure and a major research and development capacity.

Of these constraints, the first must be overcome. It will be argued in this section that the involvement of employers and their organizations and a proper state infrastructure will be needed to achieve both this and the ET desiderata set out above. To see why this is the case, we look first at why 16 year olds choose to leave education and training, and with this in mind examine the experience of 16–20 ET in other countries.

Why do such a large proportion of young people choose to join the labour market or YTS at 16? There are two main reasons. The first is financial. On YTS or social security young people get a small income. If they remain in full-time education they receive nothing (their parents receiving child benefit). There are therefore strong inducements to leave full-time education at 16. The demographic shrinking of the 16-plus age group (while it will make reform easier) will, in the absence of reform, strengthen the incentive to leave; this is because employers are accustomed to recruiting from this age group, directly or nowadays through YTS, since it provides relatively cheap and pliable labour, so that relative earnings at 16-plus may be expected to rise.

In the second place, staying on in full-time ET has not been seen as a bridge to stable employment. The best route to employment for most 16 year olds today is via YTS, which is used by many employers as a screening device for the choice of permanent employees. YTS trainees who show themselves to be cooperative have a high probability of securing permanent employment; and that probability will rise as the demographic decline in the 16-plus age cohort sets in.

Foreign experience can give an idea of different possible systems of 16–20 ET, as well as identifying some of the problems these alternative face.

- One country often cited as an exemplar is the US. About 75 per cent of the relevant age group graduates from high school by age 18 after a broadly based

course, more academically geared for those going on to HE, more vocational for those going directly into the labour market. Over 40 per cent go on to two-year junior colleges or university, producing a remarkably educated population. But there are problems with the education and training of those who do not go on to HE. In many areas, lack of coordinated employer involvement has meant there is no clear bridge between education and employment. The 'Boston compact', under which a group of companies guaranteed training and employment against good high school performance, acknowledged this need. And lack of involvement by companies in 16–20 ET has limited firms' provision of training for manual workers and low level white collar workers.
- France has a more highly structured system of initial vocational training. Less able children can go to vocational schools from 14–18, and end with craft level qualifications. More emphasis in the future is being placed on the various higher level vocational *baccalaureat* courses, from 16–19, which turns out technician engineers with managerial skills. Compared with the UK, both routes are impressive, especially the second. But, as in the US, there is limited employer involvement. One consequence is staying on rates at 16-plus well below the Northern European and Japanese, and a higher rate of youth unemployment. A second is limited training for manual workers in companies.
- In the Germanic (Germany, Austria, Switzerland) system, those going on to higher education spend two years from 16 to 18 in a high school before taking the *abitur*. Those working for vocational qualifications become apprenticed at 16 for three or four years and follow a highly structured, carefully monitored system of on-the-job and off-the-job training and education, with external exams on both practical and theoretical subjects.
- In the Scandinavian (Norway, Sweden) system, young people remain in the same college between 16 and 18, specializing in vocational or academic areas; vocational education is then completed in vocational centres post-18.
- Denmark has been actively experimenting with post-16 ET in the last two decades. The Danes have been moving towards a system in which all young people remain within the same educational institution between 16 and 18, more or less a tertiary college. If they choose the vocational route, they move into a two-year apprenticeship at 18, for which much work will have already been covered in the college.

Both the Germanic and Scandinavian systems succeed in attaining very high participation rates for the 16–18 age groups, and in delivering high quality vocational training as well as good general education. There are, however, arguments against both Germanic and Scandinavian systems as the optimal model for the UK, despite the fact that both systems are greatly superior to our own. The main argument against applying the Scandinavian system to the British context is that Britain lacks the infrastructure to make it work: the close involvement of employer organizations with the public system of vocational education. Moreover, in these countries there is powerful union and state pressure on companies to maintain training standards. The Germanic system also has disadvantages, in part because it would be based too strongly on employers if transplanted to the UK. There are four reasons why we should be wary of advocating a German-type division at 16 between academic education and an employer-based three- or four-year apprenticeship.

- The greater the employer involvement (unless restrained by powerful organizations and unions as in Germany), the more the apprenticeship will reflect the short-term needs of the employer. This is illustrated by the otherwise excellent EITB engineering apprenticeship scheme in the UK: broken into modules, employers select those modules most relevant to their own needs, rather than to the longer-term needs of the trainee.
- Few UK employers are in a position to run quality three- or four-year apprenticeships; but these would be needed across the board in public and private sectors, and in industry and services.
- If young people were to move into employer-based apprenticeships at 16, it would *de facto* close them off from higher education.
- Equally, by dividing the population at 16, the opportunity to reduce class distinctions would not be taken.

How, then, should 16–20 ET evolve in the future? We believe a system very roughly along Danish lines is the most feasible model to aim for, given the current UK position.

A common educational institution from 16 to 18 Apart from the Germanic countries, the US and Scandinavia, as well as Japan (more or less), have a common institution from 16 to 18. France and Denmark have both been moving towards it as a matter of conscious choice. It is an obvious vehicle for encouraging a rising percentage of young people to go on to higher education at 18. Equally it has a necessary part to play in reducing class differences. In practice, the high cost of constructing a new tertiary college system would dictate that some areas would, in the short term, provide a common offering for 16–18s through a consortium of existing institutions.

Accelerated apprenticeships post-18: the bridge to employment The Germanic and Scandinavian systems, and Japan and South Korea, provide at least four years of ET post-16. This could be done in the UK by short, highly structured apprenticeships for 18 year olds, which would at the same time build clear bridges to employment. The next section discusses how companies could develop high quality training capacities: it is evident that if they can the benefits would go beyond 16–20 ET; the need for companies in both public and private sectors to develop effective training capacities is central to the management of change.

Linking post–18 apprenticeships with pre–18 ET In order for two-year apprenticeships to be of high quality, considerable preparatory work towards them will need to have been completed pre-18. It is also important to make clear to students the link between what is expected from them in the 16–18 period and their subsequent training opportunities. Preparatory work covers both general and vocational education. The role of a good general education, covering technical subjects and the humanities, has already been stressed, as has the parallel need for vocational education to include the acquisition of broad skills including communications and decision making competences, with emphasis on developing individual initiative and teamwork through projects. Vocational education will also be focused in part on the chosen apprenticeship area. Thus, for those who choose it at 16, there will be a 'vocational' route, with specific and general requirements for particular apprenticeship areas.

Modules and certification Vocational qualifications would be awarded and HE entrance requirements satisfied by successfully completed modules. In the case of HE the modules would all be taken in the common institution; it would be natural to think of AS levels as a first step toward the modulization of HE entrance requirements. To gain a vocational qualification, and to fulfil the condition for entry to an apprenticeship, a substantial proportion of the necessary modules could and should be completed pre-16. A modular system in a single institution provides considerable flexibility. Most students would choose early on a vocational or an HE route; but if some proportion of AS modules were allowed for vocational qualification purposes and some proportion of vocational modules for entry into HE, those students who wished to do so could keep their options open for longer. Modules could thus be used to broaden HE entry requirements, and to increase the general education component in vocational qualifications. There might in addition be a case for a college graduation diploma, as in many countries, based on successful completion of modules.

Employer coordination and involvement A high degree of employer coordination and involvement will be needed to make this system work. This is the positive lesson of Northern Europe. Local coordination is necessary to link 'training' employers with educational institutions and with students. At a regional and national level, employer involvement is needed to help develop curricula, monitoring of 'trainers', assessment procedures, and so on. This will require more powerful employer organizations, nationally, sectorally and locally, than the UK has now. How this might be achieved is further discussed below.

Role of unions Many 'training' employers, especially in the public sector, are unionized, so that union cooperation will be needed. Union involvement in curriculum development and the like will also be important in balancing the power of employer organizations. This again is a lesson from the experience of Sweden and Germany.

Local and national government Government has played a key role in providing a coherent framework for the 16–20 ET system at local, regional and national level in each of the countries discussed, with the exception of the US. The UK lacks institutional coherence in this area, and has only a limited research and policy making capacity.

Education maintenance allowance and financial incentives A central purpose of the reform strategy suggested above has been to construct a clear bridge from education to employment so that young people stay within a well structured ET system from the age of 16 to 19 or 20. This is in line with the instrumental view of education taken by most young people who leave at 16 (Brown 1987). But to be successful in raising the 16-plus participation rate, it is also necessary to ensure that leaving at 16 is less attractive than staying on. This will require, first, an educational maintenance allowance for those who stay on, at least equal to state payments for those who leave. More fundamentally, it raises the question of reducing employer incentives to hire 16 year olds, and convincing them to stop seeing the 16-plus age group as its main recruiting ground for unskilled and semi-skilled labour (Ashton, Maguire and Spilsbury 1987). This is discussed in the next section.

Developing the training capacity of employers

International comparisons suggest that UK employers devote a smaller share of value-added to training expenditures than any other major advanced country. For radical reform to be successful, the attitude of employers will have to change, as has been seen in the discussion in the last section of post-16 ET and restructuring: specifically, the development by employers of a training capacity is necessary for a system of accelerated apprenticeships. This training capacity will also facilitate restructuring within organizations, by training and retraining existing employees.

In looking at restructuring, it is useful to distinguish between retraining by the existing employer, which will be referred to as internal retraining, and retraining elsewhere, primarily in state/union/employers' organization or private vocational training centres. This will be referred to as external retraining and will be discussed below. Roughly the internal/external retraining distinction corresponds to that between internal (e.g. changing product composition within a company) and external (e.g. closures/running down an industry) restructuring.

With internal restructuring companies meet declining demand through product innovation. In countries where product innovation strategies are emphasized, such strategies are associated with reliable sources of long-term finance and long-term relations with suppliers which the company does not wish to disrupt. More important, they are associated with internal training capacities in companies, a retrainable workforce with on-the-job flexibility and a high perceived cost to making workers redundant (Streeck *et al.* 1985; Sorge and Streeck 1988; Hotz-Hart 1988). The high perceived cost may arise from legal requirements, as in Germany, or collective bargaining power, as in Sweden, or from a basic communitarian view of the enterprise, as in Japan (Dore 1987). Cost reduction strategies under these circumstances will tend to focus on reducing capital or material or financing costs, rather than labour saving changes. Again, retraining capacities are critical.

In the UK much more use has been made of external restructuring. This reflects the lack of the institutional preconditions for internal restructuring present in countries such as Germany, Japan and Sweden. Instead the UK is characterized by:

- The organization of production around relatively standardized goods and services, with low skill requirements and cost cutting rather than technically competent management; aggravated by the public goods problem; and the pressure of financial institutions or in the public sector, cash limits against long-term investment activity.
- The lack of pressure from employees to maintain training; and the ease with which companies can make workers redundant without being required to consider product innovation and retraining as alternative ways of maintaining employment.
- The lack of an effective infrastructure. Few sectors of the economy have well developed training structures, with worked out systems of certification, training schools, and information and counselling for companies. Employers' organizations are weak, and unions are seldom equipped to provide good training services to their members.

The difficulties involved in increasing company expenditure on training and ensuring the training is of the right quality are thus substantial. In a longish-term perspective two general points may be made:

- The increase in the educational level of young people entering the labour force and a different attitude to adult education and training will make it easier for companies to move to a higher skills equilibrium.
- Policies to change company behaviour on training should be one part of a coordinated strategy to help companies focus on marketing, product innovation, new technology, high quality production, and provision of long-term finance. Education and training policies should be closely linked to industrial and regional policies; but to trace out these links would be beyond the scope of this paper. Four main policy directions are set out here: how they might be financed, where not implicit, is discussed below.

Financial incentives There is little question that companies in both public and private sectors need financial incentives (positive or negative) if they are significantly to increase their training activities. This is because, for the foreseeable future, there will be a divergence between private and public returns because of the public good problem and the low skills equilibrium. (The general strategy advocated in this paper is designed to reduce the divergence over time, but specific incentives will be necessary until then.)

The form of the incentives is critical. A minimum legal requirement is unlikely to be productive, at least by itself. It might take one of two forms: a requirement to spend a certain minimum percentage of value added or payroll on training; and/or a requirement to carry out certain types of training, e.g. to take so many apprentices, with a significant enough penalty to gain compliance. One problem with both approaches is that some companies may be better placed to carry out effective training than others. In addition, the minimum percentage approach (by itself) says nothing about who gets trained: in France this approach led to senior managers being sent to expensive hotels in the French Pacific to learn English. And the 'minimum number of apprentices' approach poses formidable quality problems.

A sensible way forward is to give financial incentives to companies (private and public) who are prepared to train and undergo the monitoring and other conditions necessary to ensure both quality and coverage (i.e. that training covers apprenticeships and semi-skilled workers as well as managers, etc.). The further conditions are discussed in the next paragraph. These incentives would not need to be uniform across industries, regions or types of training.

Meisters and certification How are we to ensure that companies train to the right quality and over the desired coverage? In Japan, Germany and similar countries, the role of the supervisor in both industry and services is different from the UK supervisor (see e.g. Prais and Wagner 1988). In those countries supervisors (in German, *meister*) are technically skilled as well as playing a management role; moreover they have major responsibility for training. In the German system, they have themselves to pass a rigorous training after having gained a technician or craft level qualification. The above suggests ideas along the following lines:

- A distinction should be drawn between certified skills and non-certified skills. This would be similar to the distinction between marketable and firm-specific skills. In practical terms it would reflect those that the NCVQ included as certifiable.

- Companies wishing to participate in the training of employees for certified skills would be required to employ certified 'training supervisors', i.e. similar to German *meisters*.
- The government could then negotiate with employer organizations tariffs for different certified skills, and use this as one means of influencing the size and distribution of training. Those companies would then get automatic payments for certified training, subject to periodic inspections and subject to satisfactory results of trainees in external assessment.

In summary, financial incentives should be used, not just to produce a desired amount of training, but also to ensure that companies acquire a training capacity and supervisory staff with a professional commitment to training.

Changing the age structure of hiring Specific disincentives will be needed to dissuade businesses from hiring 16–18 year olds over the next decade.

Employee representation Again, as in Northern Europe, it is sensible to give employees a role in decision making on training within companies. They have an interest in the acquisition of certified skills. For this role to be effective, decisions on training would need to be codetermined between management and employees. In addition, continental experience suggests that employee representatives need union expertise if they are to challenge low spending management with any chance of success.

In particular, it is important to enable employees to challenge management decisions on redundancies. In the German model, management is required to reach an agreement with the works council on how redundancies are to be dealt with. The cost to management of not reaching an agreement means that managers emphasize innovation and retraining in their long-term planning.

External infrastructure Both the second and third impose strong demands on an external infrastructure. Companies will in practice rely heavily on the advice of employer organizations, whom they can trust at least to give advice in the interest of the sector they represent, if not in the interest of the individual company. Employees need the advice of unions if they are to challenge company decisions on training and redundancies. Public or tripartite bodies will be required to provide R & D on training technology and labour market developments (e.g. skill shortages); to run a system of certification; and to provide training where it is needed to complement company training. How this can be done is discussed below.

A culture of lifetime education and training

There is an apparent lack of interest by adults in the UK in continuing education and training. In countries with good training systems, a strong belief by individuals in the benefits of ET reinforces the system: parents can see the value of education and training for their children; employees put pressure on laggardly employers to provide training; the public good problem which companies face is reduced by individuals paying for the acquisition of marketable skills. Yet in the UK little adult training takes place which is not paid for by the employer, this is in particular the case for unskilled and semi-skilled employees and for the unemployed. Why is human capital theory wrong in asserting that individuals will be prepared to pay for the acquisition of marketable skills? Why especially is this the case when vacancies for skilled jobs coexist with high unemployment and insecure semi-skilled employment?

In the first place, individuals seldom have access to financial resources sufficient to finance any extended period of vocational training:

- Financial institutions are reticent about lending without security for training, except for a few cases where returns from the training are high. This is not particular to UK financial institutions. Banks in most countries will not lend for ET purposes to individuals, unless the loans are guaranteed or subsidized or unless the bank has close connections and knowledge of a community. This probably reflects both moral hazard and adverse selection problems.
- There is limited access to state subsidy for most adult vocational training, particularly for maintenance, but also for tuition. Individual expenditure on training is in general not tax deductible. The unemployed likewise have limited access to funds: their retraining possibilities seldom relate to those areas in which there are vacancies.
- Major reductions in income are seldom feasible for those who are employed; *a fortiori* for those who are unemployed.

Second, the individual return from much vocational training is not high. There are several reasons for this:

- The low skills equilibrium organization of work means that the marginal productivity of skills for individual workers is below what it would be in an economy where a large enough proportion of the workforce was skilled to permit a high skills pattern of work organization.
- For a large proportion of the workforce (manual and low level white collar) this reflects the organization of work discussed. Second, differentials for skilled workers were heavily compressed in the 1970s, and though they have widened since, they are still not high in comparison to high skill countries (Prais and Wagner 1988).
- A large proportion of the workforce does not have the basic education required to proceed to craft level vocational training; so a major prior investment is necessary.
- The existing system of certification is unhelpful, as the NCVQ has emphasized. Apart from being confusing, it fails to give employers real guarantees in many areas as to the competences of the certified employee, because of the lack of proper assessment procedures. In addition, and more important, portability is limited. In the modern economy skills obsolesce. The acquisition of new skills should not involve returning to square one, as it frequently does today.
- Finally, for those who are currently employed, and wish independently to take leave to pursue education or training, there is seldom a guarantee that they will be able to keep their job.

This means that major self-financed training or retraining is not seen as a realistic possibility, if it is considered at all, by most unskilled or semi-skilled workers or those who are unemployed. Moreover, with the exceptions of a few unions who provide good counselling services, little advice is available.

In response to these problems, thought needs to be given to specific issues, such as guaranteeing employment at the end of a period of training. There are two major policy areas to which we will now turn.

A comprehensive external training system Those who seek, or might be persuaded to seek, external training fall into two categories with some overlap: people with clear goals and courses in mind, adequate previous education and training, but held back by unavailability of finance or employment insecurity; and the unskilled, semi-skilled and unemployed with little belief in the possibility of effective retraining. For both groups adequate financing is necessary. There is a strong case for formalizing a system of education credits for adults. These credits would be intended for training not covered by companies. The general question of financing is considered below, but it should be noted here that if individuals had their own 'training accounts', into which education credits were put, these credits could be added to by saving, perhaps topped up by public funding. For most people in the second group, additional financing will be necessary, since it will not be reasonable to expect them to save enough. It is of great importance that those threatened by redundancy or made redundant are given sufficient resources for long periods of ET. Along Swedish lines, a reasonable income might be conditional on, in effect, a contract to train for a given range of skills in which there are vacancies or in which employment is likely.

For this group, much more is required than financing. Counselling, an information system covering vacancies and future areas of demand, structured basic education if necessary, training and retraining facilities (though they might be in the private sector and hired by the state), and a support system to facilitate mobility are also needed. How an external retraining system might be set up is discussed in the next section.

Returns to skills This is an important problem to which there are few easy solutions. We argued above for policies to encourage the development of a supervisory grade with technical qualifications: if successful, that would help the concept of a career ladder based on skills. It is harder for the government to intervene in the process of wage determination to widen skill differentials even if there is case for doing so. In our view, the more sensible approach is to give incentives to employers to increase training, on the one hand, and to develop an external training policy to help redundant and potentially redundant workers, who have less need of incentives to acquire skills, on the other.

Institutional infrastructure

Radical reform of ET requires a more effective institutional infrastructure than presently exists. It was argued above that the old constraining infrastructure has broken down; and that the government has used this opportunity to increase centralized control via the MSC (as was) and the DES, combined with the use of contracts with training agents. The centralization of policy making has not been accompanied by a significant expansion of the very limited research and information gathering capacities of the MSC and the DES. A parallel can be drawn between this system and large conglomerates controlled by a small financially oriented headquarters. The deficiencies of the new system will become more pronounced as: (i) local education authorities have a diminished role in post-16 ET, with the removal of polytechnics and the larger CFEs from their control; with the decline in importance of TVEI; and with the possible opting out of secondary schools; (ii) the wide variety of course development, assessment and accreditation bodies are encouraged to behave more competitively; and (iii) the NCVQ becomes more a body carrying out government instructions, especially in relation to certification of YTS trainees, than a forum in which different points of view, of the business community, of unions and of educationalists and trainers can be expressed.

The new system is hardly adequate for dealing with YTS and adult training; it has major drawbacks if it is to carry through radical reform. We will argue that a different system needs to be developed in which employers' organizations, unions, educationalists and the regions should all ideally play a more important part; and in which the role of government should be more concerned with the provision of information, research and development, and coordination, than with unilateral policy making.

The need for better information, R & D and coordination The reforms discussed in the preceding subsections involve major course developments: for 16–18 year olds; for accelerated apprenticeships; for those at work; for *meisters*; for those undertaking external retraining; together with development of assessment procedures, certification and accreditation of examining bodies. It will be necessary to coordinate academic examining boards with vocational training institutions such as BTEC; and to coordinate the activities of the vocational institutions themselves. Also, it is important to allow experimentation and thus course development by individual teachers or trainers, and a mechanism is needed to permit the diffusion of best practice innovations. All this demands a much greater role of government in the R & D and coordination process. This might perhaps be on the lines of regional labour market and regional education boards in Sweden.

For two broad reasons, a more effective ET system also requires involvement by the social partners (employers' organizations and unions) as well as educational institutions and the government. The first is to ensure that policy making is conducted in a balanced way (see below). The second is to bring about the participation of companies and employees.

Multilateral participation in ET governance Running a complex ET system is a problem in principal–agent relationships. However clear the ideas of the government (the principal) and however effective its own research and development activities, the cooperation of teachers and trainers as agents is essential to efficient course development, assessment, etc. But educators will have their own interests. (Japan is a case in point, where educationalists dominate the development of 16–18 education, business has no influence, and where rote learning still plays a major role.) A tempting solution is for governments to use expert civil servants as additional agents; of course it is important that government experts should be involved, but there is a danger: if detailed policy making is left to government experts and educationalists, the former may over time assimilate the goals of the latter, particularly if governments change.

A more effective solution is to balance the interests of educators against the interests of employers and those of employees. Hence the case for involving their representatives as additional agents, to bring about more balanced objects. If this is to be successful, both employers' organizations and unions need expertise; here again Northern European experience, where the social partners have their own research institutions, in some cases financed by the state, is suggestive. Moreover, as employers' organizations and unions acquire expertise, so a common culture of understanding and agreement on a range of training issues gets built up by professionals on all sides. Thus the agents, with their different interests but shared culture, become players in a cooperative game over time in which compromise and flexibility are available to meet changing conditions. (For a broader use of this type of approach, see the insightful Lange 1987.)

A similar case can be made for involving representatives of regions in addition to central government. Individual regions will have their own economic goals, and more political stability than central government. Again, effective involvement requires expertise. This reinforces the argument for regional labour market and regional education boards.

Employers' organizations and the participation of companies Most companies see no gain in participating in training in marketable skills and associated activities to a socially optimal degree. This is both because of the standard prisoner's dilemma problem and the low skills equilibrium. As a partial solution to both problems we suggested the use of financial incentives to encourage the building up of a training capacity within companies. Important though that is by itself, its effectiveness can be greatly enhanced through employers' organizations. First, getting companies to train in the right way is difficult for government, because of an asymmetry of information: the company knows much more about how good its training is than the government. Companies are often loathe to be monitored by, or give detailed information to, government, because they distrust the use to which the information will be put. Employers' organizations are in a better position to engage the cooperation of companies, because they are seen to be on the side of companies as a whole. Second, powerful employers' organizations, as in Germany, can sanction free riders more cheaply than the government. This is the case where employers' organizations distribute a range of valued services to companies, not necessarily just in the training area; and have a degree of discretion over their distribution. One of these services may be training; others might be, say, export marketing advice. This gives the organization potential sanctions, which might enable it, for instance, to organize local coordination of companies with respect to the bridge between education and employment; or to prod companies into increasing training activities.

Employees and unions Unions have several important roles to play in an effective ET system, as mentioned above. Here we want to stress the role of unions in promoting employee involvement in training decision making. Such involvement is a critical component of high skill economies. If it is to be effective, employees must be properly backed up by union advice and expertise.

Much of the argument of this subsection is influenced by the study of why the Scandinavian and Germanic ET systems have been successful. There is an important research agenda here for the UK. We do not want to suggest the type of powerful employers' organizations or union confederations in those countries, or regional government as in Germany is transplantable; it is not. But there is a strong case for giving muscle to employers' organizations and unions, and to regions and perhaps metropolitan areas, in the training field. Unions are moving in the UK (some much faster than others) to consider training as a core area of their interests. Business organizations are moving less fast, but in the right direction. Radical reform of ET will need a push by government. One possibility, for a radical reforming government, is to give the social partners the resources to develop major expertise in training. A second is to consider whether chambers of commerce can play a more significant role at local level, so as to enable them to develop local employer networks. Third, to consider the possibilities of regional labour market and regional education boards as quadripartite institutions, with educationalists and regional representatives as well as the social partners.

Macro-economic and financing implications

The preceding four subsections have looked at the micro-aspects of policies needed for transforming the post-16 education and training system. They have suggested how to change incentives facing individuals and organizations; how coordinating and providing institutions could be built up; and how training policies should be seen as part of a broader micro-economic strategy directed at changing ways in which companies operate. If successful these changes carry great benefits in terms of macro-economic performance. But to be successful they require a major injection of resources.

In a steady state, the benefits can be assumed to outweigh the resource cost. But in the process of transforming the system, resource costs would be likely to precede the benefits of additional resources. There is not the space in this article to discuss in detail the financing of this gap. But we want to make some brief points to indicate why we believe that increased expenditures in this area can be more easily managed than in many others.

The increased resources needed for ET can be found in one or more of three ways:

- an increase in GDP;
- a reduction in other expenditures;
- an increase in imports.

There are two reasons why some part of the resource cost can be met by reduction in other expenditures. First, specific forms of taxation or quasi-taxation can be exploited with minimal economic damage.

- A training levy on companies who do not undertake certified training. It will be difficult for these companies to pass on the levy in the form of higher prices if some competitors are undertaking certified training and hence not paying the levy. And since most of the non-training companies are likely to be in the sheltered sector of the economy, any reduction in their activity levels as a result of the levy will have the beneficial effect of transferring business to training competitors.
- Individual training accounts. If individuals choose to contribute to an individual

training account, it will come from a voluntary reduction in consumers' expenditure.

Second, other government expenditures will be reduced:

- Reduction in government expenditures on YTS and other MSC related activities which would be phased out as a new system of 16–20 ET developed.
- Reduction in government expenditures on education and training post-16 as a result of demographic decline.

Thus some part of the necessary resources can be met from reduced expenditure elsewhere without relying on an increase in general taxation. The damage caused by the latter is not only political, but also, via its inflationary potential, economic. But there are limits beyond which it may be unwise or impossible to push these reductions.

This means that the resources to finance a training programme will have to come in part from increased GDP and increased imports. The point to be made here is that the standard problems associated with an expansionary policy can be more easily handled within the context of a training programme than in other cases. The first problem is that of inflation caused by the increased bargaining power of employees as employment rises. Appropriate increases in the skilled workforce can reduce inflationary pressures in two ways. Directly, it reduces skilled labour bottlenecks and the power of 'insiders' relative to outsiders. Indirectly, it facilitates wage restraint, especially if unions are involved in the training institutions.

The second problem is financing the external deficit and the public sector deficit, at least without a fall in the exchange rate or a rise in the interest rate. Avoiding these consequences requires that inflation does not increase; and that the increase in the PSBR and the external deficit are seen as eventually self-correcting. The last paragraph was concerned with inflation. A training programme can, more easily than most programmes involving increased government expenditure, be credibly seen as self-correcting in its effect on the PSBR and the external deficit.

Concluding remarks

The UK has long suffered from a low skills equilibrium in which the ET system has delivered badly educated and minimally trained 16-year-old school leavers to an economy which has been geared to operate – albeit today more efficiently – with a relatively unskilled labour force. Some companies have broken out of this equilibrium with the aid of strategic managers, who see training and innovation as core activities. Most have not.

Despite the much vaunted reforms of the ET system of the last few years, major improvements are unlikely to be brought about:

- The majority of children will still leave school at 16 and will gain a low level training in YTS; referring to the certification of YTS by the NCVQ, Jarvis and Prais argued that it would lead to 'a certificated semi-literate under-class – a section of the workforce inhibited in job-flexibility, and inhibited in the possibility of progression' (*Financial Times*, 1 July 1988, quoting Jarvis and Prais 1988).

- There are no substantive policies to remedy the vacuum in training in most companies.
- There are no measures to undertake the depth of education and training frequently needed in a rapidly restructuring world economy to enable those made redundant to acquire relevant skills.

We have argued the case for full-time education to 18, with 'accelerated' apprenticeships thereafter, for those not going on to higher education; building up training capacities within companies; and an external retraining system to deal with restructuring between companies and industries.

Instead of summarizing these proposals, we want to underline certain points which have not always been adequately brought out in discussions of reform.

- It is important to think in terms of the incentives which face individuals, rather than make the mistake of some educators of just talking about institutions or educational innovations. But equally the economist's mistake, of treating of incentives as only financial, must be avoided. We lay stress on the idea of enabling individuals to see career progressions: thus importance is attached to the bridge from education to employment for 16–20 year olds.
- Companies should be seen not as profit maximizing black boxes, but as coalitions of interests, particularly among managers. We argue that, rather than incentives being used to increase the amount of training as such, they can more effectively be used if they increase a company's training capacity, by giving companies an incentive to train or hire *meisters*, or training supervisors. This produces a stake in training as a company activity.
- Along similar lines, employees should be given a role in training decision making within the company. Here, there are lessons to be learned from industrial democracy procedures in Germany and Sweden. This reinforces the idea of groups within the company with a stake in training.
- More generally, the problem of moving companies from a low skill to a high skill equilibrium involves much more than training and education. It requires changes in management style, R & D, financing, marketing, etc., so training policy should be seen as part of a wider industrial strategy.
- Countries with successful ET systems devote substantial resources to research on education and training and labour market developments. In the UK today, policy making has become highly centralized but based on limited information and research.
- Successful countries also place great reliance on employers' organizations and unions. In the UK their role in the governance of training has been progressively reduced. If radical reform is to be successful, it will be important to build up the expertise and involvement of the social partners.

To conclude, the UK is becoming isolated among advanced industrialized countries, which have either attained or are targeting a far higher level of generalized education and training than is being considered here. This should be worrying enough in itself. What makes it more so, is the progress made by other countries with substantially lower labour costs: South Korea has currently 85 per cent in full-time education to the age of 17 or 18, and over 30 per cent in higher education (*Financial Times*, 30 June 1988).

Acknowledgements

The authors would like to thank Kay Andrews, Geoffrey Garrett, Ken Mayhew, Derek Morris, John Muellbauer and Len Schoppa for helpful comments; and to acknowledge intellectual indebtedness to Chris Hayes and Professor S. Prais. Research on comparative aspects of training was financed in part by a grant to D. Soskice from the ESRC Corporatist and Accountability Research Programme.

Notes

1 'Equilibrium' is not meant to imply that all British firms produce low quality products or services, or that all individuals are poorly educated and trained. A number of companies (often foreign-owned multinationals) have succeeded in recruiting the educational elite and offering good training programmes.
2 An excellent discussion of the differences in each of these dimensions between British and German companies is contained in Lane (1988).
3 The government announced significant changes to YTS including the abolition of the scheme's name, after the completion of this chapter.

References

The authors and editor are grateful to Oxford University Press for allowing their revised article to be reprinted from *Oxford Review of Economic Policy*, Vol. 4, No. 3, 1988.

Anderson, A. (1987). 'Adult training: private industry and the Nicholson letter' in A. Harrison and J. Gretton (eds), *Education & Training UK*, London, Policy Journals, 67–73.

Ashton, D.N., Maguire, M. & Spilsbury, M. (1987) 'Labour market segmentation and the structure of the youth labour market' in P. Brown, and D.N. Ashton (eds.), *Education, Unemployment and Labour Markets*, London, Falmer.

Brady, T. (1984). *New Technology and Skills in British Industry*, Cambridge, Science Policy Research Unit.

Brown, P. (1987). 'Schooling for inequality: ordinary kids in school and the labour market' in P. Brown and D.N. Ashton (eds), *Education, Unemployment and Labour Markets*, London, Falmer.

Business Week (1988). 'How the new math of productivity adds up', 6 June, 49–55.

Callaghan, J. (1976). Ruskin College Speech, *The Times Educational Supplement*, 22 October, 72.

Centre for Contemporary Cultural Studies (CCCS) (1981). *Unpopular Education*, London, Hutchinson.

Chapman, P. and Tooze, M. (1987). *The Youth Training Scheme in the UK*, Aldershot, Avebury.

Clegg, H. (1972). *The System of Industrial Relations in Great Britain*, Oxford, Basil Blackwell.

Clement, B. (1986). 'Industry threatened over training lapses', *Independent*, 29 November, 3.

Coopers and Lybrand Associates (1985). *A Challenge to Complacency: Changing Attitudes to Training*, MSC/NEDO, Moorfoot, Sheffield.

Crowther Commission (1959). *15–18*, Report to the DES, London, HMSO.

Dale, R. (1983a). 'The politics of education in England 1970–1983: state, capital and civil society', Open University, unpublished.

Dale, R. (1983b). 'Thatcherism and education' in J. Ahier and M. Flude (eds), *Comtemporary Education Policy*, London, Croom Helm.

Dale, R. (1985). 'The background and inception of TVEI' in R. Dale (ed.), *Education, Training and Employment*, Milton Keynes, Open University Press.

Dale, R. (forthcoming). *TVEI: From National Guidelines to Local Practice*.

Daly, A. (1984). *Education, Training and productivity in the US and Great Britain*, London, National Institute of Economic and Social Research (NIESR) No 63.

Davies, S. and Caves, R. (1987). *Britain's Productivity Gap*, Cambridge, Cambridge University Press.

Deakin, B.M. and Pratten, C.F. (1987). 'Economic effects of YTS', *Department of Employment Gazette*, 95, 491-7.

Department of Education and Science (1987). Education Reform Bill, 20 November.

Department of Education and Science (1988). *Tax Concessions for Training*, London, HMSO.

Department of Employment (DE) and Department of Education and Science (DES) (1984). *Training for Jobs*, White Paper, London, HMSO.

Department of Employment (DE) (1988). *Training for Employment*, London, HMSO No. 316, February.

De Ville, H.G. et al. (1986). *Review of Vocational Qualifications in England and Wales*, London, MSC and DES; April.

Donovan, Lord (1986). *Royal Commission on Trade Unions and Employers' Associations 1965-1968* London, HMSO.

Dore, R. (1987). *Taking Japan Seriously*, London, Athlone Press.

Fenwick, I.G.K. (1976). *The Comprehensive School 1944-1970*, London, Methuen.

Fonda, N. and Hayes, C. (1988). Education training and economic performance: positioning for turbulent times. *Oxford Review of Economic Policy*, Vol. 4, No. 3, Oxford, Oxford University Press.

Gapper, J. (1988). '£500,000 scheme to boost training in tourist sector', *Financial Times*, 17 March.

George, K.D. and Shorey, J. (1985). 'Manual workers, good jobs and structured internal labour markets', *British Journal of Industrial Relations*, 23, 3, 425-47.

Giddens, A. (1979). 'An anatomy of the British ruling class', *New Society*, 4 October, 8-10.

Gow, D. (1988a). 'Fury at A-level rejection', *Guardian*, 8 June, 1.

Gow, D. (1988b). 'Teaching shortage catastrophe feared', *Guardian*, 16 June, 4.

Gow, D. and Travis, A. (1988). 'Leak exposes Thatcher rift with Baker', *Guardian*, 10 March, 1.

Greenhalgh, C. (1988). *Employment and Structural Change: Trends and Policy Options*, Oxford, mimeo.

Hall, P. (1986). *Governing the Economy*, Oxford, Polity Press.

Harland, J. (1987) 'The TVEI experience' in D. Gleeson (ed.), *TVEI and Secondary Education*, Milton Keynes, Open University Press.

Hotz-Hart, B. (1988). 'Comparative research and new technology: modernisation in three industrial relations systems', in R. Hyman and W. Streeck (eds), *New Technology and Industrial Relations*, Oxford, Basil Blackwell.

Howell, D.A. (1980). 'The Department of Education and Science: its critics and defenders', *Educational Administration*, 9, 108-33.

Hyman, R. and Streeck, W. (eds) (1988). *New Technology and Industrial Relations*, Oxford, Basil Blackwell.

Independent (1986). 'Managers "a decade out of date" ', 11 December.

Jackson, M. (1988). 'More leavers shun youth training scheme', *Times Educational Supplement*, 19 February, 13.

Jennings, R.E. (1977). *Education and Politics: Policy-Making in Local Education Authorities*, London, Batsford.

Jones, I. (1988). 'An evaluation of YTS', *Oxford Review of Economic Policy*, Vol. 4, No. 3, Oxford, Oxford University Press.

Keep, E. (1986). *Designing the Stable Door: A Study of how the Youth Training Scheme was Planned*, Warwick Papers in Industrial Relations No 8, May.

Keep, E. (1987). *Britain's Attempts to Create a National Vocational Educational and Training System: A Review of Progress*, Warwick Papers in Industrial Relations No. 16.

Lane, C. (1988). 'Industrial change in Europe: the pursuit of flexible specialisation', *Work, Employment and Society* 2, 2, 141-68.

Lange, P. (1987). *The Institutionalisation of Concertation. International Political Economy*, WP No 26, Duke University, Unpublished.
Leadbeater, C. (1987). 'MSC criticises standard of youth training', *Financial Times*, 13 May, 1.
Locke, M. and Bloomfield, J. (1982). *Mapping and Reviewing the Pattern of 16–19 Education*, London, Schools Council.
Lynn, R. (1988). *Educational Achievement in Japan*, Basingstoke, Macmillan.
Manpower Services Commission (MSC) (1981). *A New Training Initiative, a Consultative Document*, London, HMSO.
Manpower Services Commission (MSC) (1986). *Skills Monitoring Report*, MSC Evaluation and Research Unit, Sheffield.
Maurice, M., Sellier, F. and Silvestre, J.J. (1986). *The Social Foundations of Industrial Power: A Comparison of France and West Germany*, Cambridge, MA, MIT Press.
Mayer, C. (1987). 'The assessment: financial systems and corporate investment', *Oxford Review of Economic Policy*, Winter.
Mayhew, K. (1986). 'Reforming the labour market', *Oxford Review of Economic Policy*, Summer.
McArthur, A. and McGregor, A. (1986). 'Training and economic development: national versus local perspectives', *Political Quarterly*, 57, 3, 246–55.
McCulloch, G. et al. (1985). *Technological Revolution? The Politics of School Science and Technology in England and Wales since 1945*, London, Falmer.
MacFarlane, N. (1980). *Education for 16–19 Year Olds*, report to the DES and Local Authority Associations, HMSO.
Moon, J. and Richardson, J. (1985). *Unemployment in the UK*, Aldershot, Gower.
Morton, K. (1980). *The Education Services of the TGWU*, Oxford University, Ruskin College Project Report.
National Economic Development Council (NEDO) (1978) *Engineering Craftsmen: Shortages and Related Problems*, London, NEDO.
NEDO/MSC (1984). *Competence and Competition: Training in the Federal Republic of Germany, the United States and Japan*, London, NEDO/MSC.
New, C. and Myers, A. (1986). *Managing Manufacturing Operations in the UK, 1975–85*, Brighton, Sussex University, Institute of Manpower Studies.
Nicholson, B. (1986). Press conference at 'People and Technology Conference', London, November.
OECD (1975). *Educational Development Strategy in England and Wales*, Paris, OECD.
OECD (1985). *Education and Training After Basic Schooling*, Paris, OECD.
Page, G. (1967). *The Industrial Training Act and After*, London, Andre Deutsch.
Perry, P.J.C. (1976). *The Evolution of British Manpower Policy*, London, BACIE.
Postlethwaite, N. (1988). 'English last in science', *Guardian*, 1 March.
Prais, S.J. and Wagner, K. (1983) *Schooling Standards in Britain and Germany*, London, NIESR Discussion Paper No. 60.
Prais, S.J. and Wagner, K. (1988). *Productivity and Management: The Training of Foremen in Britain and Germany* No. 12, 3 February.
Raffe, D. (1984), *Fourteen to Eighteen*, Aberdeen, Aberdeen University Press.
Rajan, A. and Pearson, R. (eds) (1986). *UK Occupational and Employment Trends*, IMS, London, Butterworths.
Ranson, S. (1985). 'Contradictions in the government of educational change', *Political Studies*, 33, 1, 56–72.
Reich, R. (1983). *The Next American Frontier*, Middlesex, Penguin.
Reid, G.L. (1980). 'The research needs of British policy-makers' in A. McIntosh, *Employment Policy in the UK and the US*, London, John Martin.
Riddell, P. (1983). *The Thatcher Government*, Oxford, Martin Robertson.
Salter, B. and Tapper, T. (1981). *Education, Politics and the State*, London, Grant McIntyre.
Scarbrough, H. (1986). 'The politics of technological change at BL', in O. Jacobi et al. (eds), *Economic Crisis, Trade Unions and the State*, London, Croom Helm.

Shirai, T. (1983). *Contemporary Industrial Relations in Japan*, Madison, University of Wisconsin Press.
Sorge, A. and Streeck, W. (1988). 'Industrial relations and technological change' in R. Hyman and W. Streeck (eds), *New Technology and Industrial Relations*, Oxford, Basil Blackwell.
Steedman, H. (1986). 'Vocational training in France and Britain: the construction industry', *NI Economic Review*, May.
Steedman, H. and Wagner, K. (1987). 'A second look at productivity, machinery and skills in Britain and Germany', *NI Economic Review*, November.
Streeck, W. (1985). 'Industrial change and industrial relations in the motor industry: an international overview', Lecture at University of Warwick, 23 October.
Streeck et al. (1985). *Industrial Relations and Technical Change in the British, Italian and German Automobile Industry*, discussion paper 85-5, Research Unit Labour Market and Employment, Wissenschaftzentrum, Berlin.
Taylor, R. (1980). *The Fifth Estate*, London, Plan.
Tipton, B. (1982). 'The quality of training and the design of work', *Industrial Relations Journal*, Spring, 27–42.
TUC Annual Reports, 1980–1986.
Walton, R.E. and Susman, G. (1987). 'People policies for the new machines', *Harvard Business Review*, Vol. 65, No. 2 March–April, 98–106.
Wiener, M. (1981). *English Culture and the Decline of the Industrial Spirit*, Cambridge, Cambridge University Press.
Wilensky, H. and Turner, L. (1987). *Democratic Corporatism and Policy Linkages*, Berkeley, CA, Institute of International Studies.
Woodall, J. (1985). *European Trade Unions and Youth Unemployment*, London, unpublished Kingston Polytechnic mimeo.
Worswick, G.D. (1985) *Education and Economic Performance*, Aldershot, Gower.

David Raffe 3

The context of the Youth Training Scheme: an analysis of its strategy and development

Overview

'So far as young people are concerned' the most significant training development since the Second World War took place with the launching of the Youth Training Scheme (YTS) in April 1983' (DES/DE 1985 p. 3). YTS owes its existence to the political opportunities created by youth unemployment and it retains unemployment-related as well as training-related objectives. This chapter investigates the tensions between these two sets of objectives.

Because YTS attempts to innovate from the bottom up, it risks entrapment in a 'vicious circle' of low status. The current YTS strategy assumes that the employment prospects of YTS trainees, and the effective dissemination of YTS and its training philosophy, both depend primarily on the content and quality of YTS training. In the second part of this chapter I argue, by contrast, that both depend primarily on the context of YTS – its relation to the structure of educational differentiation and to processes of recruitment and selection in the labour market – and very little on its content. High quality training alone is unlikely to enable YTS to break the vicious circle of low status and achieve its broader training objectives. This is likely to be achieved only through one of two strategies: either through providing specific skills, credibly certified, in demand in the local labour market; or through giving trainees privileged access to the employment networks through which employers recruit, thereby enhancing the context of YTS.

YTS is internally differentiated. In the third part of this chapter I outline a typology of four sectors, distinguished by their different labour market contexts. The development of YTS, and its success in breaking the vicious circle of low status, can be analysed in terms of the relative size and significance of the sectors; and the fourth part discusses the progress of YTS to date and its prospects in the light of recent policy developments and the changing demographic and economic environment. The chapter's main argument is that market models are inadequate to guide the development of training policy; it concludes by briefly discussing the wider application of this argument.

The context of YTS

YTS is an ambitious programme. It seeks, within a very short time, to reverse Britain's chronic inferiority in the way it prepares its young people for employment. In pursuit of the second objective of the New Training Initiative (MSC 1981a, p. 4) it aims to move Britain 'towards a position where all young people under the age of 18 have the opportunity either of continuing in full-time education or of entering training or a period of planned work experience combining work-related training and education'. This aim embraces both quantity and quality. The training effort is not to be focused merely on areas of specific skill shortage or on an elite of skilled workers: instead it reflects a (perceived) consensus 'that *all* young people entering employment need good quality basic training as a foundation for work and for further training or retraining' (MSC 1981b, p. 7, original emphasis). The emphasis is on the training needs of all young workers, and in particular on the needs arising from the fast changing, unpredictable and unreliable world of employment in which many traditional narrowly based skills are redundant. YTS, and the philosophy it represents, seek to provide transferable skills for a versatile and adaptable workforce, capable of responding to changing types, patterns and indeed levels of employment; a foundation on which subsequent more specific training inputs can more effectively build.

In addition to its training objectives, YTS also pursues a second 'unemployment-related function. The scheme has developed incrementally from a succession of special programmes, most recently the Youth Opportunities Programme (YOP), which have sought to redress or at least alleviate the problem of youth unemployment. YTS continues to provide the 'safety net' for school leavers who cannot find jobs, and its availability has been used to justify the withdrawal of benefit in 1988 from unemployed 16 and 17 year olds. YTS is not only the government's main instrument for the reform of youth training; it is also its main response to the socially and politically damaging problem of youth unemployment.

That YTS came to pursue these two objectives, concerned respectively with training and unemployment, was the end result of a particular configuration of events: the collapse of youth employment after 1979; the growing unpopularity and perceived inadequacy of YOP; the government's need to be seen to be doing something about youth unemployment, together with the inefficacy of most policy options consistent with its political priorities; the political weakness of the training lobby, and its consequent willingness to exploit the opportunities created by youth unemployment; the government's dislike of union-regulated forms of training and its wish to reduce youth wages; and the genuine desire of a wide range of people and bodies to help young people and alleviate their sufferings. All these factors led the government, the MSC, education and training interests and other groups to agree to the redefinition, in the early 1980s, of the problem of youth unemployment as a problem of education and training, and to develop a policy whose political appeal, reflected in a substantial level of support if not a consensus, lay partly in the very ambivalence of its objectives.[1]

In public debate the two objectives of YTS, to do with training and unemployment, are often assumed to be congruent. This is because much of the debate is framed by what may be termed the modified market model of training. This model accepts, on the one hand, that the supply of training needs to be stimulated by government interventions such as YTS. On the other hand, the demand for training (from young people) or for its products (from employers) is seen as less of a problem. The model assumes that trainees' employment prospects are largely determined by the content and quality of their training. If the content is appropriate and the quality high, the productive potential of YTS trainees will be enhanced, they will be more attractive to employers and they will have better employment prospects. The scheme will thus not only improve economic performance (its training objective), it will help to reduce youth unemployment, by enabling more young people to get jobs as well as by removing many under-18s from the unemployment record.

The modified market model gained influence partly because it matched the arguments of many of the scheme's original proponents. On the one hand, the supply of training was clearly deficient; something needed to be done. On the other hand, by assuming a reasonably competitive market for the products of training it was possible to claim (or at least, not energetically to deny) that the proposed scheme would reduce youth unemployment – the necessary condition for political support. The continued power of the modified market model is illustrated by the fact that it is accepted by many of the scheme's critics as well as by its supporters. In the views of the supporters, quality will out: so, in the eyes of the critics, will poor quality. Thus, just as supporters of the scheme point to employed YTS graduates as evidence of high quality training, so do critics point to unemployed YTS graduates as evidence of low quality.

The modified market model is also a model of the dissemination of YTS and of its training philosophy. The content and quality of training are seen as the key to the scheme's long-term success. If the content is appropriate and the quality is high, YTS will help young people to get jobs – and good ones. It will thereby create the market signals that encourage future cohorts of young people to enter the scheme or to enter other forms of education or training based on the YTS approach. Because the scheme will attract recruits of high calibre, employers will want to recruit through it. The future dissemination of the YTS philosophy will be assured. As the MSC's Youth Task Group wrote: 'our aim has been to design a scheme so attractive to employers and to young people that [only] a minority of young people enter jobs outside the scheme or remain unemployed rather than join the scheme' (MSC 1982, para. 48).

There are, however, at least two serious problems with the modified market model. First, it assumes that the training contributes to productive potential with respect to the individual trainee and in the short term. This assumption is questioned by recent government and MSC thinking which reflects, perhaps unwittingly, a more sociological perspective on training. This points out that the contribution of any form or content of training cannot be judged in isolation from the prevailing culture, values and organization of work and the labour market (IMS 1984). It follows that a change in training provision alone may have little effect on economic performance unless accompanied by changes in these cultural and organizational variables. The individualistic assumption at the heart of much economic (human capital) and psychological thinking about training is therefore called into question: it is possible that YTS might yield a positive long-term social return, when acting with and through broader cultural and organizational changes, but show few returns at the individual level in the short run. The returns to training, especially to universal foundation training, may therefore be collective, conditional and long-term.

The second problem with the modified market model is its assumption that employers have perfect information on the potential job performance of young people seeking employment, and can therefore discriminate in favour of those whose potential performance has been enhanced by quality training. The assumption is false. The partial closure of employment relationships, the tendency for wages to be fixed for the job, and the costs of induction and training of new workers make initial selection decisions important for employers (Sorensen and Kalleberg 1981; Thurow 1975); but it is very costly if not impossible to obtain reliable information on the potential performance 'especially' of new entrants to the workforce.[2]

Employers adopt two tactics in response to this problem. First, they use available indices and signals which offer cheap if imprecise measures of an individual's potential performance (Spence 1973). Educational credentials are important criteria in the selection of young people – and may have been made more rather than less important by high youth unemployment (Payne 1985; Roberts et al. 1987). Their value is largely unrelated to the specific content of an individual's education. Instead credentials provide a crude indicator of such personal qualities as ability, perseverance, motivation and conformity to the social and behavioural demands of (school) work, all of which are assumed to correlate with potential performance in a job. A corollary of this is that credentials tend to be used largely as a measure of an individual's position in a single dimension, the hierarchy of educational attainment, which correlates with potential performance. They tend also to be used (in effect) to measure pre-existing differences among young people more than the differences contributed by the education itself. This is particularly the case for relatively short courses such as YTS: the pre-existing variation among young people in the qualities sought by employers is likely to be far greater than the variation contributed by the course itself, particularly if, as suggested above, much of the course's effect is long-term, collective and conditional. In a hierarchically differentiated system entry to any course is likely to be correlated, positively or negatively, with the qualities which indicate potential performance. The credential awarded on the course is likely to be a much better measure of pre-existing qualities than of the net contribution of the course.

The second tactic which employers adopt is to restrict recruitment to groups for whom reliable information on potential performance can be more easily or cheaply acquired. This is one reason why employers often recruit through 'information networks' rather than through more formal channels; the networks not only restrict the availability of information about vacancies, but also supply the employer with information about potential employees. Recruitment from the internal labour market – of workers whose performance has been directly observed by the employer – is an important special case of the use of information networks (Jenkins et al. 1983), as is the use of government-funded work experience schemes such as YTS to screen and select potential recruits.

The use of credentials and information networks constitutes rational behaviour on the part of employers. Nevertheless, their effect is to create a set of market signals *to* young people which distort the modified market model of dissemination outlined above. The main influence on young people's decisions with respect to

YTS (and other options) is the perceived probability that it will lead them to desired jobs. The content or quality of the training is of little intrinsic significance; 'training for training's sake' is, after all, a contradiction in terms. Young people therefore tend to choose education or training options which transmit favourable signals to potential employers (Spence 1973) and which give them access to the information networks through which employers locate potential recruits. Both of these extrinsic criteria may vary independently of the intrinsic relevance or quality of the education or training.

Young people's decisions regarding training or education are therefore influenced by its context more than by its content. The notion of 'context' has been discussed elsewhere (Raffe 1984a); applied to YTS it refers to its articulation with structures of educational and occupational differentiation and, in particular, with selection and recruitment in the labour market. The argument that context influences individual aspirations and behaviour runs parallel to Roberts's (1981) notion of the determining influence of opportunity structures. However, the main theme of this paper concerns the implications for change and development at a macro- rather than a micro-sociological level. The long-term development and success of YTS and the training philosophy it embodies depend crucially on its context, specifically on how it articulates with processes of selection and recruitment in the labour market.

One of the main impediments to the success of YTS in these respects arises from the fact that it is attempting to innovate from the bottom up. When education performs an important screening or signalling function, and when this function is dominated by a single, vertical dimension of status, educational change tends to spread from the top downwards. Students press to join, or to emulate, those courses which carry high status; conversely, employers (and selectors in later stages of education) tend to value individuals' educational experiences largely as measures of their position in the educational hierarchy, and to favour those at the top of the hierarchy. The decisions of students and employers are mutually reinforcing. A vicious circle is created whereby employers stigmatize students on low status courses as less able, less motivated and less employable; the more able, motivated and employable students, being higher in the educational hierarchy, have more options, and avoid the low status courses; the stigmatization is thereby reinforced. Provided that access to the higher levels of the hierarchy tends to be restricted in favour of those who have pre-existing qualities more favoured by employers this pattern can stabilize independently of the curricular content of the high status and low status courses (Spence 1973). In the case of YTS, the vicious circle may apply to employers not only as potential recruiters of YTS graduates but also as potential recruiters of young people through YTS schemes: they will avoid using YTS to recruit to 'good' jobs if it does not attract recruits of the desired calibre.[3] The vicious circle is intensified at a political level if the low status courses are perceived as unsuccessful by virtue of their unpopularity and the low employment rates of their former students. This phenomenon has already been observed with respect to YOP, to mode B schemes on one-year YTS, and to premium places on the two-year scheme.

It is here that the unemployment and training functions of YTS come into conflict (see also Ryan 1984). YTS was introduced as a direct successor to YOP, a low status and in parts remedially oriented scheme designed to enhance the 'employability' of young people. Moreover, YTS must focus a substantial part of its energies on the unemployed, since it is committed to providing places for 16- and 17-year-old school leavers who remain out of work. YTS therefore risks being stigmatized as a scheme for the less able, the less motivated and above all the less employable, and thereby being sucked into the vicious circle of low status described above. Were this to happen, it would not succeed in its aim of spreading its training philosophy across the whole age group. Even if the scarcity of jobs drove many school leavers into the scheme, it would still be perceived as a second best, it would be avoided by students further up the educational hierarchy for whom there remained educational or employment alternatives, its curriculum and philosophy would be perceived as of low status and would not be emulated, and the scheme would be perceived as a failure and lose political and consequently financial support. Conversely, if jobs became more plentiful, the scheme would shrink; it would be deserted by school leavers and also by employers who would need to offer 'real' jobs to attract good young recruits. These consequences would follow regardless of the scheme's possible contribution to the long-term economic or social regeneration of Britain.

Consistent with the modified market model, the MSC's current strategy rests primarily upon improvements in quality (MSC 1985).

> Hardened sceptics in the education and training fields are beginning to believe that the Manpower Services Commission is really determined to see that the new two-year version of the Youth Training Scheme is a genuine high quality training programme ... Both the Commission's chairman, Mr Bryan Nicholson, and Mr Geoffrey Holland, its director, are saying at every possible opportunity that the scheme must give overriding priority to quality, without which it will fail ... 'If the two-year YTS fails then we are at the end of the road. There will be nowhere else to go' [said Geoffrey Holland].
>
> (*TES*, 13 September 1985)

It is unlikely that YTS can escape the vicious circle of low status merely by improving the quality of training. The general problem is that the vicious circle arises from the context of YTS, not its content, and that quality improvements alone cannot transform this context. At least five obstacles may be mentioned. First, the strategy presupposes a demand for the skills produced by the training. But employers remain sceptical of the value of the kind of 'foundation' training provided by YTS (Chapman and Tooze 1985; Bevan and Hutt 1985; Roberts *et al.* 1987); and as for more specific occupational skills, most of those provided by YTS are not in short supply in most labour markets (Deakin and Pratten 1987). Experienced adults will retain their competitive advantage as well as their entrenched positions. Second, to the extent that the returns to YTS training are (as suggested above) collective, conditional and long-term, YTS will not enhance the potential job performance of individual trainees under present conditions and in the short term. To this extent YTS training will not make its trainees more attractive to an individual employer with short-term horizons. Third, YTS must not only enhance potential performance but provide a credible certificate or other means of persuading an employer that it has done so for a given trainee. There are considerable problems in devising any reliable form of assessment for the domains covered by YTS, let alone one that has credibility with more sceptically minded employers (SCOVO 1982). Given the reluctance of employers to take risks in recruiting, it is unlikely that the mere knowledge that YTS is often effective will offset the perceived risk involved in taking on a trainee from a low status scheme. Fourth, to the extent that the YTS curriculum continues to emphasize foundation skills the stigmatization of the scheme will be reinforced, given the recent history and organization of training in Britain. Foundation or non-specific training is still associated with low skilled jobs (for which no specific skills can be identified), with provision for the unemployed (for whom job-specific training may be inappropriate) and with courses for those judged incapable of learning specific skills. The emphasis on foundation training therefore serves to reinforce the vicious circle of low status. Fifth, to break this circle YTS must not only enhance the potential performance of young people but do so to such an extent that the pre-existing disadvantages of young people entering the scheme – who are drawn from the bottom of the educational hierarchy – are outweighed, and seen to be outweighed. YTS must be so effective that it more than compensates for the combined effects of the genetic, social and educational disadvantages of its low status entrants. Given the existing state of knowledge about skill transfer or how to train for it (Annett and Sparrow 1985) this is unrealistic.

There are, it seems, two ways by which YTS might hope to break the vicious circle. Both are likely to apply, at least in the first instance, to particular schemes or places rather than to YTS as a whole. The first is to provide occupationally specific skills in demand in the local labour market and to certify these in a way that retains the confidence of potential employers – relying either on recognized vocational certificates or on the reputation of the scheme provider. The scarcity value of the skills might then outweigh the effects of the low status of trainees in the minds of potential employers; and in time the more favourable context would attract higher status entrants to the schemes concerned.

The second strategy is to enhance the context of YTS by giving its trainees favoured access to the information networks through which employers recruit. Here the emphasis is not on whether YTS enhances young people's employability in the eyes of a potential employer, but on whether it gives them a better chance of being considered by an employer in the first place. Information networks are defined broadly here (as above) to embrace the recruitment of trainees by managing agents or work experience providers. An important limiting case is where an employer guarantees employment to trainees when they enter YTS – although from the trainee's point of view this might be little different from entering an ordinary job.

Differentiation within YTS

I have suggested that these two strategies are likely to apply, at least in the first instance, to particular schemes or places rather than to YTS as a whole. However the analysis has so far only examined YTS in the aggregate. Schemes and scheme places vary enormously, particularly with respect to their attractiveness to young people; this variation reflects differences in context, that is, different modes of articulation with recruitment and selection in the labour market and consequent differences in access to desired employment opportunities (Lee *et al*. 1987; Roberts *et al*. 1987).

YTS trainees who find jobs may do so in any of five ways. They may:

- be kept on by their scheme employer as a result of commitments made when they entered the scheme;
- be kept on, but not as a result of any prior commitment;
- find jobs elsewhere, because of marketable skills acquired on YTS;
- find jobs elsewhere, through information networks to which they gained access on YTS; or
- find jobs elsewhere for reasons unrelated to YTS.

YTS places vary according to which of these processes is most likely to lead their trainees to jobs. There is no precise one-to-one correspondence of scheme places to job finding processes. The following typology of scheme places, based on these processes, is primarily a heuristic device to illustrate the implications of differentiation within YTS for the scheme's impact and development. The second and fourth of the job finding processes listed above are both contained within the notion of 'information networks' discussed earlier. With these two combined the five processes point to four sectors within YTS. These are summarized in Table 3.1.

Young people entering the *sponsorship sector* either have employed status from the start of their YTS training or have a guarantee, or a very strong prospect, of a permanent job at the end of it. This sector includes long-term traineeships brought within the scheme, typically apprenticeships in construction and engineering. Other YTS places in the sponsorship sector may provide no training progression after YTS but nevertheless offer progression into employment with the managing agent, so that young people joining them know they will be retained. The sponsorship sector has several distinctive features. Young people entering it are likely to stay on their schemes for their full duration; there is no employment-linked incentive to leave early. Because trainees are expected to find employment in the jobs for which they are trained, and with the employers who have been primarily responsible for their training, the content of the training is likely to emphasize both occupationally specific and employer-specific skills. Above all, trainees in the sponsorship sector are relatively sheltered from the pressures of the external labour market: once selected to their schemes, sponsorship trainees are assured of employment subject only to minimal levels of performance. The crucial selection occurs on entry to the schemes, which thereafter perform no significant screening function. For this reason, and because many of the jobs concerned require lengthy training, the initial selection criteria tend to be stringent. Young people in sponsorship places, especially long-term trainees, are the most likely to have employed status or to have their YTS allowance topped up by employers. This may partly reflect trade union pressure (Randall 1986); but it also reflects the desire of employers to attract high calibre entrants to the skilled jobs concerned.

Young people entering the *credentialling sector* of YTS do not themselves expect to find employment with their scheme employers, but their prospects of employment are good. Their YTS training provides them with occupationally specific skills and experiences that are in demand in the local labour market and certifies them in a

Table 3.1 YTS sectors

	Sponsorship	Credentialling	Contest	Detached
Expected progression	Job with YTS employer	Job through external labour market: marketable skill	Compete for job with YTS employer or for access to external information networks	Unrelated to YTS
Progression depends on	Minimum level of performance on YTS	Adequate performance	'Good' performance plus 'luck' (opening available at right time, etc.)	Largely unrelated to performance on YTS
Relation to pressures of labour market competition	Sheltered	Exposed but advantaged; competition external to YTS	Exposed; competition brought within YTS	Exposed; competition external to YTS
Relation of training to future job	Occupationally and company-specific 'skills'	Occupationally specific 'skills'	Often slight: general or company-specific 'skills'	Often slight: general 'skills'
Inducement to complete scheme?	Yes	Yes	No	No
Bias of recruitment	Males, well qualified	Females, fairly well qualified	Females	Low qualified, labour market disadvantaged
Screening function	Minimal	May be implicit in concept of skill: blurred borderline with contest sector	Dominant: emphasis on motivation, personal qualities	Minimal

way that is credible to potential employers. Like the sponsorship sector, the credentialling sector offers an incentive to complete the scheme and tends to focus on occupationally specific skills which are expected to be used directly in subsequent employment. It therefore presupposes the existence of occupational labour markets (Marsden 1986) in the relevant skills. Unlike the sponsorship sector its trainees are not sheltered from labour market pressures, although their competitive position in the market is enhanced by YTS. A theoretically and practically important feature of the credentialling sector is that, unlike the other sectors, its articulation with labour market selection and recruitment practices – and thus the job chances of its trainees – are directly related to the quality and content of the training. But quality and content are necessary but not sufficient conditions. They must also be certified in a way that is credible to employers; given the initial low status of YTS the source of credibility may need to be external to YTS, such as the reputation of the managing agent or a recognized occupational qualification. The skills must also be in local demand. In principle, the credentialling sector of YTS performs no screening function, except through the certification of skills acquired on the schemes. In practice many schemes or places which appear to belong in the credentialling sector might more appropriately be classified in the contest sector, described below, as their main contribution to the trainee is to offer privileged access to employment information networks: the main benefit derived from the scheme is not the skill itself but the managing agent's willingness to confirm that the trainee has the personal characteristics required in the job. (Many 'skill shortages' reported by employers may in fact reflect perceived deficiencies in the personal qualities of applicants rather than in their skills (Ashton and Maguire 1986).) The number of places in the true credentialling sector may be very small, particularly in local labour markets where few if any of the skills to be obtained through YTS are scarce.

Young people enter the *contest sector* in the knowledge that their YTS experience might help them find employment but that nothing is certain. Such help might take one of two main forms. First, many employers use YTS to screen potential recruits; their trainees cannot therefore be guaranteed employment when they enter YTS, since this depends on their performance on the scheme. Even if recruitment is not a main reason for running a scheme, the availability of tried and tested workers, familiar with a firm's practices, may make YTS a suitable source of recruits should vacancies occur. Subcontracted work experience providers, many of them small firms, make particular use of YTS as a source of recruitment. Second, schemes may give access to the information networks through which jobs elsewhere can be found; this may come about either casually or through a deliberate effort to find jobs for a scheme's trainees. Young people are thus screened for employment with employers not directly involved in the schemes (Knasel and Watts 1987). Trainees in the contest sector are the most exposed to the pressures of the labour market; not only do they enter YTS with no guarantee of future employment, but the competition for jobs is brought into the YTS schemes, whose dominant function is a screening one. The content of the training is not central to this screening process and may not be closely related to a trainee's future employment; motivation and personal qualities, as revealed by performance on the job, are typically the main criteria for selection. So is 'luck': trainees in the contest sector are particularly vulnerable to chance factors which influence the probability of vacancies occurring in sufficient numbers and at the right time and place; this unpredictability for the trainee is the corollary of the flexibility which attracts many employers to recruit through the contest sector. There may be little inducement to complete the scheme; many young people finding employment through the contest sector of YTS are likely to leave their scheme early, particularly if the jobs are found with external employers or with work experience providers who are only responsible for part of the scheme.

Finally, the *detached sector* is so called to indicate its detachment from the processes of selection and recruitment in the labour market. Young people entering this sector have a negligible chance of being kept on by their YTS employer or of being given privileged access to information networks. The sector includes several mode B places under one-year YTS and premium places under the two-year scheme. It also includes many places on schemes which are set up largely as an expression of social responsibility by the employer and kept separate from the firm's ordinary recruitment. However, there may still be a chance that such trainees might be recruited by their YTS employer or gain access through YTS to external information networks. It may be more appropriate to regard the detached sector as one extreme of the continuum of YTS places which makes up the contest sector. The detached sector lies at the least attractive end of the YTS hierarchy, but unemployed young people may still improve their job prospects by entering it: at the very least they probably avoid the worse stigmatization that continued unemployment would involve. Attending any YTS scheme may be seen by an employer as evidence of motivation or of willingness to do something to avoid unemployment. Although trainees in the detached sector of YTS are, like their counterparts in the contest sector, at the mercy of labour market competition, this competition is external to their schemes: trainees' performance on the scheme will have relatively little effect on their employment chances. The detached sector provides the safety net for YTS: it recruits young people who are unable to enter the more sought after sectors, all of which may impose entrance criteria of varying stringency, and its trainees are therefore less qualified and less 'employable' than those in other sectors.

The sectors comprise a hierarchy closely related to the hierarchy within education and to the employment prospects of trainees. However the sectors are not unidimensional. They are ideal types, in which several dimensions of variation – such as employment chances, exposure to the external labour market, screening functions – are combined. The higher status sectors are likely to lead to the more skilled and more sought after jobs, partly because these jobs are more likely to require the occupationally specific training input associated with the sponsorship and credentialling sectors, and partly because employers recruiting to these jobs wish to attract the most employable (or trainable) school leavers and therefore recruit through the YTS sectors most likely to attract such school leavers. The hierarchy of sectors tends to be correlated with the 'employability' of recruits as indicated by qualification levels and local labour market conditions (high unemployment areas have proportionately more YTS places in the low status sectors). Males predominate in the sponsorship sector and females in the credentialling and contest sectors.

The context of YTS places – that is, the sector they belong to – may influence the orientations of trainees and the effectiveness of training. Young people's orientations to their YTS training may well depend on such factors as the extent to which trainees are sheltered from the pressures of labour market competition; their perceived chances of employment; the perceived probability that subsequent employment will be related to the occupational content of the training; the extent to which employment chances are affected by skill acquisition on the scheme (that is by the content of the training), the extent to which employment chances are related to trainees' behaviour and performance on the scheme; and whether trainees expect to complete the scheme or search for jobs in the expectation of leaving early if successful (see also Knasel and Watts 1987). Thus trainees' orientations towards YTS, and consequently the quality and effectiveness of the learning experience, may vary across sectors, irrespective of the quality or content of the training input.

This poses problems for the evaluation of YTS schemes. On the one hand completion rates and job placement rates are increasingly used to evaluate the success of training schemes, for example those run by the proposed training and enterprise councils (DE 1988 p. 42). But these outcomes tend to reflect the sector (labour market context) within which scheme places are located much more than the quality or relevance of the scheme's content. The highest quality training on YTS may often be found on schemes with the least favourable context, where the pressures to distort the YTS curriculum are least strong (Roberts et al. 1987). It might therefore seem appropriate to discount the influence of context when evaluating the quality of schemes. On the other hand this context, by influencing trainees' orientations, may itself influence the effectiveness of a given training input. At the very least any evaluation of the training provided on YTS schemes must try, as far as possible, to separate the respective influences of the content of the training (the quality and relevance of the curriculum, work experience, pedagogy, and so on) and of the context in which it is provided.

The internal differentiation of YTS also has implications for the scheme's position in the machinery for occupational selection. A majority of young people entering the labour market directly from school now go through YTS, and they are in various ways screened, sorted and certificated by the scheme. This is sometimes seen to herald a new structure of opportunity, in which traditional criteria for selection in the labour market cease to apply. Qualifications played a less important role in determining the employment chances of young people screened by YOP (Raffe 1984a), and the same is likely to be true for YTS. The scheme allows employers to observe young people's performance on the job so that other criteria of selection such as qualifications, gender or race need no longer be used. However, the argument is only valid to the extent that initial selection to YTS sectors is not based on these criteria; for a young person's opportunity to demonstrate good performance on the job, and the type of job involved, will vary widely across sectors and places. The major occupational selection, in other words, will continue to be made at 16 rather than 17 or 18, and concerns the YTS sector to which young people have access.

The development of YTS

Over its first four years YTS appeared to consolidate its position in the labour market. In January 1984, in its first year, 25 per cent of 16 year olds in Britain were on the scheme. Two years later this figure had risen to 27 per cent, and it remained at that level in January 1987, in the first year of the two-year scheme (DE 1987, p. 460). These figures are 'snapshots' and underestimate the total proportion of 16 year olds who ever went on YTS. Over the same period the status of YTS, as measured by the relative school qualification levels of its entrants, increased slowly but steadily. YTS trainees still tended to have lower qualifications than 16-year-old entrants to 'ordinary' jobs, but the gap was slowly narrowing (Raffe 1988). The two-year YTS, with its improvements in length and quality, its more rigorous demands on employers, and its extension of certification opportunities seemed set to enhance its status and acceptability still further.

However two external factors may have interrupted this picture of slow but steady consolidation. First, the labour market has begun to recover, if slowly and unevenly. As in previous cycles the youth labour market has recovered faster than the general labour market (Raffe 1987), and its recovery is encouraged by the demographic decline among the age group (NEDO 1988). This confronts YTS with its most critical test. Has it escaped the 'vicious circle of low status' sufficiently to prevent school leavers deserting it for the jobs that are more readily available, or employers from abandoning it on the grounds that it no longer attracts recruits of the required calibre? The early evidence suggests that it has not. Between 1986–87 and 1987–88 the number of new entrants fell from 360,000 to 327,600, more than demographic trends alone would account for.[4] The decline was steepest in the more prosperous south-east where the impact of economic recovery was greatest. YTS has always been skewed towards areas of higher unemployment, but the skew has become more pronounced. Several employers, especially in the south-east but including some national companies, notably in retailing, have left YTS (Finn 1988).

The second external factor is the removal of benefit entitlement from most unemployed 16 and 17 year olds. While this has helped to stem the decline in entrants to YTS – temporarily disguising the underlying decline – it has also threatened the status of the scheme by reinforcing its function, and its image, as a scheme for the unemployed. Moreover it has increased the geographical skew of YTS towards areas of higher unemployment.

However the transition to a two-year scheme, the recovery of the labour market and the changing benefit entitlements may also intensify the differentiation within YTS. More than ever it is necessary to discuss the development of YTS, not in aggregate, but in terms of the four sectors described earlier.

The sectors correspond to the two strategies, discussed above, by which YTS might hope to break the vicious circle of low status and achieve its broader objectives. These are, respectively, through providing occupationally specific skills, credibly certified, in demand in the local labour market, and through giving its trainees privileged access to the information networks through which employers recruit. The first strategy corresponds to an expansion of the credentialling sector; the second corresponds to an expansion of the sponsorship and contest sectors, and to an upward move within the continuum that comprises the contest sector.

An analysis of one-year YTS estimated that only 11 per cent of trainees found full-time jobs in the external labour market on the strength of the 'content' of YTS (Raffe 1989a). Even this figure probably exaggerates the scale of the credentialling sector, for reasons discussed above. A much larger proportion, 39 per cent, found jobs on the strength of the context of YTS; most of these were kept on by YTS

The context of the Youth Training Scheme

employers but some found jobs externally, for example helped by YTS to gain access to informal recruitment networks. This suggests that one-year YTS mainly pursued the second strategy, of enhancing the relative importance of its sponsorship and contest sectors, and upgrading the contest sectors.

The introduction of two-year YTS further encouraged this trend. The permanence of the scheme encouraged more employers to build it into their regular training and recruitment arrangements. The longer commitment entailed by the two-year scheme, and the effort involved in obtaining approved training organization status, discouraged some employers from participating *unless* they saw a clear tie in with their own recruitment and training. This trend will intensify if the government's belief that 'the time has now come for employers progressively to assume a fuller share of the costs of YTS' (DE 1988, p. 47) is reflected in future funding arrangements for the scheme. Moreover, the funding arrangements for two-year YTS discourage employers from offering detached or lower status contest places: it is harder to recruit trainees to such places, and harder to keep them on the schemes once recruited, so sponsors risk having unfilled and therefore unfunded places.

Economic and demographic trends have had two main effects on the relative scale of the contest and (especially) the sponsorship sectors. On the one hand in areas where it is difficult to recruit 'good' young workers employers need to enhance the status of their YTS places, often by offering employed status within YTS. The proportion of employed status places within YTS has increased rapidly since 1986, especially in the south-east. On the other hand, if employers have to offer real jobs and wages to attract young trainees (as employed status YTS entails) they may feel that the bureaucratic restrictions of YTS, and especially the loss of freedom to train to their own specifications, is no longer justified; another effect of economic and demographic trends is for places in the contest and sponsorship sectors to be lost to YTS. Which of these two effects proves stronger in the long term remains to be seen.

At the other end of the spectrum the detached sector of YTS is also growing. It is the sector most affected by the influx of socially and educationally disadvantaged young people who fail to find jobs in a strongly (and perhaps increasingly) selective labour market (Roberts *et al*. 1987) but are now denied the alternative of supplementary benefit. As a result YTS is becoming increasingly polarized and differentiation within the scheme is assuming a spatial as well as a social dimension.

One problem for YTS is that the bottom end of this increasingly polarized hierarchy is likely to remain the most visible part of the scheme. Many employees on YTS are unaware that they are even on the scheme, and schemes which seek to attract high calibre recruits do not emphasize their YTS connection. The signals emitted by YTS are still largely negative. This is reflected in the failure of attitudes to the scheme to 'improve' to any great extent among successive year groups of young people (Raffe 1989b).

But what of the first strategy for raising the status of YTS – through providing occupationally specific skills, credibly certified, in demand in the local labour market? This would be reflected in an expansion of the credentialling sector which, as mentioned above, was a relatively unimportant sector of one-year YTS. At face value the two-year YTS would appear to give this sector a substantial boost. It increases the emphasis on occupational skills, it offers all its trainees the chance to gain recognized qualifications, and the competences they attest will be those specified by 'industry' itself. At the time of writing it is too early to seek evidence of the effect of these changes on the credentialling sector, but it is doubtful whether the credentialling sector can ever become a very large part of YTS. Some of the reasons for this were discussed above. For example, even if 'industry' specifies the competences to be certified, the credible certification of the assessment of these competences will remain a problem, particularly given employers' scepticism about the 'transferable' elements of the training and the continuing stigmatization of YTS trainees as low status. Perhaps most importantly, the size of the true credentialling sector, and thus the effect of the extension of certification on the context of YTS, will be restricted by the market for skills. Even if all trainees are offered a formal opportunity to obtain marketable qualifications, surplus skills will be devalued by the market itself. Most of the occupational skills obtainable through YTS are not in short supply in most labour markets (Deakin and Pratten 1987); those in short supply tend to be the skills traditionally acquired through apprenticeships, which tend to be incorporated within the sponsorship rather than the credentialling sector of YTS. There may be a need for the broader based skills which YTS aims to develop, but this need tends not to be recognized by employers or communicated through the market.

Part of the problem is that the demand for skills may not necessarily reflect the long-term need for them. This is partly because, as described above, the returns to training are often collective, conditional and long-term, and therefore not experienced by an individual employer in the short term; and partly because British employers tend not to recognize or value the more general and transferable skills that YTS is supposed to provide. Moreover, the British youth labour market is simply not geared to recruiting young people with skills gained in pre-entry education or training courses. With a few exceptions, it prefers to provide its own skills on the job, or to buy them in the form of experienced workers trained elsewhere (Raffe 1988).

For these reasons, although economic recovery may increase the demand for skills and therefore the size of the credentialling sector, this effect is likely to be limited; there is unlikely to be a major growth in the demand for the kinds of skills which YTS mainly provides. One implication of the continued small size of the credentialling sector is that the modified market model of training, whose assumptions only hold (if at all) in respect of this sector, will continue to be a poor guide to the development of youth training.

Alternatives: beyond the modified market model

In this paper I have argued that market forces will not ensure the development of YTS or the success of its wider training objectives. Even the modified market model, which acknowledges the need for intervention on the supply side, is inadequate. And the recent White Paper's proposal that 'employers should progressively take over from Government the ownership and development of youth training' (DE 1988, p. 47) threatens to reinforce, rather than challenge, the market distortions outlined above.

I have argued from the perspective of YTS, and judged its prospects in terms of its claim to be 'first and last a training scheme' (DE 1981, p. 9) rather than a social or educational measure. But the argument can, and should, be applied more widely. For just as market forces will not provide for optimal developments within YTS, even on purely economic criteria, neither will they bring about the best balance between YTS and alternative forms of education and training for 16–18 year olds. We need something more than a policy of letting the market decide. The lack of the necessary strategic thinking is embodied in the competition between YTS and the Technical and Vocational Education Initiative (TVEI). Both run by the Training Agency (formerly the MSC), their aims and objectives are at least superficially similar. But they represent very different principles of delivery, and they compete for 16–18 year olds, The current evidence is that YTS is winning this competition, on balance, not because its content is more valid on either economic or educational grounds, but because it has the more favourable context. Not only does it give young people an allowance and at least a surrogate 'worker' status, but its higher status schemes offer favoured access to recruitment networks that TVEI cannot match (Bell et al. 1988). This distorting effect of context may particularly affect well qualified 16 year olds, marginal leavers who might most easily be persuaded to stay on at school, but who are also most likely to find places in the sponsorship sector of YTS and enjoy the favourable context they provide. Ironically the formal egalitarianism of TVEI has often hindered its ability to appeal to these relatively advantaged young people, in comparison with the highly differentiated YTS. A further irony is that these are precisely the young people whose continuation in full-time education is so often seen as desirable on purely economic grounds.

The argument can be taken one step further. Debates about education and training for 16–18 year olds are often premised, if implicitly, on the assumption that economic and labour market objectives conflict with social and educational ones. This assumption is shared by many conservatives, liberals and radicals, even if their practical conclusions differ. I have sought to show that the demands of the labour market are not necessarily the same as its needs, particularly if the latter are understood in a more long-term and societal sense. Although the demands of the labour market may conflict with social and educational values, this may not be true of its needs. I have described the strong pressures towards internal differentiation and selectivity within YTS. These pressures originate from the operations – and thus the demands – of the labour market. But the long-term needs of the labour market may be for a more general, longer and less differentiated system of education for this age group (Weir 1988).

The context of education and training must be recognized as a legitimate target of policy – to be shaped in a way that removes its distortions or remoulds and redirects them to encourage desired developments within the education system. It must not be made the arbiter of policy through a misguided wish to leave decisions to the market.

Notes

An earlier and longer version of this chapter was published in the *British Journal of Education and Work,* Vol 1, No 1, 1987. It is reproduced by kind permission of the publishers, Trentham Books Limited (revised January 1989).

1 A more detailed account of the political and economic events leading to the establishment of YTS is provided by Raffe (1984b).
2 It matters little to the present argument whether 'potential performance' is understood to refer to potential (marginal) productivity in an individualistic, human capital sense, to the relative training costs for the individual (Thurow 1985) or to the set of traits, skills, knowledge and dispositions (including 'conformity') which employers seek in their recruits. An individual's potential performance may vary across jobs, although there is an underlying dimension. The important assumption in the present argument is that potential performance cannot be measured cheaply and reliably and that indices and signals, notably credentials, are used as proxy measures.
3 See Roberts *et al.* (1987) and Dutton (1986). This stigmatization is reflected in the tendency for some managing agents to disguise the fact that the training places on offer are part of YTS. In some promotional literature for a recent CITB scheme, the words 'youth', 'training' and 'scheme' all appear, but nowhere in that combination.
4 Figures from *Youth Training News,* September 1987 and November 1988. The *Employment Gazette* shows a steeper decline, from 372,577 to 316,249 (Table 9.1, May 1987 and May 1988).

References

Annett, J. and Sparrow, J. (1985). *Transfer of Learning and Training,* Research and Development Series No 23, Sheffield, Manpower Services Commission.
Ashton, D.N. and Maguire, M.J. (1986). *Young Adults in the Labour Market,* Research Paper No 55, London, Department of Employment.
Bell, C., Howieson, C., King, K. and Raffe, D. (1988). *Liaisons Dangereuses? Education-Industry Relationships in the First Scottish TVEI Pilot Projects,* Sheffield, Training Agency.
Bevan, S. and Hutt, R. (1985). *Company Perspectives on the Youth Training Scheme,* IMS Report No 104, University of Sussex, Institute for Manpower Studies.
Chapman, P.G. and Tooze, M. (1985). *Youth Training in Scotland: A Review of Progress,* Dundee University, Department of Economics.
Deakin, B.M. and Pratten, C.F. (1987). 'Economic effects of YTS', *Employment Gazette,* October, 491–7.
Department of Education and Science (DES) and Department of Employment (DE) (1985). *Education and Training for Young People,* Cmnd 9482, London, HMSO.
Department of Employment (DE) (1981). *A New Training Initiative: A Programme for Action,* Cmnd 8455. London, HMSO.
Department of Employment (DE) (1987). 'Education and labour market status of young people', *Employment Gazette,* September, 459–64.
Department of Employment (DE) (1988). *Employment for the 1990s,* Cm 540, London, HMSO.
Dutton, P.A. (1986). *Engineering Apprenticeship and YTS in Coventry,* University of Warwick, Institute for Employment Research.
Finn, D. (1988). 'Why train school-leavers?', *Unemployment Bulletin,* 28, 1–8.
Institute for Manpower Studies (IMS) (1984). *Competence and Competition,* London, MSC/NEDO.
Jenkins, R., Bryman, A., Ford, J., Keil, T. and Beardsworth, A. (1983). 'Information in the labour market: the impact of recession', *Sociology,* 17, 260–7.
Knasel, E.G. and Watts, A.G. (1987). 'Timing of selection within the Youth Training Scheme', *British Journal of Education and Work,* 1, 91–102.
Lee, D., Marsden, D., Hardey, M., Rickman, P. and Masters, K. (1987). 'Youth training life

chances and orientations to work: a case study of the Youth Training Scheme' in P. Brown and D.N. Ashton (eds), *Education, Unemployment and Labour Markets*, Lewes Falmer.
Manpower Services Commission (MSC) (1981a). *A New Training Initiative: A Consultative Document*, London, MSC.
Manpower Services Commission (MSC) (1981b). *A New Training Initiative: An Agenda for Action*, London, MSC.
Manpower Services Commission (MSC) (1982). *Youth Task Group Report*, Sheffield, MSC.
Manpower Services Commission (MSC) (1985). *Development of the Youth Training Scheme*, Sheffield, MSC.
Marsden, D. (1986). *The End of Economic Man?* Brighton, Wheatsheaf.
National Economic Development Office (NEDO) (1988). *Young People and the Labour Market: A Challenge for the 1990s*, London, NEDO and Training Commission.
Payne, J. (1985). 'Changes in the youth labour market, 1974-1981', *Oxford Review of Education*, 11.
Raffe, D. (ed.) (1984a). *Fourteen to Eighteen*, Aberdeen, Aberdeen University Press.
Raffe, D. (1984b). 'Youth unemployment and the MSC: 1977-1983', in D. McCrone (ed.), *Scottish Government Yearbook 1984*, Edinburgh, Unit for the Study of Government in Scotland.
Raffe, D. (1987). 'Youth unemployment in the UK: 1979-1984', in P. Brown and D.N. Ashton (eds), *Education, Unemployment and Labour Markets*, Lewes, Falmer Press.
Raffe, D. (1988). 'Going with the grain: youth training in transition', in S. Brown and R. Wake (eds), *Education in Transition*, Edinburgh, Scottish Council for Research in Education.
Raffe, D. (1989a). 'The transition from school to YTS: content, context and the external labour market'. Paper submitted to Annual Conference of British Sociological Association, Plymouth.
Raffe, D. (1989b). 'Longitudinal and historical change in young people's attitudes to the Youth Training Scheme.' *British Educational Research Journal*, 15.
Randall, C. (1986). *Manpower: Serving Whose Interests?*, Bath, Centre for a Working World.
Roberts, K. (1981). 'The sociology of work entry and occupational choice', in A.G. Watts, D.E. Super and J.M. Kidd (eds), *Career Development in Britain*, Cambridge, CRAC/Hobsons.
Roberts, K., Dench, S. and Richardson, D. (1987). *The Changing Structure of Youth Labour Markets*, Research Paper No 59, London, Department of Employment.
Ryan, P. (1984). 'The New Training Initiative after two years' *Lloyds Bank Review*, April, 31-45.
Scottish Vocational Preparation Unit (SCOVO) (1982). *Assessment in Youth Training: Made to Measure?* Glasgow, Jordanhill College.
Sorensen, A.B. and Kalleberg, A.L. (1981). 'A theory of the matching of persons to jobs', in I. Berg (ed.), *Sociological Perspectives on Labor Markets*, New York, Academic Press.
Spence, M. (1973). 'Job market signaling'. *Quarterly Journal of Economics*, 87, 355-74.
Thurow, L. (1985). *Generating Inequality*, New York, Basic Books.
Weir, A.D. (1988). *Education and Vocation: 14-18*, Edinburgh, Scottish Academic Press.

Ken Roberts, Sally Dench and Deborah Richardson

Youth labour market processes, outcomes and policies

The stress points

During the 1970s youth unemployment became one of Britain's headline issues and it remained so throughout the early 1980s. At that time the shortage of well qualified young people to train for higher level occupations attracted far less attention. Yet better qualified school leavers remained in demand, even in parts of Britain with well above average unemployment. Our 1984 surveys of employers in Chelmsford, Liverpool and Walsall found that the majority of those seeking recruits with five O-levels or better were experiencing problems, though few were broadcasting their difficulties. The employers expected less sympathy than the young unemployed. Unfilled vacancies were not always being notified to the statutory agencies. In any case, nearly all the employers felt able to cope, at least temporarily.

During the second half of the 1980s Britain's shortage of well qualified entrants to the labour market has surfaced as a public issue. Official reports have begun publicizing this problem (NEDO 1988). The new demographic trend – the contraction of school leaving cohorts by approximately a quarter between 1984 and 1985 – seems to be turning some firms' difficulties into a crisis. Banks, insurance companies, the health and education services, and high technology manufacturers are all wondering how they will possibly cope. It seems remarkable that they should be facing such apparently intractable difficulties after a decade of successive initiatives intended to enlarge and strengthen Britain's system of vocational preparation. After all, the Technical and Vocational Education Initiative (TVEI), the Certificate of Pre-Vocational Education (CPVE), the General Certificate of Secondary Education (GCSE), and the creation of the National Council for Vocational Qualifications (NCVQ) were supposed to increase the proportion and the size of the pool of young people suitable for further training. The Youth Training Scheme (YTS) was supposed to offer generic training and transferable skills to all 16-year-old school leavers.

During the late 1980s youth unemployment seems to have disappeared from Britain's agenda of urgent problems. This is partly because joblessness among 16 and 17 year olds has declined alongside the introduction of sufficient courses and schemes to accommodate the entire age group. During 1988 the 'residual' youth unemployment problem was abolished by legislative fiat and virtually all members of this age group lost their entitlement to register even if they were neither in employment, training nor education. We no longer even count the numbers of 16 and 17 year olds who are unemployed. They have become officially invisible. Actually the bulk of Britain's earlier youth unemployment problem has now been transferred to the 18–25 age group. Their unemployment may have ceased to be news, but in many parts of the country their rates of joblessness are still above 20 per cent despite almost a decade of steady economic growth. Many of the 1980s' school leavers have discovered that Britain's new transitional arrangements have operated only as temporary refuges from unemployment. Despite the succession of measures starting with Job Creation Projects (JCPs) in 1975, from which a Work Experience Programme (WEP) for 16–18 year olds was detached in 1976, which was replaced by the larger Youth Opportunities Programme (YOP) in 1978, which was superseded by the still larger one-year YTS in 1983, which became a two-year scheme in 1986, unemployment is still the main threat facing less qualified school and scheme leavers in *most* parts of the country.

Our mid-1980s' research into the changing structure of Britain's youth labour markets identified two major stress points. One was being experienced by less qualified young people and the other by employers who were seeking the better qualified. The main descriptive findings from this study have been published elsewhere (Roberts *et al*. 1987). The fieldwork consisted of interview surveys during 1984 and 1985 among quota samples of 308 firms in Chelmsford, Liverpool and Walsall, and random samples totalling 854 17–18 year olds from these same areas who had completed full-time education and entered the local labour markets. The results of this research explain how on–going economic, technological and occupational changes have been creating and deepening the stress points identified above. These stresses would probably have arisen even if general unemployment in the UK had remained low, and had there been no regional imbalances. In addition, the findings explain how and why the educational and training initiatives then in operation, which have since been extended but not replaced, have been shaped by, instead of curing, the stresses.

Demand for well qualified young people to train for technician, management and professional careers was relatively strong in all three areas. Such school leavers could expect training, within or outside the YTS, leading to progressive and relatively well paid employment. Others were literally surplus to economic requirements. Even in Chelmsford, where just 8 per cent overall were unemployed when interviewed (compared with 28 per cent in Walsall and 41 per cent in Liverpool), the rate for males who had left school with no qualifications was 43 per cent. For less qualified young people in all three areas, though even more so in Walsall and Liverpool than in Chelmsford, the YTS was often proving only a temporary alternative to unemployment. Moreover, the jobs for which these young people were eligible were deteriorating in quality. Many ports of entry once open to the less qualified had closed. Craft apprentice training was declining. Large firms that once offered modest careers in internal labour markets even to unskilled staff were generally contracting and not recruiting, or were submerged by experienced adult applicants whenever jobs became available. Firms still hiring young people to non-skilled jobs had often remained in youth labour markets mainly because of the ease with which cheap and dispensable teenagers could be hired. Polarization was evident in Chelmsford, Walsall and Liverpool, though whether it was due mainly to the growth of opportunities at the top, or to a collapse at the bottom, varied from place to place.

Throughout the 1980s the government retained faith in market forces restoring equilibrium between labour supply and demand. Its main initiatives to promote youth training and employment – the YTS, the Young Workers' Scheme (YWS) and its successor, the New Workers' Scheme (NWS) – were designed to work with and through rather than to override the market. In particular, government measures were intended to reinforce employers' demands. So the YTS became an employer-led scheme. Industry wanted financial support, but resisted the degree of external regulation that West German employers accept, without equivalent subsidies, in their apprenticeship system (Raggatt 1988). Our evidence explains exactly why these initiatives have proved inadequate, and indicates the additional measures that are needed to rebuild school leavers' transitions and to resolve firms' skill shortages and training problems.

Market signals and responses

Our research was spread across three areas partly to illustrate how national trends can have different consequences in different regions, and also to permit analysis of the interaction between supply and demand within local youth labour markets. Whatever the original sources – loss of customers, technological change, occupational restructuring or regional decline – there is a body of economic theory which explains how imbalances between supply and demand should be corrected by labour market mechanisms, provided the actors signal their difficulties, and are able to read and prepared to respond to market forces. It is argued that employers who are short of well qualified applicants, who indicate their requirements by raising starting salaries and publicizing the immediate and longer-term rewards on offer, can expect to attract a larger share from the pool of potentially suitable labour. High starting pay and bright career prospects should entice recruits from areas where equally rewarding jobs are less plentiful. Employers could make migration more attractive with resettlement allowances or assistance with housing. An alternative would be for firms to relocate or transfer some business to sites where qualified labour was more abundant. Employers who were still unable to attract enough labour with the preferred qualifications could redesign jobs or post-entry training so as to accommodate recruits who would formerly have been considered unsuitable. The YTS was originally intended to assist firms to make this kind of adjustment.

The generally less qualified young people who cannot find jobs have been expected to play their parts in the labour market. Indeed, the solution to Britain's youth labour market imbalances has been seen as depending on young people being educated to realism in their expectations and demands. If they will accept lower pay, then, it has been argued, this will enable firms to reduce costs and selling prices, to widen their markets then create more jobs. Lower wages could tilt the balance in favour of youth labour against experienced staff and new technology, and could enable employers to provide more training so as to bring otherwise substandard recruits up to the firms' requirements. Cheap labour might operate as a magnet drawing firms into otherwise declining regions. The YWS and NWS have been intended to reinforce the YTS and market forces in producing solutions to youth unemployment via the pay mechanism. If they wished to avoid low paid solutions, unemployed school leavers might consider migration to areas where jobs were more plentiful. They might also consider upgrading themselves, and making their labour more attractive to potential employers by acquiring skills and qualifications in demand. On encountering market realities, or earlier if they received prior warning from friends, families or in careers education, young people at risk of unemployment have been expected to see the wisdom in working harder and remaining at school or college to earn useful credentials. School leavers without jobs have been expected to see the sense of joining the YTS, obtaining work experience, basic skills and vocational qualifications so as to strengthen their likelihood of impressing employers. The YTS, the TVEI and the CPVE were promoted to enable young people to respond to market forces in just these ways.

Are young people adequately prepared?

Making youth labour markets operate more effectively has generally been seen as requiring measures to make young people more aware of and responsive to market forces. However, our evidence suggests that the 1980s' school leavers have been generally well aware of, and have been prepared to be flexible in the face of labour market realities. The spread of unemployment in the late 1970s and early 1980s was accompanied by a battery of criticism, much of it aimed at school leavers. They were accused of entertaining exaggerated ideas of their immediate value to employers, of lacking entrepreneurial qualities and of a reluctance to acquire skills that firms required. They were accused of ignorance of the rewards on offer to the suitably motivated and qualified, especially in manufacturing industries. Some were criticized for 'opting' for unemployment.

Most of the 17–18 year olds that we interviewed were guiltless. They displayed all the attitudes that would have been expected of 'human capitalists'. On reaching age 16, the main consideration that had led to most decisions to stay on or to leave full-time education was the likely vocational returns. Approximately a third of the Chelmsford sample, and two-thirds in Liverpool and Walsall, had entered the workforce via the YTS. Only 6 per cent of all respondents had chosen to remain continuously unemployed despite Britain's youth guarantee of a place. Individuals who were otherwise unable to find employment were generally only too willing to have their skills and market value upgraded. Trainees' most frequent criticisms of the YTS were not objections to the principle of training but to schemes that had led nowhere.

A small minority of the young people, approximately 10 per cent of the unemployed in our samples, were drifting apathetically, apparently reconciled to joblessness. Some of these had deliberately avoided the YTS. However, the vast majority of unemployed respondents were anything but happy with the predicament. Most were YTS products, not refusers, and were actively seeking work when interviewed. Of the unemployed 86 per cent were visiting the statutory services and most of them were using additional job search methods simultaneously.

No school leaver can possibly be equipped with complete information about his or her local labour market – accurate knowledge of every job and scheme on offer, the immediate remuneration and the longer-term rewards. Knowledge is filtered selectively by teachers, careers officers and through informal networks. Many school leavers are uncertain of their own preferences. Approximately a fifth of our respondents seemed never to have possessed any definite ambitions, while the aspirations of the remainder varied in their specificity and flexibility. Young people's uncertainty and ignorance have been defined as problems to be treated. It might seem that if school leavers were more certain of their own capabilities and preferences, and of the available employment, then out of school youth would behave more rationally and labour markets would operate more effectively. Hence the alleged importance of careers work preparing school leavers to make occupational choices.

This thinking may sound reasonable, but it is incorrect. Market mechanisms will operate provided young people's *collective* knowledge is comprehensive and accurate, and the plain fact is that British school leavers' aspirations have been, and remain generally realistic. Every investigation throughout the history of research in the field has pointed to this same conclusion. According to our evidence, this state of affairs has remained unchanged in the 1980s. Collectively our samples had left school with accurate and adequate information about the awaiting labour market conditions. The young people were aware of their risks of unemployment, the value of qualifications, and what the YTS might offer. Some expressed blanket approval or disapproval, but the majority realized that schemes differed, and that some, but not all, were likely to lead directly to employment.

Young people's often imprecise and flexible aspirations do not obstruct labour market mechanisms. These mechanisms would stall if every school leaver had precise and rigid aims. Our samples had been willing to compromise. Their wage demands were not inflexible. Of those unemployed 61 per cent when interviewed were prepared to take jobs paying less than £40 per week. It was not the young people's insistence on high earnings that was preventing youth rates floating downwards in the local labour markets that we investigated. Overall, the school leavers' aspirations modestly overshot and did not precisely mirror the proportions of jobs at different levels in their home areas; but this incongruence was not obstructing the market. After all, individuals need not remain forever in their home areas or at the levels where they first enter the occupational structure. Respondents who were unemployed or dissatisfied with jobs that fell short of their aspirations were not held back by ignorance or lack of motivation. Rather, their problem was the employers' unwillingness to recognize and respond to the qualifications, training and experience that were within the young people's immediate reach.

Demand-side rigidity

It was the employers, not the young people, who were proving relatively inflexible in the face of labour market pressures. The former were neither ignorant of labour market conditions nor, in most cases, tradition bound. Rather, those who were short of well qualified applicants were reluctant to lower entry thresholds because they believed that good O-levels were their only reliable indicators of who would succeed on technician and professional courses, then prove capable of applying the knowledge in changing work environments. Overhauling induction and training in ways that might have accommodated the less qualified and talented would have required broader changes in management styles and working practices, and training was rarely accorded such priority to let it dictate other aspects of business. Short-term survival seemed to depend on giving priority to customers' immediate requirements, technological innovations, plus changes in tax and other government regulations. Only a minority of employers saw any benefit in reducing their youth rates of pay to local market levels because, however cheap beginners became, the firms could see no way of absorbing additional numbers, given their existing work practices.

The different ways in which firms were using the YTS (Roberts *et al.* 1986) and their equally selective responses to the YWS, meant that the government measures in operation were reflecting rather than reducing the stresses that were polarizing the local youth labour markets. Whether employers were using these measures and, if so, how, depended primarily on the compatibility between the schemes' incentives and the firms' normal recruitment and training practices. Firms that were predisposed to hire cheap teenage labour were using the YWS while other employers ignored the subsidy. Few employers were prepared to reconsider and possibly change their ways merely because the government had introduced yet another scheme.

At the time of our fieldwork certain segments of the local youth labour markets were being recasualized. The dead ends and bind alleys that became infamous before World War 2 were being re-created. The starkest examples were youth training schemes where employers derived some benefit from their labour before trainees were discarded. These were closely followed by low wage jobs, often subsidized under the YWS, that young people were expected if not required to leave once they had outgrown the subsidies. For some young people, mainly the better qualified, the YTS was leading to extended careers in primary segments of firms' workforces. Other young people's training was leading nowhere. Sixteen year olds who had chosen to remain unemployed three months after leaving school had proved as successful in establishing themselves in the workforce by the time of our interviews, another 15–21 months later, as those who entered the YTS but were not retained by the firms where they were based or placed. The YTS was becoming a dual scheme, and the main stratifying processes were external, not internal to the training. As Raffe (1986) has argued, 'context' tends to override 'content' in determining youth training outcomes. Subsequent prospects depend less on the character of whatever on- and off-the-job training young people receive than the state of their surrounding labour markets, particularly the level of unemployment, the links between schemes and firms' own recruitment and training, and the qualities with which trainees enter the scheme, especially their school leaving qualifications.

Locked out

Low paid youth jobs that could never make satisfactory long-term occupations are not new; but in times of full employment these jobs enabled beginners to acquire the experience that then strengthened their chances of proceeding to better things. Young adults become eligible for a wider range of jobs, some involving shift hours, driving, alcohol and other features that exclude teenagers. However, at the time of our fieldwork many out-of-school young people were being denied the experience that employers could demand when recruiting to jobs where the terms and conditions attracted adult applicants. All firms were questioned on the qualities sought when recruiting 19–25 year olds. When filling skilled vacancies most employers expected applicants to have completed full apprentice training or to possess exceptional qualifications. According to our evidence, ascent to skilled status usually still needs to begin very early in working life. When filling office and unskilled manual jobs, the firms looked for 'relevant experience' rather than specific training and skills. The latter could always be offered and learnt in the new companies. Above all, the employers were impressed by stability in applicants' job histories. Employment records showing career progression were especially favoured. The employers did not expect individuals to have remained in low paid jobs for years; but neither did they want personnel who had leapt frequently and haphazardly from job to job.

We asked how a history of unemployment affected young adults' chances when applying for work. Only 10 per cent of the employers gave blanket negative responses. Twenty-eight per cent claimed to be especially sympathetic towards unemployed applicants. Sixty-two per cent said that being unemployed made absolutely no difference. However, the employers' sympathy and tolerance were usually conditional. Short spells out of work may not have diminished applicants' credibility, but long-term unemployment tended to be viewed differently: 'those unemployed for over six months obviously lack motivation'. Many employers took account of whether the unemployed had brought the condition upon themselves unnecessarily by quitting jobs or earning the sack. 'We treat them as normal if they've been made redundant, but it's different if they've been dismissed.'

At the time of our interviews 37 per cent of the Liverpool 17–18 year olds and 25 per cent in Walsall were still awaiting their first jobs. Most of these were products of the YTS. Their local youth labour markets were denying these respondents the experience to meet employers' requirements for stepping into adult occupations. Throughout the late 1970s and early 1980s, unemployment was lower among the over-25s than in younger age groups, but individuals then in their late 20s began their working lives when jobs were relatively plentiful. We cannot assume that the 1980s' school leavers will be equally successful, eventually, in establishing themselves in adult employment.

Now the fact that 17–18 year olds are not already settled in jobs consistent with their aspirations need not be a calamity. Even episodes of unemployment may not prove long-term disasters. The cause for concern in our findings is not that so many respondents had been unable to fulfil their goals with their first steps, but that they had been unable even to discover pathways towards eventual adult employment. Many victims of polarization felt locked out, apparently for ever. Possible routes out via education, training, low wage stopgaps, self-employment and migration were proving either non-existent or blind alleys.

Returning to education

Just 30 of our 854 respondents had left school or college and entered the labour market, then returned to full-time education sometime afterwards. Every 16 year old in Britain has the nominal option of continuing in, or returning to education. Colleges and most sixth forms will nowadays accommodate virtually all comers. Staying on or returning to education to obtain better qualifications may appear obvious remedies for 16 year olds who are unable to progress in their local labour markets. So why were the majority of unemployed respondents, and those whose jobs offered no prospects, not seizing their educational opportunities? Some wanted to avoid any further contact with formal education. School had turned them off. However, even those who were acutely disappointed with their lack of progress since leaving school and who had seriously considered returning to education had mostly decided against. Grants were not automatically available. Parents were not always able and willing to finance the teenagers' pursuit of further qualifications. Moreover, the vocational returns were uncertain. We found that staying on for an extra year to earn additional qualifications had strengthened the chances of those respondents, mostly females, who were aiming for office jobs. In contrast, individuals seeking craft apprenticeships, technician or professional training were likely to have found any additional qualifications devalued by the extra time spent earning them. For young adults who had failed to cross the 'good O-level' threshold at 16-plus, the returns from further qualifications were uncertain and sometimes non-existent, unless they were already in careers where educational credentials would assist at promotion hurdles.

Migration

Moving to another part of Britain could have improved many Liverpool and Walsall respondents' propsects. Unemployment was lower, and qualifications were earning better vocational returns in Chelmsford, and presumably in other relatively buoyant areas. Many Liverpool and Walsall respondents were aware that migration could widen their opportunities, and only a minority were so attached to their home districts that any employment had to be local. Two-thirds of all respondents said that they would move for the 'right job', and 34 per cent had 'seriously considered' migration. However, only 9 per cent had taken any active steps such as visiting or making written applications for work in other areas. Even these had realized that they would be unable to afford independent accommodation. Education, employment and training for Britain's 16–18 year olds operate on the assumption that the individuals will have family support. Not a single firm in our employers survey was offering resettlement allowances or assistance with housing to the 16–18s. The one company that once ran a hostel had closed it some years earlier in a cost cutting drive. Nor was any firm considering relocation to where youth labour was more plentiful. Location was often treated as fixed, and decisions on where multi-site companies would expand were more responsive to the state of other markets – for their products, and for skilled and experienced adult labour.

Self-employment

Twenty respondents had branched into self-employment without the assistance of the enterprise allowances which were available only from age 18. Some young entrepreneurs felt unjustly excluded and argued that 16 and 17 year olds who were keen to set up on their own accounts deserved official support. The self-employed respondents were not all thriving. Four had given up by the time of our interviews. The enterprises of another two had not progressed beyond the part-time stage. One of these individuals, a part-time cabinet maker, was officially unemployed, but the remainder, those whose businesses were reasonably secure, were among the most satisfied and optimistic members of our entire sample. Many were keen to spread the news and argued for the careers service to orient more young people towards creating their own, instead of searching for ready made jobs. In practice, however, nearly all the successful self-employed respondents had other advantages apart from their own enterprise. Of the 20 examples 10 were in Chelmsford, the area with the most buoyant local economy. Few of the self-employed owed anything to educational qualifications, or to skills and knowledge acquired at school or college. They owed far more to family and other social contacts. Several had simply been absorbed within family businesses but were classed as self-employed. Others had been set up in separate enterprises that were affiliated to their parents' businesses. Some had branched out in partnership, or with advice and support from friends, neighbours or relatives. Only two respondents had started businesses entirely on their own independent initiative – a free-lance photographer and a secretary. They had gone independent with skills acquired very early in working life.

Polarization

The above discussion has concentrated on the 17–18 year olds who were locked out because they are everyone's main problem group; but the concentration would be misleading if allowed to convey an impression of our enquiry having uncovered an all round deterioration in young people's opportunities. For everyone who was disadvantaged, others were advantaged by their educational attainments, places of residence and youth training schemes that had led to progressive careers in which the individuals were keen to settle. School leavers' prospects were not generally deteriorating but polarizing. There were more opportunities for some young people, generally the better qualified, particularly if they lived in areas well stocked with service sector and high technology manufacturing employment, to launch into careers leading towards primary segments of the occupational structure. Meanwhile, other young people were quickly finding themselves locked out, sidetracked into blind alley training schemes and youth jobs, or excluded from all employment.

Since our fieldwork in 1984–85, Britain's youth labour markets will have changed, not least because government measures for assisting beginning workers have been overhauled. In 1986 the YTS was extended from 12 to 24 months. When our 17–18 year olds, the fifth-form classes of 1983, entered the labour market, the Young Workers' Scheme (YWS) applied to 16 year olds and, in effect, competed against the YTS. The YWS was subsequently transferred to 17 year olds, thus creating the option of an end on relationship with youth training. In 1986 this scheme was phased out alongside the advent of the two-year YTS, but a new job subsidy scheme for 18–20 year olds, the New Workers' Scheme (NWS), was launched simultaneously. These measures will have altered the opportunities awaiting school leavers; but they are unlikely to have changed the manner in which, at the time of our fieldwork, government interventions were being shaped by prevailing trends and rigidities, and were reflecting rather than ameliorating the twin stress points in youth labour markets thereby contributing to the polarization of young people's prospects.

These comments are not meant to imply that all the policies and provisions operating at the time of our fieldwork were irrelevant or mischievous. Quite the reverse: our evidence suggests that all Britain's recent initiatives would have proved necessary, at least desirable, even in the absence of the spread of general unemployment and regional imbalances. A youth training initiative would probably have proved necessary, given employers' inability to satisfy old and new skill requirements by recruiting the types of young people customarily sought, then training them in the traditional ways. So would a job subsidy scheme to check the decline in demand for less qualified school leavers. The fact that the wage mechanism was being overwhelmed by the sheer scale of unemployment, especially in Liverpool and Walsall at the time of our fieldwork, is no reason for ignoring the costs of hiring beginners. The case for educational initiatives to align courses and qualification with changes in technology and job requirements would have been as persuasive even if full employment had been maintained in all parts of Britain. The persistence of the stresses identified in our fieldwork is a case for complementing rather than abandoning existing measures.

Regenerating employment

The persistence of high general unemployment and even higher levels among young adults, especially in areas such as Liverpool and Walsall, but also in pockets even within generally buoyant districts as among unqualified males in Chelmsford, seems certain to strengthen arguments not so much for faster economic growth as for direct job creating public spending. There can be no question that regions such as Merseyside and the West Midlands need more jobs, given their current populations. Unemployment among young adults in these areas is likely to remain high whatever education and training they receive unless the general quantitative imbalances between labour supply and demand are remedied.

However, our evidence casts doubts on whether efforts to re-create the demand for youth labour of the 1960s and 1970s will resolve young people's transition problems in the 1990s. Economic growth alone, whatever the pace, will not necessarily revive demand for less qualified school leavers. If most of the overall growth in labour demand is for part-time or temporary employees, as was the case between 1981 and 1988, or in the higher occupational grades, the young people currently at greatest risk of unemployment are unlikely to benefit directly. Creating jobs specifically for less qualified unemployed young people could exacerbate the problems associated with too many blind alleys and insufficient primary employment. Experience in the 1980s has undermined assumptions that if only young people are better educated and trained, jobs will automatically follow. Assuming that the jobs generated by economic growth will be filled by currently unemployed young adults is equally unrealistic.

Vocational preparation

Our findings suggest that the current stresses in youth labour markets will not be relieved solely by quantitative changes, but only by making each side, especially employers, more responsive to the other. Efforts to improve the efficiency of youth labour markets up to now have concentrated on the supply side – on making young people more aware of market realities and offering education and training to enable beginners to meet employers' requirements. The evidence that our samples of young people were generally aware of labour market realities, and were keen to use any old or new opportunities to enhance their employability, could be interpreted as signs that existing efforts were succeeding. The obstacles that were continuing to prevent the young people adapting to demand were not rooted in their own motivations and aspirations but in their environments; the issues for the 1990s concern how these barriers can be removed.

Our samples of young people were being thwarted by a qualification barrier. GCE O-levels, the most prestigious public examinations at 16-plus, evolved from an educational tradition designed to reserve success to a minority. Economic trends that demand parallel educational reforms have been acknowledged for over a generation. Despite this, secondary school curricula remain geared to standards that only a minority can achieve. These curricula and examinations have now entered a period of flux. A new 16-plus examination, the GCSE, replaced CSEs and O-levels in 1988. New courses have been developed under the TVEI and for the CPVE. Vocational qualifications are being systematized. The two-year YTS has created more opportunities for young people to continue in part-time education, working towards academic and vocational qualifications while in training or employment. The impact of all these changes in youth labour markets is likely to hinge on whether employers can be persuaded to treat other qualifications as alternatives to, rather than inferior to those GCSE results that are considered equivalent to grades A–C at O-level.

Some obstacles to young people meeting employers' requirements arise within education, others from their family and ethnic backgrounds, and gender divisions. Redrafting secondary school curricula, redefining standards of success and creating new qualifications are of little value when young people are held back by social class, racial and gender barriers. Our enquiries found all these old predictors of success and failure in sound working order. The case for greater equality of opportunity extends far beyond improving labour market efficiency. Social justice and harmony alone, especially in multiracial inner cities, justify steps to reduce the hold of ethnic and family origins on young people's prospects. New courses and qualifications alone will not necessarily raise standards among the young people currently at the tail of the educational procession. This tail end clearly needs to be drawn in. Otherwise, as our Chelmsford evidence indicates, these young people are in danger of being rendered vocationally obsolete.

School leavers' prospects still depend on their social origins as well as their educational opportunities, and also on where they live. Successive regional policies have failed to redress inequalities between the relatively prosperous south and most provinces, though these policies may have prevented wider imbalances. It is obviously difficult to persuade employers to relocate, whereas our surveys found that most of the young people would have been willing to migrate if there were worthwhile jobs at the destinations. The main barrier to migration was the sheer impracticality of resettlement on youth wages, training allowances or social security. There are mechanisms to facilitate uprooting and resettling young people who proceed through full-time higher education. Is there now a case for extending similar provisions, like housing and resettlement allowances for those whose training or employment do not permit them to remain home-based, to the remainder of the age group at 18-plus?

Employers

Britain's youth labour market problem has been generally seen as requiring new measures to mould young people to fit employers' requirements. Prime Minister Callaghan's 1976 Ruskin speech (*TES*, 22 October) struck a chord. It harmonized with earlier thinking that had defined work entry problems in terms of ensuring that school leavers were adequately prepared but modified the definition of adequate preparation. Hence the subsequent search for solutions to a 'youth' problem. This entire set of questions and the attempted solutions have been as much blind alleys as some young people's opportunities. The structure of these opportunities, of labour-demand, not supply, has always been the main determinant of school leavers' trajectories, and this structure is the real crux of their current problems. The key issue is this: how can employers be persuaded to offer enough jobs with the right training to enable the British economy to benefit from new technologies, and from young people's abilities and aspirations, then compete in international markets?

Most of the obstacles to supply and demand balancing in our local youth markets were on the demand side, in employers' practices. Training was still restricted to specific age groups in most firms. Boys and girls respectively were expected to apply for men's and women's jobs. The same 'good qualifications' were being demanded for entry to jobs with training to technician status or higher even when firms were desperately short of such applicants. Beginning workers were still being divided into separate castes – those given just basic inductions, then others who were trained in specific crafts, office skills, or for professional, management and technician careers. Few firms were responding to the opportunities presented by market forces to reduce wage costs, then discover new uses for less qualified school leavers. The YTS was originally intended to erode some of these rigidities, especially the divisions between different grades of beginning workers. Training for all was to dissolve the division between future skilled workers and the rest.

Generic training in transferable skills was to undermine demarcations between formerly separate trades. At the time of our fieldwork these radical aims were being smothered by existing patterns of work organization.

Earlier attempts to modernize Britain's vocational training met a similar fate. In 1945 there were hopes of treating all beginners as trainees and making continuing education universal (Ministry of Labour and National Service 1945). In practice, however, apprentice training was revived only in traditionally skilled occupations. The 1964 Industrial Training Act led to the creation of Industrial Training Boards with levies and grants to induce firms to align their quantity and quality of training with each industry's projected skill requirements. This new regime was initially hailed as a revolution (Williams 1969), but in the event most firms either welcomed the grants for, or resented the levies and bureaucratic interference with, their normal methods. During the 1970s Unified Vocational Preparation was piloted with the intention of giving all young people a better start in working life by enriching the inductions of those who formerly received neither systematic on-the-job training nor further education. This initiative was overwhelmed by rising youth unemployment and superseded by special measures: WEP in 1976, YOP in 1978, then the YTS in 1983. The YTS was launched as a training initiative to become a permanent bridge between schooling and employment, not as just another temporary alternative to unemployment; but otherwise unemployed 16 year olds were the majority of the initial intakes. It would have been difficult to select a less promising springboard for new ideas, given that diffusion normally works best from the top downwards.

Training for young adults

The proportion of Britain's large army of young adults aged 18–25 with experience in only non-skilled employment, if any, and who left school without good qualifications, who would be prepared to invest in their own further training, is uncertain. Some of our respondents had been prejudiced by YTS experiences that had led nowhere. Only 12 per cent of all respondents complained of having received too little training in their most recent jobs. Sixty-nine per cent of those in sales, and 70 per cent in unskilled occupations, expressed no interest in any further education, full-time or part-time. Some were vehement in proclaiming disinterest. However, 40 per cent of males and 30 per cent of females who were unemployed or still on the YTS when interviewed expressed a preference for employment with training that lasted three or four years rather than jobs that could be learnt more quickly.

Whether such individuals are offered opportunities to enter jobs with training at 18-plus may depend on whether employers in the 1990s can continue to cope with shortages of ready trained skilled labour, and of school leavers whose qualifications make them appear safe bets within existing training regimes. The long-term upgrading of firms' workforces that was in process at the time of our fieldwork, largely an outcome of technological change, and the consequent growth in demand for well qualified recruits to train for higher-level occupations, could combine with the decline in the size of school leaving cohorts during the 1990s and become the screw that turns some firms' difficulties into serious crises. They could then be forced to consider new ways of attracting females into skilled occupations, into modifying their methods of on-the-job and off-the-job training so as to accommodate the less qualified, and into seeking trainable recruits among young adults who missed out earlier in working life.

New patterns of transition

If a combination of the measures discussed above enables young people and employers to better adapt to each other, the end product is unlikely to be a return to Britain's levels and patterns of youth employment in earlier decades. The evidence from our enquiry warns against judging youth labour market policies in the 1990s against standards from the past. The chances are that in the future most young people will commence full-time permanent employment at a later age, following phased transitions involving various combinations of earning, training and learning.

It could be sensible to recognize a convergence that is already under way. Part-time employment is becoming the norm in the 16-plus age group. School leavers who obtain relatively secure and progressive jobs spend part of their time in formal education and training, and are only part-time producers. Young people who are locked out of such careers tend, at best, to be part-time employees, in practice. Their typical early work histories now consist of intermittent employment and unemployment. Part-time employment is also becoming normal for young people who continue in nominally full-time education. Fourteen per cent of the firms that we surveyed used 16–18 year olds in part-time jobs. These businesses, mainly in distribution, and hotels and catering, were rarely interested in the young unemployed. They preferred school and college students. The employers often valued the bright, up-market atmospheres that these young part-timers helped to create. Many were equally impressed by the young people's willingness to work for straight cash incentives with no long-term commitment on either side. Among our samples of young people, part-time employment while still at school or college had been more common in Chelmsford than in Liverpool or Walsall. Within all areas such employment was related to educational success, not failure. Many aspiring young people and their parents were treating part-time employment as a source of economic and social independence that allowed and, indeed, encouraged the teenagers to remain in education. The sums that the students earned in evening and weekend jobs often rivalled the amounts they could have expected as youth trainees.

Recognizing a norm of part-time employment until, say, age 19, would harmonize with current trends, and could be a more practical way of closing the job deficit than attempting to roll back industrial history and regenerate more full-time employment for young school leavers. Until the recent collapse of the youth labour market, Britain had a higher rate of employment among 16–18 year olds, and a lower proportion in education and training, than most other advanced industrial countries.

Acknowledgement

The research on which this chapter is based was funded by the Department of Employment, but the views expressed are solely the authors'.

References

Department of Education and Science (DES) (1977). *Education in Schools: a Consultative Document*, Cmnd 6869, London, HMSO.
Ministry of Labour and National Service (1945). *Recruitment and Training of Juveniles for Industry*, London, HMSO.
National Economic Development Office (NEDO) (1988). *Young People and the Labour Market: a Challenge for the 1990s*, London. National Economic Development Office.
Raffe, D. (1986). *The Context of the Youth Training Scheme: an Analysis of its Strategy and Development*, Working paper 8611, Centre for Educational Sociology, University of Edinburgh.
Raggatt, P. (1988). 'Quality control in the dual system of West Germany', *Oxford Review of Education*, 14, 163–86.
Roberts, K., Dench, S. and Richardson, D. (1986). 'Firms' uses of the Youth Training Scheme', *Policy Studies*, 6, 37–53.
Roberts, K., Dench, S. and Richardson D. (1987). *The Changing Structure of Youth Labour Markets*, Department of Employment Research Paper 59, London.
Williams, G. (1969). 'The revolution in industrial training', *Sociological Review Monograph*, 13, 89–103.

Joan Chandler and Claire Wallace

5

Some alternatives in youth training: franchise and corporatist models

Radical approaches to training have tended to come from the New Right in recent years, reflecting philosophies of entrepreneurship, free enterprise and the private market. This is in contrast to the approach previously offered in Britain and in other countries. In order to consider what alternatives might be desirable we critically assess developments in training both here and in West Germany before considering the foundations for a progressive training strategy in Britain.

In this chapter we examine two alternative models of youth training – the 'corporatist' model in West Germany involving a high degree of collaboration between industry and the state and the 'franchise' model in England whereby youth training has been subcontracted to small and mostly private agencies but at public expense. Models of training need to be set within the political economy of the nation and of the capitalist system as a whole and are crucial in the social reproduction of class, race and gender divisions. The organization and delivery of youth or adult training needs to be seen in its historical and cultural context. However, this does not mean that particular systems are determined entirely by external factors; 'better' and 'worse' models still exist according to whether they are able to meet training needs nationally and the needs of young people more specifically.

The value of comparison

Youth unemployment became an issue in most industrial societies in the 1970s and 1980s and those countries – such as West Germany, Austria and Switzerland – which already had established training schemes, expanded them, whereas others which had no such schemes – such as Australia, Britain and Canada – started to construct them. In all these countries young people in the unqualified, bottom end of the school spectrum were identified as the 'problems', the ones least likely to get jobs. Likewise, other traditionally disadvantaged groups such as young women and migrant workers or those from ethnic minorities were also identified (OECD 1981).

The various new schemes introduced were designed to 'mop up' the unemployed and compensate for their disadvantages. However, this needs to be set within the context of pre-existing education and training systems. Table 5.1 gives some comparison of Britain and other European countries in the late 1970s, when these schemes were introduced. It can be seen that comparatively more young people entered the labour market directly in Great Britain than most other countries and the 'youth unemployment' problem was correspondingly greater. (Youth unemployment is in inverted commas here since to some extent it is an artefact of the education/training system. Thus, in West Germany, and now in Britain, too, there is no official unemployment for young people who have not worked before.)

Table 5.1 Occupation of young people immediately after the end of compulsory education (%)

	Switzerland	Austria	Netherlands	Federal Republic of Germany	Denmark	UK
Grammar school courses	10	13	10	25	60	10
Technical and vocational courses	16	25	65	15	60	10
Vocational training (apprenticeship)	60	50	3	40	10	20
At work and unemployed	14	12	22	20	20	60

Source: Council of Europe 1981.

Despite differences in national economic performance, certain themes remain in common to all such schemes: first, there is the issue of whether training should be universal or selective in its approach (Benn and Fairley 1986; Dale 1985). Second, there is the extent to which youth training programmes should recruit on a voluntary or compulsory basis; and third there are debates about the status and quality of training and skills imparted (Ainley 1988; Cockburn 1983; Peck and Haughton 1987). The structure and legitimation of youth training may also respond differently to the ebb and flow of economic and demographic tides.

Sheldrake and Vickerstaff (1987) devised a classification of the relationship between vocational training systems and their funding structures and philosophies. In their classification, the German system is seen as embodying a 'corporate' solution to training provision. West Germany has a long tradition of vocational training for young people, an apprenticeship system which is a product of the close alliance of public and employer interest. The USA relies on the free market where it is left to companies to fund the training of their employees or individuals to fund their own vocational development. By contrast, France has followed a more interventionist path in the provision of state funding and provides a legal entitlement for each individual to avail themselves of training.

Sheldrake and Vickerstaff (1987) describe the infertile ground in Britain for the growth of any system of vocational preparation – the reluctance of private companies to pay for training, the commitment of trade unions to training only so long as it enhanced the position of craft workers over the rest, the state's commitment to training only in times of national emergency (such as war) or as an *ad hoc* response to unemployment. They chart the failed and half-hearted corporatist solution embodied in the Industrial Training Boards following the 1964 Industrial Training Act. According to these authors there is no identifiable training 'system' in Britain and hence it is left out of their classification. Ainley and Corney (1990) bring their historical account further forward as they chronicle the rise, the reshaping and the fall of the Manpower Services Commission (MSC). Amid the squabbling, the interdepartmental rivalry, the mercurial switches of organizational tack and the spawning of a host of vocational schemes, they argue that an approach to training is discernible. We shall begin therefore by describing the system in Great Britain.

Great Britain: the 'franchise' model of youth training

The development of vocational training in Britain needs to be seen in the context of the history of social change. Through the nineteenth century, the dominant economic model in Britain was that of *laissez faire*, whereas in Germany the state took a more active role in social policy. Britain had industrialized with a workforce largely uneducated and untrained. Educational institutions were attended by a gentlemanly elite and wedded to aristocratic, landed and imperial values. Education for the masses was largely in the hands of voluntary organizations, and trade schools served the needs of local employers. Nevertheless, it was considered important for mass education (introduced in 1870) to inculcate girls and boys with the right attitudes for working life – in the factories, farms and as domestic servants: in this sense it was 'vocational'. Although apprenticeships were selectively available, until quite recently the majority left school at the minimum age without any training and drifted between 'dead end' jobs, absorbing the culture of the workplace as they learned to labour. This situation was identified as early as the 1920s as the 'problem of boy labour'; it continued more or less until the 1970s. The expansion of education from the 1960s onwards took the form of an expansion of a more academic style education, particularly at the university level, providing an avenue of mobility for some working class young people and a source of class continuity for the sons and daughters of the middle classes. There remained the continuing problem of the 'Newsom child' who benefited little from the improved education system, felt alienated from its goals and fled jubilantly into the workplace at the first opportunity. Thus, while the mood of the times was to erode selective education at the secondary school level, it nevertheless continued to value academic routes out of school.

Further education and industrial training, despite the 1959 Crowther Report, remained the Cinderella of the education system, providing courses to meet the needs of local employers according to demand (Dale 1985; Gleeson 1985). At the same time more progressive models of pedagogy argued that children needed a broad humanistic introduction to knowledge rather than a narrow vocational curriculum. At that time, too, a range of official and academic reports decried the unsupervised and random 'floundering' into work which was characteristic of this system (Maizels 1970; Ashton and Field 1976). However, until the late 1970s the solution was always seen in terms of expanding the existing primary, secondary and higher educational provision to foster equality of opportunity by providing more avenues of upward mobility. This sort of education was seen as a 'good thing' in itself and for a short while this liberal educational ideology was influential. However, it never reached the minimum age school leavers, the working class lads who saw this kind of education as boring and irrelevant to their needs (Willis 1977; Ashton and Field 1976). Even those further up the academic hierarchy tended to have an instrumental approach to education, seeing it as a means to achieve better qualifications for a job rather than having a genuine thirst for learning (Brown 1987). Marsden and Ryan (1988) describe this situation as one of a trade off between high wages for young people and low quality training; in Germany, by contrast, there was a situation of high quality training and low youth wages.

From the 1970s however, the mood changed and mass youth unemployment together with Britain's poor economic performance led to the Great Debate initiated by James Callaghan in a speech at Ruskin College in 1976. Fears about a wasted generation of idle and rioting young men soon became a reality. The 'liberal' education system and lack of training were blamed for Britain's declining place in the world economy. The response took the form of the introduction of a new vocational rhetoric into education and later various new vocational qualifications — the Technical and Vocational Educational Initiative (TVEI), the Certificate of Pre-Vocational Education, and so on. In a sense, these were not new at all; they were no more than a return to the traditional arguments for mass education, that it should turn out well socialized workers to fit the needs of the economy. The Manpower Services Commission (MSC), set up at the beginning of the decade as a modest quango, took on the job of providing training schemes for the unemployed to overcome their disadvantages in the labour market and became the vehicle for later training strategies.

Sheldrake and Vickerstaff see this as an embryonic system of training in Britain which was swallowed up by rising unemployment, but for Ainley and Corney (1990) this was evidence of the MSC being given the scope to follow its expansionist ambitions and attempt to introduce a training culture into Britain (under the redoubtable Lord Young). The sensitivity to policy change was a virtue, permitting the rapid establishment and disbandment of schemes and the introduction of the Trojan horse of training into both the school system and the workplace. By the early 1980s the MSC commanded a budget twice that of the university sector; without direct responsibility to any government department or local authority, it was able to effect rapid and wide sweeping changes. It was directed by representatives from employers, trade unions and local interest groups but also enjoyed considerable autonomy. At this stage (the early 1980s) the MSC could be said to embody a 'corporatist' solution to youth training. Its move into education was later followed by an attempt to set up a unified and compatible system of national qualifications under NCVQ.

Some alternatives in youth training

In 1981, with the introduction of the New Training Initiative, the MSC was able to replace the existing mish-mash of temporary schemes with a broad training initiative available to everyone; the Youth Training Scheme was born. Athough many aspects of this initiative were never in the end implemented, the Youth Training Scheme was expanded into a two-year scheme in 1986 and absorbed most of the older apprenticeship training, along with many of the Industrial Training Boards, to provide a full-time bridge between school and work. The increasing intervention of the state in the youth labour market was also linked to undermining craft privileges and union control of skills. Attempts to drive down youth wages at the same time (and thus allow young people to 'price themselves back into work', in the phrasing of the 1985 Employment White Paper) perhaps indicated an attempted shift towards what Marsden and Ryan might call a low wage, high quality training trade off. Marsden and Ryan (1988) argue that what had traditionally existed in Britain was training for the internal labour markets of employers so that training was often informal, often job-specific and not transferable elsewhere. Germany, by contrast, trained people for 'occupational labour markets' whereby training was generalized and transferable between firms. In this way German workers enjoyed greater flexibility and the country as a whole had a highly skilled workforce. There was an attempt to introduce this in Britain under the New Training Initiative by developing training around 'core' and 'transferable skills' and by setting up 'occupational training families' within which these skills were transferable.

Superficially, youth training appeared more established than its forerunners in make work schemes or than its adult equivalents. It appeared to lack any alternatives. As Geoffrey Holland declared, 'If the two-year YTS fails then we are at the end of the road. There is nowhere else to go' (TES, 3 September 1985).

Nevertheless there are strong suggestions that youth training is shallowly planted in Britain. Ainley and Corney (1990) catalogue the political expediency and policy shifts characteristic of the history of the MSC. As the MSC has moved through Training Commission to Training Agency, the structure and constitution of the organization was – and still is – kept administratively fluid. Demographic changes have led to fewer young people seeking work and a more buoyant economy has led to shrinking dole queues. In the process, YTS is threatened and is disappearing in some areas such as the south-east (although it always involved a smaller proportion of young people there). It may well survive as a scheme for labour market 'unemployables' in depressed areas, but its regional diversity would appear to be increasing. This decline is compounded by older doubts as to whether YTS can provide good quality training or lead into jobs. Altogether, the YTS is becoming an increasingly rickety bridge to work.

When first established, YTS contained both employer-based and workshop-based schemes. When the scheme was reorganized in 1986 the shift was towards the former for both political and financial reasons. In this reorganized form a grant is now allocated to each scheme which can be either on a 'basic' or a 'premium' level, the premium funding being available for trainees with special needs and for trainees in areas of poor employment. In addition, permanent additional funding can be obtained for those with significant learning difficulties. The funding assumes that wherever possible the trainee will be receiving on-the-job training on employer's premises and that the scheme will be receiving employer contributions.

Premium funding is designed to cover the additional cost of containing first-year trainees within a workshop unit, but assumes that in the second year these will move to placement with an employer.

It was in this context that we undertook a research project into the role of managing agents and the organization of training in two contrasting labour markets: Liverpool and the south-west. The one was urban and declining, the other was rural and while it was prosperous in some parts, in others the employment prospects were similar to those in Liverpool. Altogether 56 managing agents were interviewed in Liverpool and in the south-west. This study was complemented by one of off-the-job training and a cross-sectional survey of young people themselves. These pieces of research form the basis for the discussion here.

The 'privatization' of training

In the atmosphere of accelerated 'privatization' operating since 1979, it is perhaps inevitable that the YTS should have developed in ways which increasingly prioritize the interests and influence of the private employer. However, as LeGrand and Robinson (1984) illustrate, there are many models of privatization. After the failure of extreme privatization – *laissez faire* – which characterized this area more or less until recently, and the brief moment of corporatism in the early 1980s, a new model of privatization has emerged. In the same way that schools have been encouraged to become more financially and managerially independent or even to opt out of the state education system (albeit retaining state funding), and departments within higher education have become cost centres, with their own budgets and line managers thus creating internal markets within institutions, so the YTS and employment training is 'franchised' to small local employers or managing agents. Managing agents have been moving towards this model for some time, becoming more and more like state-funded small businesses, but the creation of Training and Enterprise Councils (TEC), with the task of subcontracting training and enterprise activities to local providers on a performance-related basis, strengthens the tendency for the British state to act like a holding company (modelled obviously on the private sector) which subcontracts parts of itself at different levels.

Since the 1980s employment-based training has increasingly been favoured over workshop- and community-based training because of its lower costs and higher likelihood of leading to jobs. Financial pressures on managing agents have encouraged them to have more trainees defined as having 'employee status'; the numbers of these have risen from 9 per cent to 16 per cent. Now under proposals in the new White Paper *Employment and Training for the 1990s*, the managing agents are likely to be controlled even more by local employer interests, as is the off-the-job training element. In itself, the MSC never ran nor devised training programmes, but set broad guidelines within which it vetted, then licensed and funded, schemes proposed by a wide assortment of bodies and individuals. Some groups had been approached by MSC and asked to submit proposals whereas others simply tendered them. Hence youth training could incorporate schemes run by employers, local authorities, private agencies and voluntary organizations and could encompass both employer-based and workshop programmes. The dominant organizational structure is thus the agency, enabling youth training to be publicly funded but privately contracted to a diverse range of sponsoring bodies. Within this franchise system, all individual schemes were routinely monitored for cost, recruitment, occupancy and performance. With changes in funding, administration began to take a primarily financial form.

Local employment conditions influence the structure of YTS and the job opportunities available to YTS leavers. In Devon the proportion of people unemployed approaches the national average of 11 per cent, while in Liverpool the proportion rises to 18 per cent. Although the same proportion of young people enter YTS in Devon and Liverpool (43 per cent), young people in Liverpool have half the chance of getting a job at 16 and three times the chance of being unemployed. The structure of YTS differs between the two regions. In Liverpool the absence of employers to lead YTS and the reluctance of the local authority to become involved in training initiatives has meant that over a third of trainees are occupying premium places in quasi-workshop schemes, primarily run by voluntary associations. The more buoyant economy in Devon gives more scope for local employers and private training agencies and the local authority is also more involved in youth training provision. Premium funding is available for those who are 'difficult to employ', but the numbers designated as such depend upon the nature of the local economy as much as the characteristics of trainees; hence 10 per cent of young people are premium-funded in Devon as against 36 per cent in Liverpool. Raffe (1987) argues that the degree of 'attachment' or 'detachment' from employers' own internal labour markets determines the likelihood of being premium-funded and the likelihood of schemes leading to jobs afterwards. The greater detachment of schemes from the labour market in Liverpool is reflected in the poorer employment prospects for leavers, with 78 per cent of YTS leavers finding work in Devon compared with 43 per cent in Liverpool.

However, although YTS guaranteed a place to all school leavers, it could not guarantee equal quality of training, nor jobs at the end, and the scheme was regarded with cynicism by many (Raffe 1988). Attempts to counteract this with a widescale publicity programme were bolstered by changes in the social security system which abolished unemployment benefit for those under 18 (and thus official unemployment for this age group) making the YTS one of the few ways in which they could get any money. Responsibility for young people's welfare was thrown back on to the family by offering a lower benefit rate for those under 25 (Wallace 1988; Abbott and Wallace 1989).

The organization of the YTS in this way has a number of advantages. First, it allows for considerable regional diversity to meet local conditions. Second, it promotes competition between managing agents to recruit, place and otherwise 'sell' training. Third, it enables very rapid changes to be introduced.

But is this really privatization? It certainly mirrors developments in the health service, education and housing; the USA rather than West Germany is increasingly being seen as the model to emulate. However, we could argue that this is in fact a form of 'state-induced enterprise'. It enables an ideology of market capitalism in terms of market trading and financial management to be introduced and a similar business ethos to permeate the franchised sections of the welfare state. In fact, however, the whole system exists because of state subsidy and state intervention and does not therefore represent the withdrawal of the state. In other words 'privatization' is introduced as an organizational principle rather than because there is a genuinely free market. This organizational principle means that problems can be privatized, too. The state accepts no responsibility for the shortfall in places or their quality at the level of delivery. Control can, however, be exercised by withdrawing the franchise if targets are not met and this is a very powerful sanction. In this way, while responsibility is decentralized, power is further centralized.

This leads in turn to an 'enterprise ideology', with managing agents seeing themselves as 'selling trainees'. It is not just the labour of trainees which is commodified but the trainees themselves, as they are the product to be sold. This is embodied in the 'buy two and get one free' approach and in the idea expressed by one managing agent that you could have one (trainee) for £10 or two disabled for £5 each. Indeed some at the Adam Smith Institute tend to see this kind of franchising – which has just been suggested for primary health care – as a form of interim arrangement on the way to full privatization.

Since early this year (1989), this model of training has applied not just to youth training but to adult training, which has been subsumed under Employment Training (also to be run by managing/training agents).

Problems with the British system

The operation of managing agencies as profit centres can serve to compromise the quality of the vocational training provided, since more global concerns about training are replaced by getting and keeping placements or making enough money to survive. The schemes are of differing quality, too. The hierarchy of training schemes is based upon proximity to employers' internal labour markets, so that schemes with close proximity to these recruit young people selectively for further development later, whereas those schemes which are relatively detached from private sector internal labour markets – particularly those being sponsored by local authorities and voluntary organizations – tend to recruit the less able (Raffe 1987). As Raffe points out, while YTS works in relation to internal labour markets, it has yet to prove itself in external labour markets; employers are not yet showing sufficient preference for YTS trainees in their recruitment practices and until they do so, the YTS will continue to suffer from a lack of legitimacy (Raffe 1988).

As we move down the training hierarchy and further from internal labour markets, placement rates for trainees fall and contributions from employers become more negotiable or non-existent. It is in this sector that employers are likely to default on their payments altogether. These issues are illustrated in the charging rates of three different schemes in Devon which were run by the same managing agent. The agent ran a forestry scheme with a regional catchment area, which obtained employer contributions of £13.50 for first-year trainees and £19 for second-year trainees. He ran a basic scheme which served a local population and obtained from £12 for first years to £17.50 for second years. He also ran a premium scheme where employer contributions would be individually negotiated within the range of £8–15 per week. The greater number of detached schemes with premium trainees in Liverpool and the fewer employers offering placements amplifies the scope for negotiation and increases the chances of employers defaulting altogether on their contributions. In this type of competitive market, managing agents start to see themselves as 'selling trainees', charging what the market will bear for the qualities under consideration, forming price cartels through managing agents' associations and, where there is a scarcity of placements, undercutting other agents.

The managing agents therefore have a strong financial interest in pleasing the employer. If a trainee loses a place, the employer may look elsewhere and to avoid this schemes engage in rigorous pre-placement screening. This is especially the case with young peple who are less attractive to employers. Hence, whatever the requirements of the MSC, managing agents are reluctant to move trainees for fear of upsetting the employers and because they would then be less likely to be employed afterwards. Where valued training places are few, agents are forced to be as unobtrusive as possible in their monitoring and to turn monitoring exercises into surreptitious marketing.

Changes in YTS have had a marginal impact on schemes run by companies and incorporated into their own recruitment. However, for schemes less linked to employment the changes have been considerable. The moves towards employer-led schemes has led all independent schemes to regard themselves as profit centres, irrespective of whether their sponsoring-body is a private firm, local authority or a voluntary organization.

Linked to this has been the growth of the training manager, the person with administrative and accounting skills who organizes elements of training and marshals the essential support of employers. Agencies have become more uniformly business oriented. Financial self-sufficiency and the entrepreneurial approach have led many agencies to seek sources of income outside the YTS. For example, many managing agents in the sample also derived an income from the sale of scheme products and services, and here premium schemes predominated. Much of this production was described as incidental and minor, but it ranged from doing small electrical, motor or dress repairs, to the manufacture of soft toys, mirrors and furniture. Predictably it was the schemes more detached from the labour market which were thinking more seriously of income generating sidelines. Some have expanded their training to include private training for employers and adult training for the government. Others have sold the goods and services of trainees so that agents have diversified into small production or service companies.

As YTS has moved towards employer control so it has become more diversified and decentralized. Suggestions following the recent White Paper are that local boards will become more autonomous and employer-composed. This raises the question of their commitment to the low achieving youngster, the least attractive and least 'employable' trainee, and the extent to which a regionalized YTS can deliver a national training programme.

For these reasons, it can be seen that although YTS was intended to train people for 'occupational labour markets', in Marsden and Ryan's terms, it in fact trains them for 'internal labour markets', as the transferability of skills is undermined by increasing employer control (and was subverted in any case during placements). As union and craft control has already been removed by previous 'reforms' this effectively deregulates the training market. A low wage, low quality training scheme has been developed.

Another problem identified with the scheme elsewhere is the perpetuation and reproduction of gender and race divisions. Cockburn (1987) has described how, despite the commitment to equal opportunities, girls are clustered within a small range of schemes and that where they try to cross out of traditionally gender stereotyped jobs they still end up doing the more 'feminine' work.

Wrench and Cross (1989) have described how the employer-led nature of the recruitment process leads careers officers and managing agents to send the sorts of recruits they know the employer will like – and these are often not black ones. Black and Asian young people are less likely to be on the schemes at all, and where they are, are found in the more stigmatized 'premium' place schemes.

Class divisions are likewise reproduced through youth training, since it does not affect the more academically oriented young people who are headed for more middle class careers at all. Although the refrain of vocationalism is heard more and more in the ivory tower of higher education, no one has yet suggested that graduates do a compensatory course of training after they have graduated and before they enter work. Hence the divisions into 'academic" and 'vocational' training perpetuated through the schemes reflects older divisions between 'grammar' and 'secondary modern' schools, between Newsom courses and others (Burgess 1988).

As the economy has been restructured and liberalized through the Thatcher years, so a more casualized and flexible labour force has been created and the MSC and YTS are no longer needed as battering rams to break down established and restrictive practices. The form of flexible franchising is also reflected in the contractual employment relations used for trainers and trainees alike. Thus, the managing agent can be closed down almost overnight and the training organizers and tutors are all on similarly temporary and performance-related contracts.

The new employment White Paper *Employment for the 1990s* will reinforce the trends we have been describing. It will reinforce the tendency towards regional decentralization and the devolution of training into more and more localized units. This makes the possibility of a coordinated training strategy ever more remote. Second, it will reinforce the tendency for schemes to be employer-led – indeed they will now become employer-owned; the proposed Training and Enterprise Councils were set up to circumvent the more uncooperative trade unions and will have to have at least two-thirds private employers. Third, it will reinforce the link between training and unemployment by making the unemployed face even more stringent tests to provide that they are looking for work and forcing them into training schemes as an alternative.

Qualifications and education

Courses and counselling offer a concerted programme of moral training as trainees are tutored in social and life skills and personal effectiveness. Reliability and self-discipline are stressed and work experience seen as the opportunity for trainees to make themselves indispensable, as the opportunity to create a real job for themselves. Courses in enterprise are also available, designed to implant the ambitions of self-employment and promote the entrepreneurial culture among the unemployed. The content of courses and the profiling and monitoring of trainees individualizes training issues and trainees' conceptions of the workplace. Youth training contains a manifest and not-so-hidden curriculum.

Theoretically, all trainees should follow an approved training programme leading to a qualification, and this is within a hierarchy of courses and qualifications. Fifty to sixty per cent of trainees in basic places had obtained a qualification in their first year of training, compared with 40 per cent of trainees in premium places. Premium trainees were also much less likely to be attempting qualifications in their second year. City and Guilds and RSA qualifications, tied to skilled occupations, continue to dominate. Many premium scheme managers regarded vocational qualifications as beyond the capacities of their trainees and irrelevant to their needs. They preferred to concentrate on basic numeracy and literacy and had devised assessment systems where any change in the response of trainees could be marked as an improvement; these were courses which no one could fail.

These figures give an official picture of expanding credentialism, but in practice it is rather different. Vocational qualifications themselves continue to be valued only in traditional areas of skilled and non-manual work. In other areas of the occupational and training hierarchy qualifications play a more symbolic role. The management of schemes catering for the low achiever may regard qualifications as beyond their capacity and argue that they may operate as a disincentive if the trainee drops out. Hence, many of the training courses become nominal in character. The development of scheme-based competence objectives are designed as much to teach worker disciplines as specific skills, and hence (as has been observed elsewhere) this form of training has served to redefine skills behaviourally.

There has always been some tension between on-the-job and off-the-job training as off-the-job training is sometimes seen as irrelevant by both employers and trainees (for an analysis of trainer's perspectives on this see Parsons 1989). In this way the division between vocational and academic learning (job-based and classroom-based) is perpetuated. The off-the-job training is organized in skill centres and sometimes in further education colleges where there may be specific YTS tutors or where other tutors may have taken on YTS courses. The present reformulations of the YTS do nothing to integrate these forms of learning, and indeed the off-the-job element is being played down by becoming more flexible and less obligatory. Yet much of which is taught, such as basic literacy and numeracy, has direct vocational impact.

The divisions emerging seem to be those holding to traditional lines of segmentation in the labour market. There is a growing polarization between schemes which serve to lead into 'better jobs' with training and those which serve as 'workfare' for the unemployed. In this context schemes will continue to have a legitimacy problem.

Germany: the corporatist model of youth training

The vocational training and education system in West Germany rests upon ancient foundations of craft appenticeship dating back to the Middle Ages, but legally instituted under the Prussian state and Weimar Republic. The importance of the state as an instrument for overcoming factional, religious and class conflicts has to be emphasized in this context and in the context of German history and social policy. Since then a whole package of 'youth welfare' legislation has evolved. The vocational training system – known as the 'dual system' because young people had to continue in education but could also go to work and be trained – was expanded into a near universal scheme in the 1960s as a way of developing a highly qualified workforce in an export-oriented economy; it has since developed even more multifoliate layers.

This has been described as a 'corporatist' model (Sheldrake and Vickerstaff 1987) because it depends upon agreement between the different interested parties – employers, educationalists, unions, and the local and national levels of the state – and is monitored, validated and coordinated by the state centrally. The system is supported by a legal framework which, on the negative side, prohibits untrained people from passing themselves off as craftsmen or training apprentices themselves, and on the positive side guarantees the legitimacy of qualifications obtained. However, the cost of training is met largely by private industry who accept 'cheap' employees on low wages in return for training them, but also by the trainees themselves who accept lower wages while training in return for the prospect of higher wages later on.

Here we shall describe the main features of the German system before going on to look at how it has responded to the crisis of youth unemployment and industrial restructuring in the 1980s. The German system relies upon a highly stratified education system which retains young people for longer than most other national education systems (see Table 5.1). For the first nine or ten years of compulsory education young people attend one of three levels of school: a *Gymnasium*, a *Realschule* (these account for about a quarter each of each age cohort) or a *Hauptschule* (accounting roughly for the other half). Pupils are selected into these different academic tracks during their fourth or fifth year of schooling. After the first nine or ten years (which is completed at roughly the age of 16) young people are obliged to undertake another two years schooling for at least eight hours per week. They can do this at full-time school or in some sort of vocational technical college as the day release part of their apprenticeship. If they undertake no form of training at all they are still obliged to do the extra two years part-time schooling, although in practice some 'disappear' from the education system at this stage. In this 'sponsored' system of educational mobility (Hamilton 1981, 1987), the *Gymnasium* represents the 'academic' track and those who leave with appropriately high marks in their final certificate are assured a place at university (which they enter at 19 or so and which takes a minimum of five years if they do a full degree course). These students later enter professional jobs. The *Realschule* do not prepare young people for university entrance but provide another certificate which equips them for technical and white collar training at an intermediate level. At the bottom of the hierarchy the *Hauptschule* offer only a basic certificate after nine or ten years schooling leading to more manual trades and training. Those leaving *Hauptschule* are the ones least likely to obtain apprenticeship places. At vocational and technical schools their off-the-job training consists of German, social studies and theoretical and practical aspects of their trade such as book-keeping, accountancy and law. A variety of technical and vocational colleges exist where people can improve their credentials through part-time study or evening classes, or full-time pre-vocational courses of various kinds. There are some regional variations in this pattern, and there are also a few comprehensives (*Gesamtschule*) in some areas.

Only about 10 per cent manage to fall out of this dual system altogether, and the remaining school leavers undertake training lasting between two and three years, although not everyone finds a place straight away. Those not getting an apprenticeship the first time round can undertake a pre-vocational course at a college and this can count towards the off-the-job training element of their apprenticeship. Those who do *not* get apprenticeships at all are more likely to be the children of *gastarbeiters* or girls – although girls are becoming increasingly vocationally minded (Seidenspinner and Burger 1982). However, there is also stratification within the apprenticeship schemes with the less prestigious schemes – such as in catering and retail – requiring only two-year courses, having lower allowances and being more likely to be staffed by girls. We are led to speculate that if it were not for the fact that girls and *gastarbeiters* are predisposed towards the less prestigious schemes and are less likely to take up training in any case, the whole system may have generated an unbearable backlog of frustrated ambition since the majority of school leavers aspire to an apprenticeship.

The apprenticeship system is monitored centrally from Berlin by the *Bundesinstitut für Berufsbildung* where regular meetings of the interested parties for each craft meet to thrash out what is required for that skill. The BIBB is also responsible for reclassifying, realigning and even abolishing skills, in line with the changing requirements of industry. The whole elaborate system of education and training (which we have described only very cursorily here) is set up so as to offer a parallel career hierarchy to that of *Gymnasium*-higher education. The vocational technical colleges of various kinds and the apprenticeship system itself are part of a tiered structure of examinations which people can work their way through, improving their position on the job and through evening classes and eventually going on to higher education in a polytechnic type establishment (*Fachhochschule*) and obtaining a degree. Alternatively, people can work their way up through night school and professional courses into positions of senior management, bypassing the higher education system altogether. This is possible because the different vocational and academic qualifications are coordinated in a national scheme of equivalence and these are linked to internal ladders of promotion.

Employers pay for this system by losing employees for the off-the-job training element of their scheme. There is a division between small and large employers in this respect. Small employers are among the main employers of craft apprentices and they are able to offer an all round introduction to the craft but can seldom offer jobs to their trainees afterwards. In large firms, on the other hand, trainees are more likely to be trained in specialist parts of the firm.

The system is sanctioned formally by the fact that no one is able to train an apprentice unless they have the certificate of *Meister*, which requires training in addition to the basic apprenticeship. Informally, employers prefer workers with some training as they are deemed more reliable and able to turn out better quality work. The apprenticeship system enjoys a high degree of status and legitimacy in the community generally. The desirability of obtaining training is reinforced by better wages later, more secure employment, access to ladders of promotion, and consequently better welfare – such as health schemes, pensions and unemployment benefits which are all linked to employment through the national insurance system.

How did this German system cope with rising youth unemployment in the

1980s? It did so basically by expanding the education and vocational training systems, making the employment of apprentices more attractive to employers (lifting various protective legislation), by adding another year to compulsory schooling in many places to make it ten years and by threatening to apply a payroll tax to employers who did not recruit sufficient apprentices (OECD 1981). Pre-vocational courses were provided for those who did not find a place straight away (Koditz 1985). They were assisted in this by the fact that more people opted to stay for longer periods in the education system so that more went to *Gymnasium* – and therefore university – and more to *Realschule* where they stayed for longer. The *Hauptschule* started to empty of all but the migrant workers' children in many areas. Where young people were unable to enter the apprenticeship of their choice, they undertook another and then took a second apprenticeship later (Heinz and Krueger 1987). Thus while there was a trading up by many trying to improve their chances through spending longer in academic education, there was also a trading down as people took courses which were lower than those they had hoped for and those (especially girls) leaving *Gymnasium* started to undertake apprenticeship training rather than going straight to university. This tended to inflate the entrance qualifications, making entry to schemes more competitive. Instead of a 'first phase' transition problem – from school to training – a 'second phase' transition problem was identified – from training into work. It is still not certain how this will affect German youth since the bulk of them are still at present absorbed within the expanded education and training system. Other alleged flaws in the system are in terms of youth attitudes: a number of surveys have tended to show that young people are becoming disillusioned and cynical about work and tend to no longer see work as a central life goal (Shell 1981). Whatever the value of such surveys, they tend to provoke wide publicity in a country where the political allegiance of the younger generation has been a point of concern since the war.

Critics have argued that the German system is not as ideal as is supposed because it rests upon highly stratified divisions within education and work (Holt and Reid 1988). Indeed, the whole process is highly bureaucratized – and some would say, rigid. Hence, in West Germany, far more trades can be classified as 'skilled' and this social construction of skill is heavily reinforced at all levels. Classroom learning plays an important part in this construction of 'skill' and this perhaps avoids the mental/manual divide of the kind found in Britain (Browne 1981; Wallace 1987). However, the gulf between the elite 'academic' track and less prestigious 'vocational' ones is nevertheless wide. Furthermore, since young people can remain at university into their 30s this means that at the academic end of the spectrum they can emerge relatively older and with no practical experience at all to take up elite jobs. Another consequence of this system is that young people are strongly socially controlled by dependence upon their parents (the training allowance does not allow them to become economically independent) and through being socialized into a hierarchical workforce from the beginning as apprentices. Finally, there are the divisions between good and less good apprenticeships which we mentioned previously.

This system discriminates against women (Heinz and Krueger 1987). Girls are less likely to go for the more prestigious trades and career ladders and they are perhaps less likely to be 'sponsored' by employers. Second, it reinforces a masculine hierarchy of waged work and the notion of unbroken 'careers', also based upon masculine models of work and skill. Despite evidence that girls are increasingly seeing their lives in terms of work roles (Seidenspinner and Burger 1982; Shell 1981) as well as family roles, this does nothing to challenge the male division of labour and merely fits girls into a world where they are sure to be disadvantaged. Finally, the system rests upon the menial and unskilled work being carried out by migrant workers who make up a significant proportion of the German workforce and have a few rights in terms of employment protection. These are the ones who end up in the secondary labour market jobs.

Thus, despite the apparent advantages of the German system it also has a number of drawbacks. Nevertheless the coordinated commitment to education and training controlled but not paid for by the state enables us to characterize this as the 'corporatist model'; for Germans it would be unthinkable for training to be run as a 'business' in itself.

Implications and lessons for the future

Raffe (1987) has indicated that the success or otherwise of the Youth Training Scheme must depend upon the *context* in which it is set rather than the actual content of the schemes. By examining these different national contexts we can speculate as to the different directions which youth training might take and the problems associated with each. In this sense, the future of youth training (as Raffe points out) will depend upon the nature of divisions within the labour market and the demand for youth labour in any given regional context.

Three main points of contrast spring to mind. First, because the German system – irrespective of its quality – was introduced at a time of full employment and relative prosperity it was built upon, and still retains, a high degree of *legitimacy* in the eyes of employers, trainers and the general public. The youth training scheme, by contrast, introduced during times of rising unemployment and as a way of concealing unemployment, has had difficulty establishing any kind of legitimacy, especially when its already fragile status is undermined by cuts in funding as youth employment starts to rise once more. We would argue, however, that the survival and legitimation of training has less to do with its effectiveness in terms of jobs than with the relationship between the state and the employers. The differences in the structure of training between Britain and Germany are symptomatic of the differences in the political economies of the two countries and the cultural valuation and definition of training and 'skill'.

Second, the crisis in training in Britain stems from rising employment rather than rising unemployment. In Germany the system is undermined when there are more trained young people than employers want – although this seems to have been solved by certificate inflation and providing people with even more training. In Britain it is the fall in unemployment which causes problems as there is then no reason to have schemes – except in a minority of cases.

Third, while the German method is to respond with a nationally coordinated strategy of integrated academic and vocational training, in Britain the solution is a variety of regionally diverse local initiatives which would seem to make NCVQ more difficult to implement. We are returning to specific locally based training designed to fit the 'needs' of local employers and reminiscent of the system which existed before the 1964 Industrial Training Act. Training in Britain will become increasingly employer-controlled, whether or not it is employer-based, and this means it will be tied to short-term economic goals rather than long-term national interests.

Finally, while the German system is based upon negotiations between a number of different interest groups – including trade unions and educationalists as well as employers – in Britain this corporatist approach has been abandoned, the educational content of courses eroded and given low priority, and the wants of employers given primary status. While the wants of private employers are important in making any scheme work, they cannot guarantee that the interests of young people, or indeed the national requirement for a trained workforce, can be met. So far, education has been blamed for not producing an appropriately trained workforce and new schemes introduced at all levels to make education more vocationally relevant. However, there is little point in improving the education and training system if, as Raffe's work (1988) suggests, employers do not recognize these skills and qualifications. It would seem that only a coordinated intervention in employers' recruitment practices – such as making it illegal to employ untrained personnel in certain capacities – would have any effect in helping to legitimate new skills.

It has been fashionable in academic circles to be sceptical of the value of youth training. It may seem strange, therefore, that we are defending it. However, a nationally coordinated series of vocational qualifications and training, providing an alternative career route out of unskilled jobs for non-academic school leavers, seems preferable to throwing them into the labour market to sink or swim at 16. This would help to integrate young people into the employment system and go some way towards mitigating the more extreme alienation of youth from the sort of 'shit jobs' which they are expected to do (Wallace 1987). The MSC almost delivered this; but the scheme was stillborn when the MSC was severely scaled down and finally abolished in September 1988. Would it have been possible to make it into something which served the needs of youth people? The MSC appeared to mainly serve the needs of political expediency, to be a way of circumventing the educational establishment. How could a better system of training have been implemented? In order to answer this question we need to be cognizant of the shortcomings of the schemes we have examined.

We recognize that the danger inherent in suggesting alternatives is that these are utopian and that any alternatives we are likely to suggest must take place within the reality of a capitalist system which ultimately serves to exploit the labour of young people for the lowest cost. We recognize that within a capitalist divided labour market, where young workers are commodified labour and the ultimate goal is profitability, there is limited scope for humanitarian alternatives. Such alternatives would need to take into account inequalities of class, race and gender which – while they may be endemic – can at least be loosened.

A nationally coordinated system of vocational qualifications built on to existing educational provision and evening classes would provide a framework for occupational mobility for those not able/or preferring not to enter academic 'tracks'. Genuine gangways between the vocational and the academic routes and re-entry tracks for those who missed out first time round would mean that there would be the possibility of movement between different levels. Age restrictions on apprenticeships would need to be removed since these make possible only a once and for all choice and discriminate against women who might like to take up a trade after having a family.

Such a national training framework would need to be negotiated with the various different members of the community in order to obtain legitimacy – trade unions, voluntary organizations, the education establishment – and in order to ensure that all views were represented. This would be achieved not by advertising hype but by consultation. Such schemes would be worthless simply as a sop to unemployment – a problem which has bedevilled them all along. They would need to be introduced in the context of an expanding labour market of the kind we may be entering in the 1990s. They would also be worthless if they were part of a 'no choice' situation such as that introduced in the recent White Paper, which linked training opportunities with forcing people off the dole.

The price for accepting some idea of skill training would be that it would have to lead to better jobs at the end of it – meaning better rewarded, more secure, linked to ladders of promotion and exchangeable in an external, occupational labour market. The creation of skills inevitably leads to the creation of segmented labour markets and, therefore, to inequality. However, our argument is that a progressive notion of skilled training would provide more open access to primary sectors instead of limiting these jobs by race and sex. Formal forms of social closure are perhaps easier to tackle than informal forms of social closure.

The dichotomy between useful (but low status) vocational training and useless (but high status) academic training would need to be broken so that a general social awareness and human understanding, as well as high standards of literacy and numeracy, can be seen as an essential part of training for jobs. However, in saying this, we would also need to recognize the antipathy which many students have to more 'academic' learning.

One problem we have identified with traditional skilled training is that it is a way of buttressing divisions of race and gender in the labour market and acts as a form of exclusion by more privileged groups. This reflects a masculine view of work and the labour market. A more progressive training policy would need to take a broader view. This use of skills would need to be challenged and the fact that a shortage of skilled workers is predicted in the 1990s gives scope to include non-traditional groups: middle-aged women training as car mechanics; young women training as North Sea divers; young Asians training for the police force and so on. Cynthia Cockburn (1987) raises the issue of the problems for men crossing to women's jobs as well as vice versa; these gender stereotypes would need to be tackled, too.

However, we can go further than this and challenge the whole way in which skill is constructed. Given that some recent research in the sociology of work raises the notion that skill is socially constructed rather than being some sort of inherent quality existing in some types of work, it would be important to redefine skill to include the sorts of activities undertaken by a variety of other groups, especially women. Hence, youth training could take into account the sorts of voluntary activities, domestic work and community care undertaken by many women and encourage young men to perceive these as worthwhile and useful. This would require some sort of training and reward for work outside of employment as well as inside.

Finally, this entire youth training scheme would need to be built upon a foundation of youth incomes policies coordinated in such a way as to afford genuine choices to young people between employment, training, and education and work outside of employment. As part of this, we would need to accept the right to be unemployed and to receive benefits as such, otherwise training and education become compulsory and lose legitimacy as time serving schemes. Thus, young people would have the right to an independent income at the age of 16 whichever course of action they pursued and if the government was concerned to encourage young people to stay in education or go into training rather than employment or unemployment it would need to offer financial incentives to do so.

So far, we have talked of national interests or national training strategies and in terms of research and policy carried out so far, that would seem to be appropriate. However, in 1992, Britain becomes part of a European labour market and British workers will need to compete against German ones for jobs. Given that they will be unqualified to legally perform many skilled jobs in Germany and that their qualifications are not transferable but job-specific, we would expect them to be disadvantaged in any European competition. It could be that they are in demand to perform the sorts of unskilled work currently carried out by migrant workers from Southern Europe or they may also perform skilled jobs illegally as *Schwarzarbeiters*. Either way they will be both exploited and disadvantaged. Surely it is now time to think of integrated and compatible training systems?

References

Abbott, P.A. and Wallace, C. (1989). 'The Family' in P. Brown and R. Sparks (eds), *Beyond Thatcherism*, Milton Keynes, Open University Press.
Ainley, P. (1988). *From School to YTS*, Milton Keynes, Open University Press.
Ainley, P. and Corney, M. (1990). *The MSC: Rise and Fall of a Quango*.
Ashton, D.N. and Field, D. (1976). *Young Workers*, London, Hutchinson.
Bates, I., Clarke, J., Cohen, P., Finn, D., Moore, R. and Willis, P. (1984). *Schooling for the Dole?*, London, Macmillan.
Benn, C. and Fairley, J. (eds) (1986). *Challenging the MSC on Jobs. Education and Training: Enquiry into a National Disaster*, London, Pluto.
Brown, P. (1987). *Schooling Ordinary Kids*, London, Tavistock.
Browne, K. (1981). 'Schooling, capitalism and the mental-manual division of labour', *Sociological Review*, 2, 3, 445-73.
Burgess, R. (1988). 'Whatever happened to the Newsom Course?' in A. Pollard, J. Purvis and G. Walford (eds), *Education, Training and the New Vocationalism*, Milton Keynes, Open University Press.
Cockburn, C. (1983). *Brothers*, London, Pluto.
Cockburn, C. (1987). *Two Track Training*, London, Macmillan.
Council of Europe (1981). *Living Tomorrow: An Inquiry into the Preparation of Young People for Working Life*, Strasburg.
Dale, R. (ed.) (1985). *Education, Training and Unemployment: Towards a New Vocationalism?*, London, Pergamon.
Fiddy, R. (1985) *Youth Unemployment and Training. A collection of national perspectives*. Lewes, Falmer.
Gleeson, D. (ed.) (1983). *Youth Training and the Search for Work*, London, Routledge.
Gleeson, D. (1985). 'The privatisation of industry and the nationalisation of youth' in R. Dale, (ed.), *Education, Training and Unemployment: Towards a New Vocationalism?*, London, Pergamon.

Hamilton, S. (1981). 'Inequality and youth unemployment: can work programmes work?', *Education and Urban Society*, 14, 1, 103-26.
Hamilton, S. (1987). 'Apprenticeship as a transition to adulthood in Germany', *American Journal of Education*, 95, 2, 314-45.
Heinz, W. and Krueger, H. (1987). *Hauptsache eine Lehrstelle. Jugendlichee vor den Huerden den Arbeitsmarkts*, Weinheim, Deutscher Studien Verlag.
Holt, M. and Reid, W.A. (1988). 'Instrumentalism and education: 14-18 rhetoric and the 11-16 curriculum' in A. Pollard, J. Purvis and G. Walford (eds), *Education, Training and the New Vocationalism*, Milton Keynes, Open University Press.
Koditz, V. (1985) 'The German Federal Republic: how the state copes with the crisis – a guide through the tangle of schemes' in D. Marsden and P. Ryan (1988). 'Apprenticeship and labour market structure: UK youth unemployment and training in comparative context', Paper submitted to International Symposium on Innovations in Apprenticeship and Training, OECD, Paris.
LeGrand, J. and Robinson, R. (1983). *Privatisation and the Welfare State*, London, Macmillan.
Maizels, J. (1970). *Adolescent Needs and the Transition from School to Work*, London, Athlone Press.
OECD Monitor (1981) Paris, OECD.
Parsons, K. (1989). 'Off the job training: tutors' perspectives.' Paper presented to the BSA Conference, Plymouth Polytechnic.
Peck, J. and Haughton, G. (1987). *Training and the Contemporary Reconstruction of a Skill*, N.W. Industry Research Unit, Manchester, Working Paper No 19.
Raffe, D. (1987). 'The context of the Youth Training Scheme; an analysis of its strategy and development', *British Journal of Education and Work*, 1, 1-33.
Raffe, D. (1988). 'Going with the grain: youth training in transition' in S. Brown and R. Wake (eds), *Education in Transition*, Edinburgh, Scottish Council for Research in Education, 110-23.
Seidenspinner, G. and Burger, A. (1982). *Maedchen '82*, Munich, Forschungsbericht Deutsches Jugendinstitut.
Sheldrake, J. and Vickerstaff, S.A. (1987). *The History of Industrial Training in Britain*, Aldershot, Gower.
Shell Survey (1981). *Jugend '81: Lebentswurfe, Altagskulturen, Zukunftsbilder*, Hamburg, Jugendwerke der Deutscher Shell (Hrsg)
Wallace, C. (1987). *For Richer, For Poorer: Growing up in and out of Work*, London, Tavistock.
Wallace, C. (1988). 'Between the family and the state: young people in transition', *Youth and Policy*, 25, 25-37.
Willis, P. (1977). *Learning to Labour*, Farnborough, Saxon House.
White Paper (1989). *Employment and Training for the 1990s*, London, HMSO.
Wrench, J. and Lee, G. (1983). 'A subtle hammering – young black people and the labour market' in B. Troyna and D.I. Smith (eds), *Racism, School and the Labour Market*, Leicester, National Youth Bureau.

Section 2

Alternatives in secondary and further education: a case study approach
Introduction

Following on from the rather more macro-oriented perspectives of the opening section, this section, drawing on case study material, examines what happens at school and college level. Without denying the powerful vocationalizing effects of government education and training policy at the present time, the papers in this section focus on the neglected ways in which participants in schools and colleges question, resist and redefine vocationalist ideology and, in so doing, search for various alternatives. Drawing on case study material both Mac an Ghaill (Chapter 6) and Avis (Chapter 7) offer different insights into the challenges posed by the sorts of academic/vocational divisions which they see as increasingly characterizing post-16 provision. Most particularly, argues Mac an Ghaill, we need to examine the old assumptions that underpin different routes through education and training, leading to different transitions from school to college to work. Particular attention needs to be given to the mental/manual division of labour dichotomy, which structures the academic/non-academic stratification of young people. According to Mac an Ghaill, the demographic downturn in the 16–19 age group provides us with the opportunity to think through the progressive political and social issues necessary for the implementation of alternatives to the present socially divisive 'new vocationalism'. It is suggested in this paper that community colleges may offer one such alternative, which provides a comprehensive programme of education and training and integrates practical and theoretical elements of learning. Similarly, Avis's analysis of further education argues that, if we wish to develop a critical and radical educational practice, we need to develop curricular forms which break down the division between academic, vocational and pre-vocational education at the post-16 level. He argues that the modularized curriculum may herald this possibility, but concludes that any alternative radical practice needs to connect with student interests and move beyond these. He seeks to demonstrate this argument via the perspectives of race, gender and class, explicit in the students' experiences and perspectives of further education and training, outlined in his case study.

How the curriculum should move beyond student interest and experience is the subject of the following chapters by Skeggs (Chapter 8) and Shilling (Chapter 9). Skeggs's position is that many vocational courses for women in further education are little more than domestic entrapments in apprenticeship. With reference to caring courses her chapter examines how the students' attempts to gain autonomy and self-esteem through earning implicates them in gender and class reproduction, leading women students to value familial roles of care over and above occupational roles. According to Skeggs, the alternatives to this process of domestic apprenticeship would involve creating real jobs with adequate financial recompense, as well as extending formal caring provision to counteract the use of young women as unpaid carers. Likewise changes in FE would involve the restructuring of the sexual division of knowledge, staff development and changes to the content of the caring curriculum. It is argued that, even in the short term, such changes would be an improvement on the provision that already exists and which has a tendency to reinforce the domestic apprenticeship system.

Shilling, in similar fashion, explores the critical potential of work experience as a valid form of educational activity. He argues that declining numbers of school leavers, the efforts of business, industry and commerce to attract them, and the integration of public and private resources, pose opportunites (as well as problems) for schools and teachers. In so doing, he explores recent developments in work experience, involving government plans to extend work-based learning to all, and the codes of practice involved. Thus, following on Skeggs's contribution, Shilling looks closely at various alternatives, including those which promote the possibility of domestic labour placements, more varied patterns of earning, learning and work, waged and unwaged work, and approaches which promote equal opportunities.

This theme is taken up in Rosie's (Chapter 10) concluding chapter, which explores various interpersonal alternatives in the teaching and learning situation between tutors and trainees. Despite Rosie's apparently individualistic account, he is at pains to demonstrate that the 'vicious circle', referred to earlier on by Raffe, can be broken. Addressing feelings of despair felt by students about unemployment, home conditions, personal and educational limitations ('I'm thick ... I am ... got shit for brains'), is an essential ingredient of any alternative curriculum. According to Rosie's study, perhaps the clearest expression of this lies in the fact that the attempt to discuss social and political issues, such as unemployment and home experiences, gave students confidence to create their own needs, demands and alternatives. While acknowledging the limitations associated with such an approach, Rosie maintains that there is much to be gained by working through students' personal experiences and the alternatives which *they* perceive in their lives.

Máirtín Mac an Ghaill

6

Beyond the 1944–88 educational interregnum: the case of Sands Community College

> The good thing about this place [Sands Community College] is that the teachers don't see you as different to them. At our last school, you had some good teachers but deep down it was us and them or really them and us. Some of us didn't want the academic way, so they thought we were part of the scrap heap. Most teachers don't really know about work, do they?
>
> (Jasvinder – student)

At present, much educational planning is underscored by demographic irony. Just as it looked as though many working class youths would continue to say 'good-bye to a working life', the situation is once again about to change. The collapse of the youth labour market in the late 1970s and the accompanying dominant explanation, in terms of faulty supply due to a 'skills mismatch' between potential employees and jobs, resulted in the setting up of a number of prevocational and vocational initiatives, including the Certificate of Pre-Vocational Education (CPVE), the Technical Vocational Education Initiative (TVEI), and the Youth Training Scheme (YTS) (see Jamieson 1985). These are now in place, just as the number of school leavers begins to fall. For example, in the Sands catchment area, where this study was carried out, there were 17,000 fifth-year students in 1982–83. This is estimated to fall by 25 per cent to 12,700 in 1989–90 (HMSO 1987, p. 23). This is reflected at a national level, with a projected fall of 26 per cent in the number of young people in the 16–19 age group between 1987 and 1994 (Finn 1988, p. 28).

There have been more organizational changes in post-16 education and training in the last 5 years than in the previous 25. In the Sands area, further education colleges have had to change in response to a decline in the manufacturing sector from 303,000 in 1971 to 159,000 employees in 1987 (Tomkins 1988, Section 3). As the main further education provision of craft training has declined, youth training schemes have grown alongside youth unemployment, which has the highest rate among any age group in the area. At the same time local sixth-form colleges, in response to labour market changes and falling rolls, are developing prevocational and vocational courses alongside the traditional academic curriculum.

There is now a growing body of critical literature concerned with the rapidly changing relationship between education, training and waged work. The debate has mainly focused on the evolution of the broad ideology about education and training that is identified as the 'new vocationalism' (see Gleeson 1984; Bates et al. 1984 and Dale 1985). Robert Moore describes the fundamental change in the restructuring of the education system in relation to production that is presently taking place:

> Essentially this reflects a shift in power of a fundamental kind – from a decentralised education system, whose agents had an *indirect* relationship to production, and consequently enjoyed a high degree of 'relative autonomy', to a centralised system, whose agents bear a *direct* relationship to production and who define their objectives specifically in terms of the needs of production. This is a shift from a liberal–humanist education paradigm to a technical training paradigm. Its most fundamental consequence is to sever the connection between practical knowledge and elaborated theoretical knowledge.
>
> (Moore 1984, p. 66 – original emphasis)

Other social theorists have been critical of such initiatives as TVEI and YTS, which they claim serve to increase academic and social divisions at state schools and colleges, thus threatening the egalitarian values of comprehensive schooling (Golby 1985; Evans and Davies 1986; and see McNeil 1989, for discussion of situation in North America).

Such theoretical arguments, which provide fresh insights, find a strong resonance within state schools and colleges among liberal teachers committed to the post-war social democratic educational consensus. However, a main weakness of the liberals' position is that in concentrating their criticisms on present educational policy, with the increasing influence of 'outside' agencies, such as the Manpower Service Commission (MSC) and employers, the teachers implicitly suggest that we might return to a non-vocationalized curriculum such as that of the 1960s, of the 'secret garden of the curriculum'. In so doing, the liberals fail to provide an adequate alternative, based on a coherent philosophy, within which to set out a set of principles and strategies for education and training. This is a vital task at a time when one of the major historical functions of mass schooling, that of the preparation of young people for the labour market, has been broken and there is much disillusionment with YTS acting as a 'permanent bridge to work' (MSC 1982).

The focus of this chapter is twofold. Its first purpose is to examine the underlying limitations and contradictions of the liberal critics of the 'new vocationalism' whom I found at a local sixth form and further education college in Sands City. There are three main areas of concern: the mental–manual division of labour, teacher–parent relations and teacher–student relations. Second, I shall explore how community colleges may operate as one way forward in overcoming these limitations, with a specific focus on class, gender and racial forms of subordination. This is illustrated with reference to Sands Community College, which is located in a working class area in an English city. It is an open access institution, both a tertiary college, providing a full range of education and training courses for everyone over the age of 16, and providing social, recreational and leisure facilities for the local community.

It is argued here, as Green (1988) suggests, that we need to reconceptualize the relationship between education, training and waged and unwaged work. At the same time we need to move beyond the present terms of the debate and to integrate the theoretical and practical elements, based on the active involvement of students and parents, in the construction of new structures and processes in the area of post-16 education and training.

Mental–manual division of labour

Until the recent establishment of the MSC, there had been little study of education and training, relative to other areas of research. Gleeson (1984, pp. 99–100) argues that this neglected area of sociological enquiry involves not only further education and training, but that 'Even at school level, it is possible to detect a certain squeamishness about vocational training and craft knowledge'. At one level this response can be seen to be related to teachers' ambiguous class position, which cannot be simply read from their economic position as wage earners. Consideration must also be given to the determinations of what Poulantzes (1973) calls the political and ideological levels. An important element of this has been the professional teaching organizations' acceptance of the 'mental–manual' division of labour and their identification with mental production. Here, professionalism can be seen as a two-edged sword. On the one hand, it has been employed by classroom teachers to maintain their autonomy as non-manual workers. On the other hand, as Finn *et al.* (1977, p. 170) comment:

> The ideology of professionalism has been used by teaching organisations to either defend their middle-class status, or to assimilate themselves into that class. Trapped between the developing power of monopoly capital and the advances of the working-class, professionalism can be understood as a petit-bourgeois strategy for advancing and defending a relatively privileged position.

It must be added that by the late 1980s the material basis of the defence has drastically altered, with the restructuring of teachers' work and the re-emergence of the increasing proletarianization of teachers in a highly centralized system (Mac an Ghaill 1988b). The liberal teachers at Sands sixth-form college displayed 'an intellectual squeamishment about vocational training' that was particularly evident in their opposition to the headteacher's promotion of such curricular areas as technology, business studies and CPVE, which they felt threatened the sixth form's academic ethos. They argued that this vocationalization of the curriculum was a veiled attempt to reintroduce a tripartite system.

However, although the liberal teachers were opposed to the perceived increased stratification of the students, they failed to see that its theoretical underpinning, which they worked with – the conception of the limited supply of intelligence – serves to reproduce, maintain and ideologically legitimate a strict stratification of 'academic' and 'non-academic' students. It is through this frame of reference that class, 'race' and gender reproduction is mediated. In the context of Sands sixth form, this division becomes synonymous with the division between working class and middle class students. So, for example, the under representation of black and white working class students in the academic examination groups has led to an over-simplistic perception of the working class, as a social group, as predominantly non-academic, with a variety of common-sense theories of social and psychological deficit suggested as the causal factor.

At this time at Sands Further Education College, there was opposition among the liberal teachers to the perceived threat posed by the involvement of the private agencies in YTS. Their main criticism of the training agencies was that they ascribed low status to the trainees, seeing them as 'factory or service sector fodder'. However, although the liberal teachers distanced themselves from the private agencies' practices, they failed to see that their own pedagogical relations were based on the same premises, such as the assumed limited intellectual capacity of the trainee students. Working with a discourse of deficit of these students, the liberal teachers adopted a narrow, instrumental approach to them. For example, it was assumed that these students would neither be interested in nor be able to cope with discussion of the wider socio-economic and political context within which their future jobs would take place.

The liberal teachers' acceptance of the ideologically constructed 'common-sense' concepts of ability, aptitude and attitude rendered them unable to see that the conventional categorization of students does not reflect class, 'race' and gender social pathologies; it is rather the case, as Lettieri (1976, p. 151) argues, that these institutional divisions reflect the labour process of capitalist societies. As Lettieri says, 'Capitalism has allowed us to get used to living under a system in which intellectual and manual work tend to be incompatible with each other'. Significantly, he adds, in relation to teachers' ideological position, 'This mutual exclusion is, moreover, a characteristic feature of petty-bourgois ideology which is horrified by the idea of manual work' (p. 151).

It may be concluded that the liberal teachers' *a priori* assumptions that underpinned their divisive day-to-day classroom practices in response to students of assumed different ability challenged the credibility and effectiveness of their theoretical rhetoric about equal opportunities for all students, and exposed the contradictions and limitations of their position in maintaining the false dichotomy between education and training.

Teachers at Sands Community College suggested that the frequently assumed juxtaposition of sixth form and further education colleges, as academic and training institutions, was historically developed to meet specific educational and training needs at specific times. They argued that this historical legacy overshadowed current curricular development in these institutions.

In contrast, they suggested that new structures and processes were being constructed within community colleges, to meet the particular needs of present day young people. Changes such as the organization of the timetable to encourage students to combine vocational, technical and academic courses were seen to challenge the false dichotomy of the mental–manual division of labour couplet. Equally important, the teachers maintained that community colleges provided the material base which enabled them to understand more fully working class students' material and social experiences, expectations and aspirations of work and adult life, from which teachers' own career biographies had cut them off.

I think what I have learned here, particularly from the mature students, is that teachers, even the sympathetic liberal ones, have no real understanding of students who do not choose traditional academic courses.

(Anne – teacher)

It's done with the best of intentions. We push working-class kids to get academic qualifications. That's right, of course, but I think that community colleges make you see that the kids on technical or vocational courses are just as bright, just as worthwhile. The way the place is organised forces you to re-evaluate all the things that you have taken for granted. Before I came here, I equated manual work with unskilled labour. I'll tell you the truth, I hadn't a clue about training. Coming from the working-class, I felt lucky to escape all that. I think that most teachers probably do.

(Iqbal – teacher)

The Sands Community College teachers also felt that they operated with a model of learning which went beyond traditional further education pedagogical responses to students on training courses, responses which tend to be based on a behavioural objectives approach to learning. They had implemented an approach that encouraged all students to be creative, critical, flexible and self-motivated learners (see Coffield *et al.* 1986, p. 223). At the same time, they have moved beyond the defensive protective attitude to traditional academic courses that many liberal teachers have adopted in response to the 'new vocationalism'.

I don't see education and training as alternatives and training can be just as intellectually demanding as academic work. And, conversely, as we know from grammar schools, so-called academic work can be reduced to skills of re-call of meaningless content in an externally based examination led and dominated system.

(Maxine – teacher)

It's incredible, five years ago, progressive teachers were the main critics of the traditional academic curriculum for failing so many kids. Now, those same teachers have been forced defensively to defend it. Here, we have tried, are trying to seriously examine ideas of relevancy, skills, standards, general education and the more specific training skills, for all students.

(Peter – teacher)

Teacher–parent relations

The second area of concern is that of teacher–parent relations. Cunningham (1988, p. 25), commenting on the latest report on *British Social Attitudes* (Jowell *et al.* 1988), writes that:

There are widespread worries about many aspects of state education ... On the vexed question of the transition between school and a first job, the report says that only one school in three teaches skills which are of use in industry. Overall parents and teachers are not optimistic about the efforts to remedy this. There appears to be a sort of resigned acceptance that school and work are far apart and that the gap seems more or less unbridgeable.

The liberal teachers at Sands sixth form and further education college did little to make contact or organize with their students' parents to discuss how to bridge this gap. More specifically, there tended to be a differential teacher response to middle class and working class parents. The latter were assumed to be educational reactionaries, who uncritically supported vocational initiatives, with their instrumental promise of success in the labour market. This dominant perception was an element in teachers' defensive response to parents, whom they caricatured as enthusiastic supporters of recent central government intervention into schools. There was little understanding or empathy among the liberal teachers of how the government's 'promise' of 'student choice', 'parental involvement', 'local control', and 'accountability' have important symbolic value for working class parents, who have been systematically locked out from participation in welfare bureaucracies, such as state schools and hospitals.

Hall (1983, p. 9) reminds us that:

> For a brief period in the 1960s and 1970s, the involvement of parents with the school was the Left's most democratic trump card. The dismantling of this into 'parental choice' and its expropriation by the Right is one of their most significant victories. They stole an idea designed to increase popular power in education and transformed it into an idea of an educational supermarket.

Teachers at Sands Community College attempted to recover the Left's earlier positive involvement of parents in educational institutions.

Working class parents at the college, some of whom attended courses there, confirmed this. They compared the college's participatory democratic structures with their former marginalization from state schools, which reduced their function to that of the provision of extra financial resources. Here at Sands Community College we see parents actively involved in the educational process, and their resulting empowerment. They challenge the caricatured images that many teachers have of working class parents. Employing a sophisticated analytical framework they discuss the difficulties of preparing young people for work and adult life, acknowledging wider socio-economic and political determinants and institutional and situational constraints. They felt that the community college's stronger links with, and accountability to, the local community will ensure genuine comprehensive education and training opportunities for all students.

> I said to the teacher at Carol's last school, what's all this about skills for work and preparing for jobs? Of course, I want her to get a good job but I think that if she can get a proper education, she has a better chance of getting one. A lot of her friends have got more training than boxers! Employers want real qualifications. Not just GCSEs, proper training as well. They wouldn't even listen at her last school. We have committees here and elections and everything, so the parents have their say.
>
> (John – parent)

> Everyone talks about what the employer is looking for in our kids. Have you ever heard a teacher ask, what are our kids looking for from the employers? I think here [Sands Community College] they do and that's the main difference to other schools and training schemes. And, I mean, for all the

kids, that's very important. When I was at school, the black kids were pushed into the low jobs and of course the girls getting the lowest.

(Rose – parent)

Parents saw the heterogeneous composition of the student population as having a number of advantages. First, that it provided a more adult atmosphere and thus a better preparation for young people in their transition to higher education, full-time waged work and adult life. Second, a number of the parents thought that the young people would benefit from wider contact with employed and unemployed adults. They were highly critical of traditional vocational courses which took place in artificial environments, with little reference to the social relations of modern employment. They were also critical of conventional school courses, with their underlying assumptions of student 'deficiencies' in their preparation for waged work.

I think that working people have always taught each other skills; fathers and mothers and the rest of the family. Like they'll try to get their kids or friends into a job. They pass on how to do the job, how to behave and the rest of it. It's like when we were discussing those life and social skills. What a laugh!

(Shubana – parent)

Our kids know more about life than most teachers. Like Jean, she's brought the rest of the kids up with me. But teachers wouldn't think of that as work which needs lots of skills. I suppose it's not their fault really, especially the male teachers. They've never had to do it.

(Susan – parent)

What I've learnt here is how complex it all is. You want your kids to have respect for authority but you also, you don't want them to be walked over. That's why it's important for them to hear from those who have worked, how you can't stand alone, you need each other, you need the unions. The kids on the training scheme are learning the hard way. And the kids will listen more to those who have been unemployed about getting on in education.

(Tim – parent)

The parents argued that it was essential at a time when state schools were suffering from government attacks and experiencing very low morale, that teachers work with parents (see Carspecken and Miller 1983). Corrigan (1988, p. 33) presents a similar argument, that teachers must combine with parents and children to attack the market mechanisms and social engineering introduced by the 1988 Education Reform Act. For the Sands Community College parents such an alliance has been of central value in improving and increasing public confidence in state schools and teachers, which in turn will increase the students' confidence in their own future.

Teacher–Student Relations

The third concern of this paper is teacher–student relations. Griffin (1987, p. 21) informs us that:

One factor which has remained relatively constant over the past hundred years is the dominance of adults in the construction of adolescence, in academic research, youth work, education and the many organizations for the regulation of young people. As unemployment extends the upper limit of youth from 18 to 21 to 25, young people themselves have little say over their own lives, with minimal access to those institutions which are designed to control and protect them.

Such a situation was dominant at Sands Sixth Form and Further Education College. The lack of teacher-parent contact at these institutions was reflected in the teacher–student relations. The dominant ethos was that of the polarization of a predominantly white middle class staff and a predominantly working class student population (see Mays 1962 and Willis 1977). This disjuncture between the teacher and student cultures was highlighted in relation to the black students of Afro-Caribbean and Asian origin.

Black students have grown up in a racially stratified society in which there is little interaction between the black and white populations. The students found that this racial division extended to teacher–student relations, with white teachers knowing little about black people, as they did not visit their homes or spend time in their community. There is now widespread evidence of racism within education, training and employment (see Mac an Ghaill 1988a; Troyna 1987; YETRU 1986; REITS 1985). Black students at Sands Community College recalled similar negative experiences at former schools and training centres. They provided detailed accounts of the operation of racist practices, which were informed by a gender-specific system of racist stereotyping (see Cockburn 1987 and Bryan *et al.* 1985).

Students felt that the non-hierarchical structures of Sands Community College provided them with the opportunity to openly discuss the racist and sexist barriers that they faced in the labour market. They thought this open discussion particularly important as a means of reinforcing explanations of unemployment that shifted away from official 'blame-the-victim' accounts.

> You know and your parents know it's not your fault but when you hear others have got jobs and you keep on being turned away, you lose your confidence and feel cut off. It's been great talking to people here who really know what it's like.
>
> (Iftikhar – student)

In a former study (Mac an Ghaill 1988c, p. 110), I found that student responses to vocational courses demonstrated that state policy intentions are not unproblematically accepted at school level but rather that students' material culture and individual biographies effectively informed their own negotiated transition from school to full-time employment, resulting in unintended outcomes. This was crystallized in the different student and teacher interpretations of 'skill', with the former demanding technical skills and the latter emphasizing the students' need to acquire social competences. It was here that we could see the inadequacy of the overly functionalist and deterministic assumptions of the 'new vocationalists' about the assumed deficiencies of working class youth, who already possessed those very skills which teachers, albeit unintentionally, systematically ignored and undermined (see Shilling 1988).

At Sands Community College students were encouraged to examine such problematic terms as 'skills', 'vocational relevancy' and 'job choice'. So, for example, the students questioned the specific benefits of work experience, when many of them had part-time jobs and experience of domestic labour. At the college career advice and discussion was extended to include the students' own cultural capital, which they acquired in their homes and wider community, in interaction with peers and in their involvement in the local labour market. For example, students were encouraged to continue with traditional working class job hunting skills, such as making personal contacts with local firms and asking relatives and neighbours to make enquiries, in conjunction with the more formal bureaucratic approach of writing letters and preparing for interviews.

Conclusion

In industrial societies the *rite-de-passage* into adulthood has always tended to be a rather ambiguous process, lacking the collective rituals, structures and support found in traditional societies. However, more recently, with the changing socio-economic conditions and the resulting government response, there has been a major fracturing in the coming of age in Britain, in the late 1980s. The concept of 'youth' now appears as a metaphor for limited and limiting opportunities. For example, Willis (1985, p. 6) speaks of how the young unemployed now find themselves in a

> new social condition of suspended animation between school and work. Many of the old transitions into work, into the cultures and organisations of work, into being consumers, into independent accommodation – have been frozen or broken ...

These transitions, which are further structured by the wider social divisions of class, 'race', gender and region, have placed increased pressure on young people as a result of the latest central government policy changes, including the new social security and YTS regulations. With a certain Orwellian rhetoric, young people are now informed that 'youth unemployment' has officially 'disappeared'.

It is argued here that progressive teachers are aware of the limitations of the official political response to the changing material conditions. It may be added that the Trades Union Congress has taken a similar stance in its critique of the new adult employment scheme. However, both groups have so far failed to articulate adequate alternatives with which to move forward. It is suggested here that community colleges offer one such alternative, and that they provide a comprehensive programme of education and training. This needs to be accompanied by the development of nationally recognized qualifications and jobs that ensure quality and equality, in terms of age, class, 'race' and gender. Sands Community College serves to illustrate the potential for a broad alliance between teachers, local communities and the labour movement to challenge the ubiquity of the present terms of the political debate, which is underpinned by assumptions concerning the 'naturalness' and 'inevitability' of the division of mental and manual labour and the resulting division between conception and execution. Such a progressive alliance will enable us to move beyond the present stage in which 'the old is dying, and the new cannot be born; in this interregnum there arises a great diversity of symptoms' (Gramsci 1971, p. 114). The demographic downturn in the 16–19 age group will undoubtedly aid the search for solutions!

Acknowledgements

I would like to thank the parents, students and teachers who cooperated with this study. This chapter has benefited from the comments of Chris Griffin and Henry Miller on earlier drafts. The names of the colleges and the participants involved in the study have been changed to maintain anonymity.

References

Bates, I., Clarke, J., Cohen, P., Finn, D., Moore, R. and Willis, P. (1984). *Schooling for the Dole? The New Vocationalism*, London, Macmillan.
Bryan, B., Dadzie, S. and Scafe, S. (1985). *The Heart of the Race: Black Women's Lives in Britain*, London, Virago.
Carspecken, P. and Miller, H. (1983). 'Parental choice and community control: the case of Croxteth Comprehensive' in A.M. Wolpe and J. Donald (eds), *Is there anyone here from education? Education after Thatcher*, London, Pluto Press.
Cockburn, C. (1987). *Two-Track Training: Sex Inequalities and the YTS*, London, Macmillan.
Coffield, F., Borrill, C. and Marshall, S. (1986). *Growing Up at the Margins: Young Adults in the North East*, Milton Keynes, Open University Press.
Corrigan, P. (1988). 'Gerbil: The Education Reform Bill', *Capital and Class*, 35, 29–33.
Cunningham, J. (1988). 'Either side of the unbridgeable gap between school and work', *The Guardian*, 2 November.
Dale, R. (ed.) (1985). *Education, Training and Employment: Towards a 'New Vocationalism'?* Oxford, Pergamon.
Evans, J. and Davies, B. (1986). 'Fixing the mix in vocational initiatives', Paper presented to the International Sociology of Education Conference, Westhill, Birmingham, January.
Finn, D. (1988). 'Education for jobs: the route to YTS', *Social Studies Review*, 4, 1, 24–9.
Finn, D., Grant, M. and Johnson, R. (1977). 'Social democracy, education and the crisis' in *Working Papers in Cultural Studies*, 10, London, Hutchinson/CCCS.
Gleeson, D. (1984). 'Some-one else's children: the new vocationalism in FE and training' in L. Barton and S. Walker (eds), *Social Crisis and Educational Research*, London, Croom Helm.
Golby, M. (1985). 'The coming crisis at 14+', *Forum*, 27, 3.
Gramsci, A. (1971). *Selections from the Prison Notebooks*, London, Lawrence and Wishart.
Green, A. (1983). 'Education and training: under new masters' in A.M. Wolpe and J. Donald (eds), *Is there Anyone here from Education? Education after Thatcher*, London, Pluto Press.
Griffin, C. (1987). 'The eternal adolescent: psychology and the creation of adolescence', Paper presented at the symposium, 'The Ideological Impact of Social Psychology' British Psychological Association Conference, Oxford University, September.
Hall, S. (1983). 'Education in crisis' in A.M. Wolpe and J. Donald (eds), *Is There Anyone there from Education? Education after Thatcher*, London, Pluto Press.
HMSO (1987). *Regional Trends*, 22, London, HMSO, 22–3.
Jamieson, I. (1985). 'Corporate hegemony or pedagogic liberation? The school–industry movement in England and Wales' in R. Dale (ed.), *Education, Training and Employment*, Oxford, Pergamon.
Jowell, L. *et al.* (eds) (1988). *British Social Attitudes* (5th Report), London, Gower.

Lettieri, A. (1976). 'Factory and school' in A. Gorz (ed.) *The Division of Labour*, Sussex, Harvester Press, 145–58.

Mac an Ghaill, M. (1988a). *Young, Gifted and Black: Student-teacher Relations in the Schooling of Black Youth*, Milton Keynes, Open University Press.

Mac an Ghaill, M. (1988b). 'Teachers: work, culture and power', Paper presented at a conference at St Hilda's College, Oxford, *Histories and Ethnographies of Teachers at Work*, 12–14, September.

Mac an Ghaill, M. (1988c). 'The new vocationalism: the response of a sixth form college' in A. Pollard, J. Purvis and G. Walford (eds), *Education, Training and the New Vocationalism*, Milton Keynes, Open University Press. 109–28.

McNeil, L. (1989). 'Teaching, the state and the curriculum void', Paper presented to the International Sociology of Education Conference, 'The State, Curriculum and Schooling', Newman College, Birmingham, 3–5 January.

Manpower Services Commission (MSC) (1982). *Youth Task Group Report: New Training Initiatives*, London, MSC.

Mays, J.B. (1962). *Education and the Urban Child*, Liverpool, Liverpool University Press.

Moore, R. (1984). 'Schooling and the world of work' in I. Bates *et al.*, *Schooling for the Dole? The New Vocationalism*, London, Macmillan.

Poulantzes, N. (1973). *Political Power and Social Classes*, London, New Left Books/Sheed and Ward.

REITS (1985). *YTS or White TS? Racial Discrimination and Coventry's Youth Training Schemes*, Coventry, REITS.

Shilling, C. (1988). 'The schools vocational programme: "Factories and Industry", a deficit project for the transfer of youth from school to work' in A. Pollard, J. Purvis and G. Walford (eds), *Education, Training and the New Vocationalism*, Milton Keynes. Open University Press, 90–108.

Tomkins, R. (1988). 'A different industrial base', *Financial Times*, Section 3, ii, 1 December.

Troyna, B. (ed.) (1987). *Racial Inequality in Education*, London, Tavistock.

Willis, P. (1977). *Learning to Labour: How Working-class Kids get Working-class Jobs*, Hampshire, Saxon House.

Willis, P. (1985). *Youth Unemployment and the New Poverty: A Summary of a Local Authority Review and Framework for Policy Development on Youth and Youth Unemployment*, Wolverhampton, Wolverhampton Local Authority.

Youth Employment and Training Resource Unit (1986). *'They must think that We are Stupid': The Experiences of Young People on the Youth Training Scheme*, Birmingham, Trade Union Research Centre.

James Avis | 7

Student responses to the curriculum: towards an alternative practice

The aim of this chapter is to bring together a number of themes that underlie the research I have been conducting on further education over the last few years. The centrepiece has been a study of students and teachers in a West Midlands college of further education.[1] In this chapter I consider student orientations to the curriculum and the vocational consequences of these. A number of issues are raised that an alternative educational practice needs to address.

Before considering the substantive material it is important to reflect on the scope of educational practice current in further education. This ranges from the academic, for example 'A' levels and to a lesser extent GCSE, to the vocational and prevocational. Reflecting those divisions Gleeson has described the tripartite structure of further education.[2]

Tertiary modern	The 'new' FE; incorporating the unqualified unemployed and unemployable. Curricular emphasis is on 'generic skills' ...
Craft	Mainly day release craft tradition (male dominated); but now incorporating female craft skills: hair dressing, beauty therapy, catering, nursing and so forth. Curricular emphasis is on training for home and non-work.
Academic-Technical	Full and part time academic/technical tradition incorporating the concept of 'educated' skilled labour. Here the curricular emphasis is on 'education' via English, maths and science. Students include those following GCE, social work, technician, management, secretarial and other courses which assume academic competence.

Though these divisions remain in place the thrust of vocationalism has continued.

A number of elements characteristic of 'the tertiary modern' sector of FE, for example the focus on social and life skills, the stress on process as opposed to the content of learning, have entered other sectors of FE including those concerned with GCSEs.[3] The 'new' FE has always been concerned with student subjectivity and has attempted to form it in ways that articulate with the needs of industry. Developments in A-level and the critiques of Higginson have introduced to A-level discussions the need for 'broadening', as has A/S-level.[4] These developments can be interpreted as an attempt to undermine the presumed anti-business bias of academic education and to ensure that students are sufficiently 'broadened' to willingly accept a market economy and their assumed position within it.

Vocationalism is not all of a piece and straddles the generic emphasis of the new vocationalism as well as the specific occupational focus of craft education. Despite these differences there is a unity that resides in the treatment of subjectivity. Craft vocationalism attempts to reproduce and socialize its charges into an appropriate occupational identity.[5] Similarly, the new vocationalism attempts to form an identity which moulds the generic worker in the image of the 'new enterprise culture'.[6] What is lacking in these versions is the development of their antithesis, a critical vocationalism. What would this look like? And how would it relate to the various streams in further education? And what interest would teachers have in the development of a critical vocationalism?

Student responses

I want to consider student responses to pedagogic relations and in particular their relation to and subjective orientations towards educational knowledge. This task poses an important question: what is the relation of these orientations to vocationalism and to the development of a critical educational practice? The students discussed in this section were pursuing A-levels, the Certificate of Further Education (a forerunner of the CPVE), BEC and TEC National Diplomas in Business Studies and Engineering.[7] All were full-time students and the research was conducted in the early 1980s.[8] While these student groupings do not represent the diversity of further education, they are important as they illustrate different trajectories in FE, the academic/non-academic and the vocational/prevocational. It is necessary to consider such groups' experiences of FE to assess the varying stances that students bring with them to college and with which a radical practice should engage.

Research that has considered students' transition from school to college has generally found a more positive orientation towards college than school. Students experience college as a more adult institution and as one that anticipates waged labour if not studentdom.[9] But their perception of college as focused towards the adult world is not necessarily translated into teachers' pedagogic practice. The form of pedagogic relations that students experience will be the result of a number of processes, departmental traditions, teachers' subject cultures, the varying constraints under which teachers labour and their solutions to pedagogic problems and subsequent survival strategies. While teachers' biographies and idiosyncrasies will have an important bearing on their practice so too will the traditions and departments in which they are located. It is at the juncture of pedagogic practice that there are variations between courses and the experiences of students following different trajectories through FE.

The Certificate of Further Education (CFE) is a prevocational qualification for students who have few, if any, qualifications. The students I studied were pursuing one of three CFE variants, two of which were specifically linked to a limited range of occupations (pre-nursing/caring and engineering); the third had a more general occupational focus (general). Students were allocated to the different course on the basis of vocational interest and academic potential; those who were perceived to be less able were directed away from the vocational CFEs to the general, as were students who were felt to be unsuited for GCE O-levels. In many colleges the CPVE has taken over the role of CFE courses.

What students on the vocationally specific CFEs valued was the practical hands on experience the courses provided. This was gained through practical classroom sessions and work experience. Thus a group of CFE engineering students when asked how they would improve the course commented:

Pupinder: I'd have more practicals.
In only one year they don't teach you...
You don't learn it properly...
you know, motor mechanics, right...
Ashvin: You don't have that much practical in the first year, if it was longer...
'cos you only have practical once a week and you can't really learn very much 'cos it's only for about an hour an' a half.

Similarly a group of pre-nursing students liked their work experience describing it as simply 'great', also enjoying the practical aspects of first aid.

On first aid we learn about putting bandages on ... all about the patient that's a good subject.

This contrasted with their feelings towards their more academic subject where, like their engineering counterparts, they suggested that more practical work would enhance the course.

JA: What would make physics more interesting?
Sheila: More practicals.
All: Yeah.
Sheila: More things we could do on our own ...
Satbir: and he just goes on with loads and loads of stuff

What is important about the orientations of both groups is that these conjoined with their vocational interests, the one being orientated towards the practical world of nursing and the other to that of engineering. In paradoxical ways these students' interests were reflected in pedagogic relations.

In marking the difference between school and college a number of CFE engineering students remarked that teachers at college treated them as adults. Students felt they had a more 'equitable' relation with their teachers.

Teachers [FE] are alright,
They're not like the teachers at school, you can have a joke with them. I mean

they don't mind, they do it themselves. I mean it's different from teachers at school ...
If you said something to them [school teachers] like a joke they would chuck you out, give you detention, tell the headmaster, but here you can joke with the teachers and they don't mind really.

(CFE engineering student)

Another group of CFE engineering students held similar views.

Robert: It's different here they treat you more like grown ups than at school, and here I reckon they're interested in what you're doing, 'cos at school it was just, they'd throw you a book and tell you what to do, what pages or exercises to do and just get on with it. At this college they explain it better and go over it with you ...
Winston: He's a teacher, not afraid of using words ...
Delroy: They have a laugh with you.

These comments not only reflect disillusionment in their relations with teachers at the end of these students' school careers. They also reflect the more open and 'adult' relationship that these male students had with some of their FE teachers. 'He's not afraid of using words' is significant as it moves away from the 'rarefied' and 'prissy' atmosphere of the school and anticipates the 'real world' of waged labour. However this world of waged labour is one that is both gendered and classed. There is a relation between the practical orientations of these male students, the pedagogic relations in which they are placed and the masculinity of the skilled worker on the shopfloor or in the workshop. This anticipation of the rough and ready masculinity of the shopfloor is consonant with a particular relation to knowledge that emphasizes the practical, the hands on experience, the ability to solve practical problems and the celebration of manual over mental labour. It poses not only a relation to knowledge but also heralds an orientation to a particular class destiny, that of the manual worker. This relation is gendered and encourages and validates the formation of a type of masculinity that is homologous with the social relations of the shopfloor. The relation of gender to a practical orientation can further be explored by considering the pre-nursing students.[10]

Bev Skeggs has suggested that low level caring courses for girls serve as a domestic apprenticeship and rather than relating to occupational destinies serve to place girls within the family.[11] She similarly argues that the types of validation of manual labour that are open to working class lads are not available to girls.[12] The girls pursuing the pre-nursing courses in my study valued the practical aspects of their course. It was this element of their studies that carried an occupational purchase and was used as a marker against which other aspects of the course were measured. Indeed, the contrast between these elements and the academic side of the course served to reaffirm their occupational orientations and push them towards the world of paid labour. As in the case of the engineering course for both students and teachers occupational focus became reflected in pedagogic practices. Here a pre-nursing course tutor reflects on her practice.

... perhaps in the first year I'm a greater disciplinarian. I don't know whether it's right or wrong but it's a matter of – in hospital there's got to be a great deal of discipline, and self-discipline, and things like being on time for classes, behaving in class, general attitudes – I'm strict about that in the first year.[13]

This teacher was also concerned with dress and appearance and required all her students to study dress at O-level. First she argued that the subject would encourage awareness of dress and appearance and therefore, 'It gives them a consciousness of clothing that helps them keep their uniform correct ... and dress themselves neatly which is another important thing in nursing'.

Second, she felt it would develop the types of manipulative skill that students would need in practical nursing and that the examination in dress echoed those found in nurse training. Clearly this teacher was concerned to encourage her students to develop the types of skills and attitudes that she deemed essential for a potential nurse. Her practices validated a particular form of femininity and also shaped a pedagogic stance that insisted on disciplined students. She emphasized the importance of timekeeping, general attitudes, classroom behaviour and standards of dress. This teacher legitimated her practice through her occupational commitment and experience as a nurse in much the same way as the CFE engineering teacher would have legitimated his freer use of language by reference to the potential occupational destinies of his students. The pre-nursing students, however, 'misrecognized' the practices of their teacher as referring back to the social relations of the school rather than as anticipating the social relations of nursing. For example Damyanti commented 'If you're away you've got to bring a note from home, a bit childish really'.

Another group of pre-nursing students whose course tutor adopted a similar stance stated:

Sheila: It's just like it [school] you're hounded around ...
Brenda: You get bullied around by some of the teachers ...
Sheila: You get hounded and hounded just like school, they [teachers] don't treat you any different.

These students perceived the teaching relations in which they were placed as relating more to school than to the hospital and therefore were seen as demeaning and childish. This misrecognition of teacher strategies paradoxically reinforced and strengthened orientations to the world of paid labour. It also encouraged a negative comparison between their work experience and the college relations in which they were placed. Consequently students' vocational orientations celebrated the practical and distanced them from the more academic elements in their course. The division between mental and manual labour was formed by the practices of these students and their interpretations of pedagogic relations.

For CFE students pursuing the engineering and pre-nursing courses educational experiences were assessed in terms of their vocational purchase. This in turn was measured against a notion of the practical, a notion that constructed the practical in terms 'of doing', with hands on experience. However a rider must be added. In the case of at least some of the CFE engineering and pre-nursing students, if their occupational desires were to be attained it was necessary to enter another course. This was particularly the case with the pre-nurses where acceptance for nurse training was dependent on passing a number of GCE O-levels. Their subjective orientation to educational knowledge was one that validated the practical and therefore other forms of educational knowledge were deemed less valid, simply hurdles to be overcome in the pursuit of occupational desires. CFE students were not alone in holding such instrumentalist orientations to educational knowledge; similar patterns were found, to some extent, among all the students. What is important is that an orientation towards practical knowledge contains an epistemology which through its focus on doing is necessarily limited. It presupposes that the world is directly knowable and therefore distances students from the potential insights of academic knowledge.

TEC students, like CFE students, validated the practical application of the syllabus they were pursuing. These students, for the most part, were oriented towards a career in engineering. The route they saw themselves following to achieve this goal was completion of the course, thus gaining access to higher education to follow a degree course, or failing that an HNC. Only after having completed their higher education did they intend to obtain a job in engineering. Most of these students were occupationally committed and used this as the vantage point from which to assess their course. Those parts of the course that did not appear to have a direct relevance to engineering were deemed illegitimate. These students extended the practical not just to include hands on experience and workshop practice but also to validate those forms of knowledge that could be used in the solution of engineering problems. However, communications and complementary studies were seen as having little direct link to the world of engineering and so were met with some hostility.

>Malcolm: The only subjects I'm not that keen on are really the communications an' complementary studies...
> I can't really see the point of doing them...
> Now I mean, like, with my project, like...
> we had to do a project while we were there [on a residential] had to do agriculture background, an' I did this project an' I thought what use was it, was that going to be for me in engineering, I mean nothing, that's the only part though...
>
>JA: Do the rest of you feel...
>All: Yeah [confused]
>John: Too much to do with people...
>Will: That's what they ought to do it on, *on engineering*!

This quote illustrates the way in which these students subjectively orientated themselves towards educational knowledge and the way in which they supported a particular and specific construction of that knowledge. Communications and complementary studies were perceived as having too much to do with people and were thought to be concerned with issues that lay outside the scope of engineering. They were a diversion from the interests of engineering. This orientation carries a very particular relation to knowledge. It constructs and conjoins with a model of engineering, technical and scientific knowledge that separates these from their social contexts. The implication is that such knowledge has universal application and that it is inherently beyond the social. By this I mean it is divorced from social relations and thus has an authority that transcends these and which is legitimated through its universality and inherent neutrality. Such knowledge becomes technicized and the social basis of scientific and technical knowledge is occluded. Thus the division between the technical and the social is sustained. Student responses to communications and complementary studies represent and collude in the division between the technical and the social. Such a division, the students, responses to it, sustains a view of the world as 'a nonsocial interconnection of things'. This division is also sustained by the curricular divisions that separate technical knowledge from other forms. Lenhardt writes:[14]

> The theme of experience, the relation between the working subject and his environment, is not just subdivided with this separation, but rather turned into a taboo. In the specialised knowledge of vocational education, the world is not presented as a relation between individuals society and the technical world, but instead a nonsocial interconnection of things.

Even when communications was valued by students it was not because it introduced the social to technological processes but rather because it developed skills that had an instrumental value.

> I thought it was a waste of time at first an' then I came to realise that it has some importance 'cos ... suppose you pass at the end of the year an' go off to university an' you get your degree or something...
> If you can't communicate to the next person you've had it, so I think it plays an important role.

While Satvinder's right he fails to make a connection between technical processes and social relations. Paradoxically the technicism of these engineering students reproduced the division between technical and 'social' knowledge. The former was validated through its presumed capacity to solve and relate to engineering problems – the practical applicability of knowledge became important: if it were not applicable it was rendered irrelevant. There is a continuity between these and the other vocational students. In as much as both were concerned with practical application they had become distanced from the more esoteric forms of academic knowledge, particularly those that attempted to place the practical within its social and political context.

The A-level students in my study were alienated from academic knowledge and appeared for the most part to endure their studies rather than being actively engaged. This was despite the fact that they had been academically successful, were following a high status course and had not only chosen to study A-levels but had also selected their subjects on the basis of interest. Peter commented, 'there's nothing interesting, sorry about this, in coming to lectures'. Other A-level students remarked:

> June: I'm alright in the hour lessons, but when it's two hours I start to fall asleep, my mind starts to wander off after an hour an' I'm just picking odd things up.
> Ranjit: An' for $2\frac{1}{2}$ hours or whatever, he just sits there an' dictates – solid dictation ... I don't think I've been to all his lessons in a week.

And Dave explained:

> It does get boring, all the time, but you have to go through patches ...

So it's the time after 12, 13 years of education people's interest is bound to wane.

The responses of these A-level students to curriculum and pedagogic relations echoed those of CFE and TEC students. They found the curriculum and pedagogic relations in which they were placed to be uninspiring. Their curricular experiences failed to develop an enthusiastic response and yet many of them remained orientated towards higher education, albeit after a year's break.[15] On occasion teachers were able to ameliorate the constraints of the academic curriculum and excite students' interest. Yet for the most part the curriculum was to be endured, accommodated and used to obtain credentials. These students' relation to the curriculum and educational knowledge was based on an instrumentalism that divorced educational knowledge from students' life worlds and rendered it meaningless. Educational knowledge was commodified, to be used and consumed in the gaining of credentials having no real validity beyond that remit.

The only group who seemed to hold an enthusiastic response to their course and educational knowledge in general were the BEC students. They consistently valued studentdom and celebrated the way in which their curriculum had encouraged them to develop an understanding of social and political issues. Gary suggested:

> It [BEC] just brings people out they're just not afraid to say what they want to say anymore...
> I think it's really good because I think it really broadens your view of life...
> I mean since I've been here, I know – you sort of read communist magazines, socialist standards, Karl Marx an' all that.

Anil, commenting on A-level students, argued:

> Ranjit only knows his sociology...
> Any current affairs, he has no idea on current affairs...
> I've talked to him an' he's totally...
> That's all he knows political history and sociology...
> an' there's another chap in science an' he just knows his science and physics an' that's it...
> An' we know bits of everything, we know law, we known economics, we know administration, an' by the time you put on options, we know insurance an' industry, an' read the *Financial Times*, read the *Guardian* an' do things like that.

There is a danger here of accepting these eulogistic tones too readily. There are two points to be made. First, students valued their ability to control and dictate the course of lessons. They justified such conduct by arguing that free flowing discussion was broadening and in some tangential way was related to their course.

> I mean with our sociology teacher Mr [ ], I mean half the time he wants to teach us something an' we say can we talk about this that or t'other ...
> an' we went through the whole lesson talking about this stuff, you know, an' it's sociology right, an' we did learn something, but it's nothing to do with the course.

Second, for a number of students, such as Gary, who valued the broadening aspects of the course and who espoused left wing sentiments there was in their stance an incipient elitism which undermined their radicalism. Gary talked dismissively of those who failed to acquire a simple understanding of Marxism.

> You can find people in the street who start going on about these commies ... but they don't know what they're on about ... So you feel really good when you say to them, 'well, what do you feel is wrong with Karl Marx?' an' they start saying, 'Oh, you know he was, you know', an' they don't really know.
>
> They just know the names an' then you start to argue them down ...
> *It's just great to argue them down.*
>
> (my emphasis)

A similar position was held by Dave, an A-level student who was dismissive of those who laboured in low waged and exploitative jobs.[16]

Towards an alternative practice

The preceding material has explored the ways in which different groups of students in FE responded to the curriculum. These responses constitute and shape different relations to vocationalism and contribute to the ongoing formation of classed, gendered and raced relations. For example, instrumentalism and celebration of the practical of the CFE students pushed them towards the world of manual labour. Similarly, the engineering students' dismissal of the social aspect of their curriculum contributes towards the formations of a section of the middle class, e.g. technician/technologists. A similar point could be made about BEC and A-level students whose practices contributed towards the ongoing formation of a generalized fraction of the middle class.[17] The notion of formation here is important, as it views classes as continually in process and as being accomplished through social practice.[18] This is an advance on the reproductive problematic which carries with it an understanding of educational relations as producing agents to fill places at the site of waged labour.[19] The notion of formation is important as it suggests that relations of class, race and gender are accomplished in and through practice. This allows interventions to be made into formative processes. Education can thus become one site of intervention and a critical educational practice is rendered possible.[20]

Curriculum divisions in further education are the result of teacher practices, institutional processes and the selection procedures used in course allocation. They are also a consequence of the 'choices' that students make when entering college.[21] The type of course students select, and their vocational interests, will have some bearing on the way in which they approach the curriculum, as will their individual histories. Similarly the social differences that divide students and which are reconstituted among them as a result of social practices will also influence their orientations to the curriculum. The key social divisions here relate to class, race and ethnicity. This chapter has been concerned with students' orientations to the curriculum, their validation of knowledge forms and the consequences of these for their vocational orientations and potential class destinies. It is important to recognize that an ongoing process is being discussed in which students have made and are in the course of making personal investments in particular identities. This investment carries a particular orientation to the curriculum and validation of knowledge. It is necessary to consider how a radical educational practice should respond to a context in which students have different orientations to the curriculum and validate different forms of knowledge.

One of the key insights of progressive education is that practice should start from where the student is. It should build upon student interest thereby moving students on to a higher level of understanding. The problem has been that much progressive education has failed to do this and has become trapped in the present, serving merely to confirm what the student already knew. Traditional academic education has been condemned for its 'banking concept', its hopeless abstraction and therefore its inability to connect with the experience or problems faced by students.[22] Technical education has similarly been castigated for its failure to recognize the social implication of its practice. These criticisms not only describe curricular divisions but are also constituted in students' responses to the curriculum. These divisions are not innocent but play a real part in the constitution of social difference. I have discussed this in terms of class destinies and to some extent in the case of gendered differentiation. Any intervention into these practices would find it necessary to challenge these curriculum distinctions. For example, a technical curriculum that allocates separate timetabled space for students to deal with issues related to the social aspects of technological processes emphasizes this distinction. In other words, the curriculum implies the technical can be separated from the social and the two thereby become separated from each other. This separation easily collapses into a technical determinism that explains technological progress through the developmental logic of a technical rationality. If the distinction between the social and the technical is to be overcome it is necessary to unite them, underlining their inseparability. This would require curriculum divisions to be transcended and, most importantly, would require teachers to rethink their educational practices. This must be an important strand in any critical educational project. For once it is recognized that technological development is not the result of an autonomous logic but is a consequence of social action, it becomes easier to realize that technological development could be subject to collective scrutiny and control.

It thus becomes important to inquire into the stakes and investments that teachers have made in particular teaching identities. For many technical teachers the recognition of the social aspects of technology would require a transformation of their practice and a realization of the political nature of education. This would require teachers to develop a new conception of what it is to be a teacher.

The introduction of a sense of history within the technical curriculum would be one way of recognizing the social. For example, the historical development of technological and work processes could be explored by indicating alternative techniques that could have been developed and were not because of social practices, interests and struggles between those involved. Here the sexual division of labour could be touched on: for example, in whose image were particular techniques and work processes designed.[23] Current production practices could be explored in terms of the available alternatives. A consideration of the international division of labour and the production processes used would enable an analysis of these. This could lead to a discussion of management and worker strategies – even

Taylorism and post-Fordism could be touched on.[24] These activities could be based around workshop practice, thus allowing students to acquire a range of engineering/technical competences at the same time as gaining an understanding of the social decisions involved in the development of labour processes. Not only would students' practical interests and their desire to understand technical processes be met, but students would be encouraged to recognize the inseparability of the social from technological development. The social decisions and interests that shape technological development would be foregrounded and students would become sensitized to the exclusions and limitations involved in changes in work processes. Such educational experiences could feed into the development of an anti-racist, anti-sexist and anti-classist education. This could emerge from a consideration of the sexual, social and international division of labour, for an understanding of these divisions would encourage a recognition of the way in which the labour process has often been used in an exploitative and oppressive way.

Teachers need to reflect on the consequences of their pedagogic practice and of the curricular divisions within which they work. These need to be transformed to provide a more educative context. Through classroom practices teachers can intervene and attempt to subvert the undesirable and anti-educative consequences of curricular divisions. Indeed in the current conjucture and the continuation of Bakerite educational policies it may become increasingly difficult for teachers to act outside their immediate sphere of influence, the classroom. At the same time it is important to reflect on the equivocations of education policy and curricular divisions. For example, the proposed changes in A-levels are doubed-edged. On one level there is a call for increasing vocationalization of academic studies. However, vocational relevance is not without its positive and critical side. Vocationalization could lead to A-levels becoming more relevant to students' lives, thereby undercutting the alienation my students experienced. Paradoxically, those elements of academic knowledge that served to alienate students – the tendency towards abstraction and distance from life worlds which served to commodify academic knowledge – could be overcome. Ironically, students' interest could then be used to introduce them to the strengths of academic knowledge which were precisely those elements that had previously served to alienate them. Students could be encouraged to use analysis and abstraction to understand society at large. They could develop systematic approaches that would encourage generalization, thereby enhancing critical facilities. Such an outcome is by no means inevitable. Alternatively an instrumental orientation to knowledge could be retained. This is partly a result of teachers' failure to understand the relation between students' collective vantage points and the knowledge they experience. It is also a consequence of a vocationalism that can very easily be trapped in the present and that accepts social relations as given, thereby positing an epistemology that fails to grasp the social construction and provisional nature of knowledge.

The gap betwen students' life experiences and the nature of academic education is wide and results in the impoverishment of the academic curriculum. Students endure and commodify the academic curriculum, treating it instrumentally. Consequently its critical potential is lost. Because of students' alienated relation to academic knowledge it is lived as it is appropriated, inauthentically, being disposed of rather than being used as means to engage the world. Academic education offers the potential for generalization, systematization and abstraction. However, when students and teachers approach this type of knowledge instrumentally this potential is not fully realized for the resulting 'knowledge' is not used in any meaningful way to engage with the world. What is important is not the designation of knowledge as academic or otherwise, but rather students' and teachers' orientations to it. It is this that renders such knowledge useful or merely fustian.

The move from student concerns to a critical educational practice must be sensitive to the nature and positionalities of the student body. Students are positioned differently in relation to gender, race, class and so on. The difference between progressivism and a critical educational project is that the latter recognizes the differential positioning of students and embodies a notion of collectivity that moves beyond the narrow individualism of progressivism. It becomes important, therefore, to consider student positionalities and the differing needs and demands that these will make of academic knowledge. If teachers fail to reflect on this and presume that an apparently neutral form of pedagogy will suffice they will merely engage in a non-reflexive practice that tends to work within existing hegemonic curricular frameworks. Educational practice assumes a model of the student and much academic practice is orientated towards white middle class male students. By taking into account student positionalities alternative practices could be developed that articulated with the needs and interests of a wider student constituency.

Within educational institutions there is a hierarchy and stratification of knowledge which is reflected in the differentiation of the student body. Students who are placed on different courses are presented with different forms of knowledge. The lower the level the more 'concrete' and 'factually' based the curriculum. Educational strategies need to be devised that work within and accept students' validation of the practical and concrete aspects of their course and yet aim to move students beyond the present so that they can develop a critical and reflexive understanding of their position within society and the course they are pursuing.

Those students who are pursuing higher level courses and have greater access to academic knowledge forms should become aware of the constructedness and provisionality of such knowledge as well as its limitations in everyday practice. For students such as Dave and Gary this relativism could challenge their elitism and presumption of superiority.

I have discussed a number of alternative practices; but what unites them is a commitment to social transformation and to the encouragement of a critical citizenship. Giroux writes[25]

> . . . citizenship in this case becomes a process of dialogue and commitment rooted in a fundamental belief in the possibility of public life and the development of forms of solidarity that allow people to reflect and organise in order to criticise and constrain the power of the state and to 'overthrow relations' which inhibit and prevent the realisation of humanity.

Some of the social differentiations surrounding FE could be undermined if the concomitant curricular divisions were removed. Current moves towards modularization herald this possibility. A modular system could accommodate the diversity present in further education and yet allow students to pursue a curriculum that was more in line with their interests. However, such a modularized curriculum would have to be designed in such a way as to break down the divisions between the technical and academic, the vocational and non-vocational. The social underpinnings of technological processes would have to be brought to the foreground and there would have to be a recognition of students differing positionalities thus enabling educational knowledge to become 'really useful'.[26]

Conclusion

An alternative educational practice needs to be attentive to students' interests and should work within these. Students' interests lead to the development of knowledge that enables some understanding of society. A radical educational practice needs to connect with these insights and develop them into a fuller understanding whereby students are encouraged to explore more systematic ways of understanding the interconnections present in the social formation.

Students are positioned differentially in relation to knowledge. A critical practice needs to recognize and work within these. Students' positionalities will have a bearing on what counts as useful knowledge and will influence the way in which students appropriate the educational knowledge they encounter. One of the insights offered by cultural studies is that people 'read' and appropriate educational knowledge differentially and therefore a critical practice must be sensitive to positional readings.

Connell argues that education disorganizes the cultural knowledge that working class students bring to school. At the same time we might add schools often seek to organize conservative forms of popular knowledge.[27] While a critical practice needs to work with students' cultural knowledge it must move beyond this to produce a fuller and interconnective understanding of the social formation.[28] At this juncture there is a convergence between those forms of empowering education which have different starting points in, for example, anti-racism and anti-sexism, and an emancipatory educational project. The recognition of students' positionalities calls forth an educational approach that incorporates these elements.

A critical educational practice can be developed at a number of levels: policy formation, institutional framework, and classroom teaching. The outcome of any radical project cannot be spelled out; all that can be hoped for is that students will have developed a fuller understanding of the interconnections and complexities within the social formation which would thus promote a critical citizenship.

Notes

1 See R.J. Avis, *Further Education in Transition: Institutional Change, Teachers and Students*, Unpublished PhD thesis, The University of Birmingham, 1988.
2 D. Gleeson, 'Further education, tripartism and the labour market', in D. Gleeson (ed.), *Youth Training and the Search for Work*, RKP, 1983, p. 38.
3 See M.F.D. Young, 'Vocationalizing tendencies in recent British educational policy: sources of exclusion or empowerment', in C. Chitty (ed.), *Redefining the Comprehensive Experience*, Bedford Way papers, No 32, London, The University of London, 1987.
4 Department of Education and Science and the Welsh Office, *Advancing A Levels: Report of a*

Committee appointed by the Secretary of State for Education and Science and the Secretary of State for Wales (The Higginson Report), HMSO, 1988.
5 See D. Gleeson et al., Further Education or Training?, London, Routledge and Kegan Paul, 1980.
6 See R. Moore, 'Education and the ideology of production', British Journal of Sociology of Education, Vol 8, No 2, 1987.
7 See Máirtín Mac an Ghail, 'The new vocationalism: the response of a sixth form college', in A. Pollard et al. (eds.) Education, Training and the New Vocationalism, Open University Press, 1988, for a discussion of student experiences of the CPVE.
8 See Avis, Further Education in Transition for a fuller discussion of these students' experiences.
9 See P. Aggleton, Rebels without a Cause, London, Falmer; 1987 R. King, School and College, London, Routledge and Kegan Paul, 1976.
10 At the time of the field work only one boy was pursuing the pre-nursing course.
11 B. Skeggs, 'Gender reproduction and further education: domestic apprenticeship', British Journal of Sociology of Education, Vol 9, No 2, 1988.
12 See P. Willis, Learning to Labour: How Working Class Kids get Working Class Jobs, Hampshire, Saxon House, 1977.
13 In the first year students studied the CFE and then in the second year studied for GCE O-Level.
14 G. Lenhardt, 'Schools and waged labour', Economic and Industrial Democracy, Vol 2, No 1, 1981, p. 204.
15 See Avis Further Education in Transition.
16 See ibid. for a discussion of elitism among A-level students and also Aggleton, Rebels without a Cause.
17 For a more detailed discussion see Avis, Further Education in Transition.
18 See A. Przeworski, Proletariat into a class: the process of class formation from Karl Kautsky's 'The Class Struggle to recent controversies', Politics and Society, Vol 7, No 4, 1977 and P. Gilroy, There Ain't No Black in the Union Jack, London, Hutchinson, 1987.
19 See for example L. Althusser, 'Ideology and ideological state apparatuses', in Lenin and Philosophy and Other Essays, Monthly Review Press, 1971; H. Bowles and S. Gintis, Schooling in Capitalist America, New York, Routledge and Kegan Paul, 1978.
20 See S. Aronowitz and H. Giroux, Education Under Siege, RKP, 1986; P. Freire and I. Shor, A Pedagogy for Liberation, London, Macmillan, 1987.
21 It is important to recognize the constraints that bear on the 'choices' students make. A better formulation would stress the negativity of choice.
22 See P. Freire, The Politics of Education, London, Macmillan, 1985.
23 See, for example, C. Cockburn, Brothers, London, Pluto 1983, for a discussion of printing which shows the way in which technology was developed with the male worker in mind.
24 See the ongoing debate in Marxism Today, 1988–89, on post-Fordism.
25 H. Giroux, 'Citizenship, public philosophy and the struggle for democracy', Educational Theory, Vol 37, No 2, 1987, p. 105.
26 A number of the themes raised in this section have been taken up and developed in J. Avis and R. Johnson, 'Education practice, professionalism and social relations' in Education Group II Department of Cultural Studies the University of Birmingham (ed.) Education Still Possible: Schooling and Training in England since 1979, London, Unwin Hyman, forthcoming.
27 R.W. Connel, Making the Difference, London, Allen and Unwin, 1982.
28 C. Mullard, Anti-Racist Education: The Three O's, Sydney, NAME, 1984.

Beverley Skeggs

Gender reproduction and further education: the case of domestic apprenticeships

This chapter falls into three sections. The first section provides a theoretical framework through an examination of the gender-biased concepts used in FE analysis; in addition the legacy of the historical development of FE and the contemporary situation are discussed; and finally the institutional location of caring courses is analysed. The second section draws on ethnographic research into the experience of 83 young, white, working class women following NAFE 'caring' courses in a northern further education college. These courses were: Preliminary Certificate in Social Care (PCSC), Preliminary Health Service (PHS) Course and Community Care. The section examines in detail the way in which the students' experience of the vocational caring curriculum both informs and brings about their collusion in the construction of their own subjectivity. This involves an examination of gender and class reproduction, and the state's attempt at restructuring social relations through vocational initiatives (Clarke and Willis 1984). Drawing on this ethnographic evidence, a third section attempts to delineate the forms and types of change needed to redress the current form of 'caring' courses. While recognizing the role of such courses in the maintenance of social order through 'moralizing' and 'normalizing' functions (Foucault 1977; Donzelot 1979), it nevertheless suggests both the short- and long-term changes that are necessary to counteract the identification of young, working class women as primarily 'caring' domestic labourers.

In the context of recent studies of vocationalism and unemployment, attention has been drawn to the increasing amount of social control being exercised through vocational schemes (Stafford 1981; Finn 1984; Bates *et al*. 1984; Walker and Barton 1986). Such methods of control are gender-specific. Gleeson (1986b) has argued that one of the functions of trainee schemes has been to condition young people to think of themselves as outside the mainstream of society. Yet such a response is dependent upon the gender of the trainees. In this ethnographic study, through their identification with caring and femininity the students come to consider their familial role, outside of the occupational structure but well inside the mainstream of society, as being of primary importance.

Similarly the mental-manual division, which Browne (1981) maintains is the central structural constraint and key organizing principle of institutional education, has limitations for explaining young women's responses to further education. The research suggests that students 'read' mental labour as being outside their aspirations, while manual labour was considered to be 'dirty' and in opposition to the culture of femininity. Most of the female students' attempts to contest aspects of either the curriculum or the teacher's interactions were informed by attempts to overcome powerlessness, rather than any positive celebration of power (as in Willis 1977). Moreover, theoretical concepts concerning the school to work transition take on new meanings or become redundant when the importance female students give to 'marriage markets' is introduced (Skeggs 1986). Likewise, historically the term 'vocational' has referred to marriage and motherhood when applied to young women (Marks 1976). Gleeson and Hopkins (1987) identify the 'new FE' as being courses not associated with employment, yet for young working class women there is nothing new about this type of provision. Thus, Blunden (1982) has documented how the early provision of domestic and caring courses centred on the assumption that the primary role for women was outside of the labour market in the family, as the next section indicates.

The structural framework

Background and development of NAFE caring courses

Whereas young working class men have been repeatedly considered by the state as a potential threat to social order (Rees 1983), young working class women have been seen as the means by which social order can be maintained, representing what Foucault (1977) and Donzelot (1979) identify as the 'means for moralising the working classes'. Johnson (1970) argues that the early provision of education for working class children was seen as compensation for a morally deficient family, able to act as a stabilizing force, imposing upon children a middle class view of family functions and responsibility. Paterson (1988) shows how the notion of 'problem families' can be seen to derive from patterns of nineteenth-century state regulated schooling. For instance, the first courses established in 1906 were not specifically related to the labour market; rather, they were concerned with the general domestic practices of young working class women (Skeggs 1986). Likewise, the teaching on the earliest courses was informed by what Summers (1979) has identified as the 'domestic ideal', in which the organization of domestic life in the middle class Victorian family was considered to be the appropriate model for all types of domestic education; an ideal which assumed that the domestic practices of the working class were somehow deficient. These general moral anxieties, Weeks (1981) and Coward (1983) have argued, were the means by which the revolutionary threat (Stedman-Jones 1971) and the hygiene-pollutionary threat of the working class (Mort 1987) became dissipated. Rose (1985) demonstrates how the relationship between the mother and the child became the means whereby nationalistic and moral issues were articulated. Thus the potential conflict between social classes was considered to be a problem of morality, rather than structural inequality; its solution being in familial regulation, primarily through the mother (David 1980) and mother-child relationship (Riley 1983; Walkerdine 1985).[1]

These moral anxieties existed alongside specific labour market demands for domestic servants (Hall 1979), and the need for fit and healthy gun fodder for the Boer War (Dyhouse 1977; Davin 1978). Moreover, they were taking place alongside changes in the forms of power deployed by the state. Using Foucault's categories, Cook (1988) identifies a change from ancient power to modern power whereby behavioural norms and techniques of surveillance were established. These conditions provided the basis for the development of caring courses, a development which was both localized and haphazard (Blunden 1982). They also provide the legacy for the more recent contemporary developments, in which caring courses have only a tenuous relationship with the labour market.

Contemporary influences

This is exemplified in the relationship between the courses and their corresponding section of the labour market, the 'personal social services', which have experienced a dramatic collapse in growth rate since 1970 and a substantial decrease in expenditure since 1976 (CSE 1979; Ungerson 1987). Nevertheless, while these cuts and contractions have been occurring, the caring courses have been expanding in a similar way to the 'explosion' of familial/parental education in schooling (David 1987); see Tables 8.1 and 8.2.

Table 8.1 National caring course participation rates

Course	1977/78	1978/79	1979/80	1980/81	1981/82	1982/83	% increase
Pre-residential/		2,017	2,068	2,016	2,261		12
PHS	–	540	970	1,062			97
CC (CGLI)	744	1,128	2,070	3,813			413
Totals	2,761	3,736	5,056	7,136			159

Source: FEU (1982).

Table 8.2 Local caring course participation rates

Course	1979/80	1980/81	1981/82	1982/83	1983/84	1984/85	1985/86	% increase
PCSC	17	28	36	42	66	75	73	329
PHS	14	23	27	34	55	30	7*	
CC (CGLI)	11	32	48	74	107	73	82	645
Totals	42	83	111	150	228	178	162	285

Source: College records* PHS moved into GCE department.

However, what is developing within welfare provision on both a local and national scale is the expansion of community care, a development many commentators maintain is equated with unpaid family care (Abrams 1977; Wilson 1977; Cousins and Coote 1981; Land 1983; Finch and Groves 1983; McIntosh 1984; Ungerson 1987). In 1983 the DHSS institutionalized the informal carer by attempting to establish support networks of which, as Croft (1986) notes, 49 per cent were voluntary, self-help support groups. Similarly Beresford (1983) and Finch (1984) note how most 'patch and community social work' is based on informal and unpaid caring, whereby roles at the bottom of the social work scale are being filled increasingly with voluntary labour (David 1985). Interestingly, in 1986 the community care course was changed to 'family and community care'. The other course titles have also become less occupationally specific: initially the pre-social care course was the pre-residential care course, while the pre-health service course was the pre-nursing course. Thus, while the courses continue to develop, becoming increasingly generic in title, their relationship to the paid labour market becomes obfuscated.

Another similarity with their historical legacy is the current increased demand for private domestic servants (euphemistically called nannies, au pairs and cleaners, see Root 1984) and public domestic servants used in the private nursing homes sector. The difference is that the contemporary courses gain educational currency from their location within further education and its associations with social mobility (Gleeson and Mardle 1980). Unlike with the earliest courses, however, the welfare state, with its agencies of corrective inspection, now operates to regulate and monitor particular caring standards.

Institutional positioning

The historical legacy and the restructuring of the personal social services suggest that the courses have only a tenuous relationship to the occupational structure but a firm relationship to the sexual division of domestic labour. This points to the location of the courses within the 'tertiary modern' sector of the tripartite FE divisions (Gleeson 1980). Thus, all of the full-time caring courses researched are classified as grade five on the Houghton scale, the lowest grade of work. There are 14 full-time staff, of which 5 are male, with an additional 8 female part-timers; only one female and two males are Lecturer Grade 2. They are frequently referred to by members of other departments as 'the stupid old women of Beesley Street'. The staff are aware of this positioning as, Sarah (community care tutor) notes: 'They'd never put the bloody bankers down here, only the courses they don't give a shit about'. The courses are taught in an old building, closed as a school because it was unfit for human habitation. There are few textbooks and access to basic teaching materials such as paper, photocopying facilities and banda machine fluid is severely limited.

It is under these conditions that these courses become involved in winning consent for the social placement of the students as unpaid domestic labourers, who are willing to sustain and regulate both their own families and provide unpaid community care if necessary, according to the already established standards of the welfare state. The courses do not just socialize students into the appropriate affectual characteristics; they also provide the framework for the construction of a gender and class identity which the students themselves negotiate. It is these issues which will now be explored.

Ethnography

Cost-benefit analysis and subject positioning

Like many young women who have been located within the 'culture of femininity', and have experienced the dominant gender coding of schools (McRobbie 1978; Arnot 1981), the students carry with them vague notions of 'working with people'. When they come on the courses they have made an assessment of the 'cultural costs' involved in such a decision.[2] Only the pre-health course students had a specific occupational commitment, to nursing. Many of the students were Nursery Nurses' Examination Board (NNEB) rejects who, while demonstrating an occupational interest, came on to the other caring courses through a process of 'default', rather than any specific caring motivation. For example:

> I couldn't get a job, it's as simple as that and this was the easiest course to get on without any qualifications, the careers officer said, he gave me the form, it was something to do.
>
> (Diane (pre-social care))

> It was either this or the dole, all me school mates are stuck on the dole, they're doing nothing, so after the summer I'd got bored so I thought I might as well give it a try.
>
> (Sally B (pre-health service))

> I applied for the NNEB but they said I wasn't clever enough, well, they didn't actually say it straight out like, but you know, when they're polite and say things like 'I think you're better suited for the CC course' ... you know what they're really saying, what they really mean is ... you're not clever, you're not good enough ... they never even give you a chance.
>
> (Michelle (community care))

These comments suggest that the 'cultural costs' are mediated by the economic possibilities that the students perceive to be available. They are all aware of the devastating costs of unemployment (through the experience of family and friends) and they perceive themselves to be academic 'failures', a point substantiated by the few academic qualifications they have gained. From the point of view of an unqualified young white working class woman in search of security and possible social mobility the choices are limited to the traditional courses of hairdressing, secretarial, catering or caring. Most already had previous experience of caring, either through their own families, similar courses at school or through paid caring work such as babysitting. They therefore feel that caring is something they are capable of doing.

Through lack of qualifications, employment opportunities or 'alternative plausibility structures' (Berger and Luckmann 1971) such young women come to utilize their previous experience as a form of educational and cultural capital. They make a realistic appraisal of both the economic and cultural possibilities open to them and come accordingly to monitor their own aspirations. Ungerson (1987) argues that carers are likely to experience an enforced motivation to care and that women, generally, are subject to considerable ideological and material pressure to be carers. The students' motivation to care appears indicative of an initial attempt, on entry to the course, to gain some 'autonomy' within class and gender structures,

Gender reproduction and further education

using the cultural resources that are available to them, and this enables them to locate themselves within a form of knowledge with which they feel comfortable.

Likewise when the students articulate their feelings about their occupational interests they are aware that paid work is a potential 'marriage market', rather than just a place where labour is performed, as students (pre-health service course) indicates:

> That's the main advantage of nursing, like it's people work, you know you're always meeting people. Me best friend Karen, she met a Rally driver on surgical ... She's engaged to him now, she goes all over with him. God, yes and he's got loads of money, she's always getting things, she gives me the things she doesn't want ...
>
> (Angela (pre-health service course))

> Like everybody knows that about nursing, mind you it's usually the doctors, they're after, although me sister says that doctors don't get much time off, so you never see them.
>
> (Sandra (pre-health service course))

> Mesself I like those gentle social worker types, all beards and soft, like you know they'd treat you well ... and they earn loads.
>
> (Marie (pre-social care))

These extracts illustrate that the students' assessments are not only in line with cultural assumptions about femininity, glamour and possible 'fun' alongside the inevitability of marriage: they are also based on an economic analysis which perceives marriage as essential for maintaining a specific cultural and economic standard of living. This emphasis on marriage prospects indicates how femininity and the inevitability of marriage can inform occupational aspirations, and acceptance or rejection of knowledge divisions. This is very different to Willis's 'lads' celebration of manual labour, which through the wage packet was seen to represent independence. Willis's (1986) contention that the wage operates as the crucial pivot for understanding social and cultural transitions fails to take into account how marriage for young women represents future economic and cultural security as much, if not more so, than the wage.

The students do, however, assess the curriculum on the basis of their own competence and the relevance of knowledge for their perceived future positioning. The curriculum is divided between practical and academic subjects. The students take three O-levels (if studying community care), five O-levels (for pre-social care and pre-health service) and one group (PCSC and PHS mixed) take two A-levels. The rest of the curriculum is divided between practical subjects (domestic science, needlework, creative skills, first aid) and caring subjects (health care, issues in caring practice, social policy). These subjects are assessed by the students on the basis of: position within the course hierarchy, whether O- or A-levels, occupational purchase or future familial use. For instance, Cath (community care course) provides a 'cost–benefit' analysis of her own perceived capabilities and cultural experience:

> It's stupid having to do all these O-levels, it's just a waste of time they know we'll never pass them, that's why they put us here 'cos we couldn't do 'em at

school, it's pointless like, we could do more placements and that ... I know we've got to have them for jobs, ... but if we're not going to get them it seems pointless anyway.

and Lynn (community care course):

... If we spent more time going out on placements and things we'd be a lot better off, then at least we'd have something to show, like lots of experience, that's what jobs always want you know.

Alternatively Mandy (pre-social care course) considers academic qualifications to have greater occupational purchase than experience:

I've come to realise that I would have been better off just doing the O- and A-levels, like the rest is OK, it's been good fun and that, but it's not going to get us anywhere. Like making all those toys [creative skills] is good, like good for my own kids, when I have them, but it's not going to be much use when I apply for a job and say, well I can make things for kids, like I want a career, not a nanny job.

These comments illustrate how in their appraisal of knowledge the students are implicated in the contradiction between what they think employers want and what they believe to be the most useful skills. For Cath and Lynn the rationalizations involved in assessing their own academic competence are weighed against their practical abilities. It is this assessment, whereby the students apply a cost–benefit analysis to the curriculum, that involves them in searching for something within the institutional parameters that can give them occupational purchase, autonomy and self-esteem. They are not prepared to waste their time, as Wendy (pre-social care course) illustrates:

I'm sick of doing all this bloody knitting, did it at school for umpteen years, it's stupid, we're all meant to sit here quietly knitting, they think we're morons, that we haven't got anything better to do, what use is bloody knitting, eh? ...

These comments show how the students decide to spend their time. Counselling, perceived by the staff to provide support for the students and give them experience of an occupational skill, is often contested by the students, as comments by Michelle (community care) and Diane (pre-social care) suggest:

He calls it counselling, I call it plain fucking nosey, I'd like to tell him where to get off, but you can't can you really?

I don't see why they should pry into your personal life, why should we tell them anything, I make up stories about problems at home to keep them happy.

Such comments indicate that the students are in no sense passive receptors of the curriculum; rather they actively assess the information that they receive, an assessment, which is ultimately informed and limited by their structural and cultural positioning. They draw on the culture of femininity while at the same time challenging its imperatives. This supports Anyon's (1983) contention that most females neither totally acquiesce with, nor totally eschew, the imperatives of 'femininity'. It is through their attempts to resist the worthlessness and low self-esteem which results from the exclusive application of femininity that the students come to endorse domestic practices when they occur in an occupational setting, while at the same time rejecting them when included on the college curriculum.

Placements (one day per week throughout the year in hospitals, nurseries, elderly people's homes) are endorsed as being worthwhile. First, they provide students with the knowledge and experience of occupational situations, indicating to them that they may be employable and useful. Second, they indicate to students that they are capable, practical and responsible; able to carry out important occupational tasks, an indication of success within a system which until now has defined them as incompetent and incapable. For instance:

> There I was left on me own in this hospital ward, just me, everyone else had gone ... and there were all the medicines to be given. They told me to give them out, measuring milligrams. I was ever so careful and I did it. I was scared at first though, now you just imagine if one of them had died, I'd have had to handle it all on me own, you know, by meself until someone came to help.
>
> (Theresa (community care course))

For Theresa the ability to handle the situation signifies more in terms of self-esteem and confidence than academic competence ever could. Although the students are aware that they are being asked to do all the dirty work, they are prepared to tolerate this for the responsibility they are made to feel. Swapping 'responsibility' stories about placement experience becomes a way of celebrating themselves as competent, practical, responsible and caring, a form of subject positioning (Donald 1986) and 'quality of being' which contains essential subjectivities of self-esteem and dignity (Willis 1983). Wallace (1986) identifies this as 'compensatory status', in which practical caring responsibility comes to take on a significance beyond itself, just as manual labour did for the 'lads'; the primary difference being that the 'lads' responded to occupational divisions, whereas the responsibility for caring for others becomes part of feminine identity and familial positioning. However, experience at being successful on placements leads students to believe that they are employable, because they can do the job. This is one of the contradictions that students sustain, in that they come to see themselves as employable through their practical capabilities; yet this location of themselves as practical, caring and responsible people takes on a significance over and above employability. Its construction involves the development of significant responsibilities for family care, and caring for others, whether paid or unpaid.

The construction of caring subjectivities

This process is also structured by the 'culture of familialism' (Donzelot 1979) presented on the courses. This defines the family as the central location for caring and the focus of good things; of relationships which are warm and deep, privileged in a way that other relationships can never be (McIntosh 1984). Such definitions facilitate student incorporation of specific caring standards. They involve the detailing of domestic practices, which are open to student assessment. However, such attempts to modify their domestic practices are frequently resisted, as Marie (pre-social care) notes in response to a bed making session:

> Oh yea, I can just see me mams face when I tell her she's been making beds wrong for the last umpteen years, she'd clatter me. She [teacher] lives in cloud bloody cuckoo land ... It's a waste of time all this stuff, they must think we're stupid ...

and as the following conversation between (Cindy and Mandy), two pre-health course students indicates:

> C: You know what we've been doing this morning, eh? ... we've been bathing dolls, yea, straight up, I bathed two dolls this morning, neither had any clothes on either!
>
> M: Come on, it wasn't dolls really, it was getting us used to babies, that's the idea, you learnt to hold their head up and that didn't you?
>
> C: Hold its fucking head up, what ... it couldn't exactly fall down, it didn't bend, you know, wallybrain. I don't know what she takes us for, we're all standing there watching her bath a doll, I just thought to meself 'what are we doing here?' like you know, coming to college to bath dolls, that's what I'm saying, playing with bloody dolls, I'm seventeen, I didn't even like dolls when I were seven ... never mind, you don't need to come to college ... now all the rest, like when we had debates on breast feeding, that's OK, that's useful 'cos where would you find out otherwise without reading a load of books, eh, but not that doll crap.

The inclusions of domestic and caring practices on the courses is not only perceived by the students as an attempt to dispute their own knowledge of domestic practices, but is also considered not to have any occupational purchase. Such pedagogy is indicative of the class-based assumptions which underpin basic skills initiatives. These practices assume students have no knowledge or experience prior to FE (Gleeson 1983) and that they are incompetent, immature and incapable (Lee 1980; Moore 1983). The concentration on these basic skills contributes further to the divisions between practical and academic knowledge in its assumption that such practices bear some relevance to the students' future lives. In reality they are ideological statements about the students' future positioning, anchoring them within vocational knowledge; a process identified as the form of control traditionally associated with ensuring the lower orders' obligation to the system and their awareness of its dominant moral codes (Willis 1977; Gleeson 1986a). Gleeson (1986a) has indicated how the hidden curriculum, with its emphasis on attitudes, demeanour and presentation, has now surfaced as the official curriculum. Such a process can be seen as training in behavioural etiquette (Cohen 1984); in this case, familial etiquette.

The resistance by students to aspects of caring practice indicates one of the inherent problems with the pedagogy of caring courses, in that although students come on the course partly because of their familiarity with caring, they see the courses as a means of securing future employment. Caring practice is not, however, just an occupational skill; it is located within the family household structure and is also a personal disposition. Ungerson (1985) identifies the general cultural confusion which equates caring *for* with caring *about*. It is this cultural equation, firmly located within femininity and family ideology, that prevents the students from making a wholesale rejection of caring, for even if they contest aspects of the curriculum and pedagogy they do not want to be seen to be uncaring.

The students become even more closely enmeshed in caring by their attempts to distinguish between good and bad caring practice (as part of the social care practice curriculum). This takes the form of an examination of case studies of 'problem' families and making assessments of family organization and methods of care. As such, some of the students are being asked to evaluate the caring practices of their own family. Although they often reject individualistic explanations, such activity often leads them to question, on a more general level, their own experience. For example Yvonne (pre-health service):

> I sometimes wonder if me mam had been different, you know if she cared more, went out less, looked after me dad more and that ... I wonder if he'd have left, still, you don't know do you? I expect you'll never be able to tell, but it makes you think. When I'm married I'm going to make sure I'm really careful about what I say, you know, not lose me temper all the time or moan like our mam.

and Fiona (pre-social care):

> ... well I thought maybe if I'd listened to our Darren he wouldn't have got into all that trouble, you know, maybe it's like he just needed someone to talk to, I never really took any notice of him 'cos he was younger than me and he'd always been a pain in the arse, now sometimes I think well why was he such a little bugger, you know, was it me ignoring him, could I have done owt to help him like, you know, you never know; me mam said it's daft to think like that 'cos you can't do nowt about it, but sometimes you just think maybe you could've made it better.

These comments illustrate that whereas the students could draw on their own domestic practices directly to set up challenges to the curriculum, it became far more difficult to use their own family backgrounds to challenge the model of good practice presented by the course: a model which is based on exclusive care, total commitment and secure financial organization. Also, because the students have come to perceive themselves as caring people, the rejection of those tenets of feminine culture which present the possibility of gaining self-esteem and confidence becomes problematic. No other subject implicates students so directly in curriculum organization as caring, for to be seen as a 'non-caring' person is an anathema to young women who are trying to gain some status from their practical caring abilities. By using caring to gain some sense of self-worth, the students become involved in self-surveillance through the continual assessment of their own and others caring abilities.

Thus, the students are locked within a paradox. They come to identify themselves as caring people from their placement experience as a consequence of which they perceive themselves as capable, responsible and employable. However, this endorsement of themselves as caring, and their location within the culture of femininity, results in judgements about caring practice which ultimately devalue their own experiential knowledge and replace it with unobtainable ideals of family life; ideals which demand such commitment and responsibility as to make occupational aspirations secondary. It is the establishment of standards and ideals which are difficult and/or impossible to obtain which Genovese (1975) describes as 'guilt culture', whereby insecurities are generated to such an extent that individuals come to control and monitor their own behaviour. Wearing (1984) and Ungerson (1987) have both demonstrated how mothers and carers continually feel guilty for not providing adequate care. Wearing (1984) argues that such guilt produces acquiescence at the 'gut' level to ideologies of motherhood and caring.

Thus, by attempting to gain some status and self-esteem while making themselves more employable, the students come to locate and categorize themselves primarily as domestic and caring labourers. Such a personal contradiction highlights the greater structural contradictions of vocational caring courses. By situating caring in an educational context, the realization of employment is considered to be possible. Yet such a realization ultimately restricts their employment prospects. The students come to prioritize familial care, reproducing a situation in which vocational caring courses become little more than domestic apprenticeships (Cohen 1982).

The abolition of these courses would deny access to FE to many young working class women. Thus changes need to be incorporated into the present structure which would arrest the domestic-labour allocation process and would enable students to move away from their primary identification with the family towards the labour market. The next section will explore these changes.

Alternatives?

The labour market

The changes proposed are divided into major structural changes; institutional changes and curricular changes. Changes in the occupational structure would, however, need to be related to a wider, more fundamental restructuring of the sexual division of labour. As this has developed from the competitive struggles between groups of workers to maintain or improve their position in the labour market (Phillips and Taylor 1980; Cockburn 1983; Brenner and Ramas 1984), consolidated by support from the TUC and the state for the family wage (Barrett and McIntosh 1982; Land 1983; Finch and Groves 1983), this change would be considerable. Although more women are being drawn into work, they remain in the secondary sector, frequently part-time without the pay, protection and security of full-time primary market employees (Beechey 1987). Thus, as the boundaries of the sexual divisions move to incorporate these workers, the conditions of those sexual divisions remain. Similar changes are occurring within the personal social services; more women are being recruited to the lower end of the scale, but their recruitment is as primarily, voluntary, part-time, unpaid of low paid workers (Croft 1986). Thus the students' options are being curtailed by the restricted employment possibilities within this restructured sector. What is required, therefore, is a massive increase in spending within the personal social services so as to provide real jobs which are well paid and have all the securities of permanent positioning, training and career structure. In this way students could perceive an economic future in which they could choose to be economically independent, rather than using men as meal tickets. As long as women are denied the access to economic independence, the meal ticket route becomes a matter of necessity to economic survival.

In this respect, Walker (1982) argues that the statutory domiciliary services should not necessarily be expanded, but that the cared for should define their needs and wants. However, this takes no account of an historical legacy that equates caring for with caring about, alongside socio-biological reductions that maintain women as naturally predisposed to care (Bland 1981); beliefs which are gaining greater currency as part of the New Right's sexual politics and family ideology (Eisenstein 1982; David 1984, 1986, 1987; Phillips 1988). The whole notion of 'community care' needs to be dropped, for as Wilson (1982) argues, community has become an ideological portmanteau word for a reactionary, conservative ideology that oppresses women by silently confining them to the private sphere without so much as even mentioning them. Finch (1984) argues that women's physical location within the community makes a non-sexist version of community care impossible. So, within the personal social services, the initial emphasis would be on an extension of formal provision and an institution framework that gave appropriate recognition to the amount of labour and knowledge involved in comparison with other sectors of the labour market. This would open up a greatly expanded network of care provision incorporating all the agencies in the voluntary sector.

Family ideologies

Another major structural and ideological change would involve challenging the historical legacy of the courses and the ideological campaigns that have been organized around the family as the site for moral regulation from which notions of 'correct' families and family 'standards' come to be defined. This would expose family blaming rhetoric as a fallacy for interpreting structural problems. There needs to be an emphasis on contradictions between the ideals and standards that are established, including the devices that are used to externally monitor and increase self-surveillance. Using McIntosh's (1984) distinction between the family household structure (FHS) as a site and location of family relationships, and family ideologies, we can see that while the state mounts ideological campaigns on many fronts, with accompanying legislative changes, the actual pressure on the FHS increases. Thus while the 'family' is continually presented as the 'haven in the heartless world', the massive cracks within it are also beginning to show, as evidenced by an increase in one parent families, the sexual abuse of children (Campbell 1983, 1988), domestic violence and marital rape (London Rape Crisis Centre 1984; Hall 1985; Stanko 1985). DSS initiatives to 'support' the informal carers indicate recognition for the need to ameliorate this pressure. Segal (1983) argues that this pressure will continue to mount as women increasingly go out to work, seek to control their fertility and continue to fight for sexual autonomy.

Exposition of such contradictions could be built into the curriculum, as could critical analysis of schemes which rely on women to constantly surveille each other's familial practice. However, before a detailed analysis of the curriculum can be made the positioning of the courses within the institutional hierarchy of FE needs to be examined.

Institutional FE organization

Again, major structural changes within the sexual divisions of the education system as a whole would appear to be necessary. For as the research shows, the students on entry to FE use their 'feminine cultural capital' and come already equipped with the gendered code of schooling. However, their cost-benefit analysis and the gender and class challenges that they made to the teachers and curriculum suggests that students would be willing to take on other forms of knowledge if they felt confident and could benefit from it. One of the tasks necessary for any form of change is to stretch the students' perception of the possibilities for action. As this study and Wolpe's (1988) recent analysis suggest, awareness of alternatives to the traditional class, gender and geographical locations is usually limited. Thus extending students' awareness of the available possibilities is one of the significant changes that could be made.

In the short term, changes could be made that would improve the positioning of the courses within the FE hierarchy. Upgrading of staff, resources and buildings would generate a significant improvement. Physical integration with the rest of the college would also challenge the courses' parochialism. A name change is imperative, so that courses are identified by occupational links. The link to real jobs could be a criterion for course validation. Placements would need to be expanded to cover a greater variety of 'people work' and the links between the college and the local labour market could be more strongly drawn. A greater variety of placements would enable students to make more personal contacts for future employment prospects. However, private nursing homes should not be used for placements, as students are drawn into a labour process that involves them in implicitly supporting cuts in the public sector. Close links need to be developed between the local DHSS to develop students' awareness of procedures and organization and to develop useful contacts. Students' prior experience of care should be drawn upon and integrated into aspects of the curriculum such as rights awareness. These suggestions would enable students to feel that they are responsible and employable and that any constrictions within the labour market should not be located at the level of individual inadequacy. Students should be discouraged from voluntary work to counteract their potential involvement in the current transition from real jobs into voluntary ones.

Staff development training would need to be implemented. Hargreaves (1984) and Hatton (1987) note that the staff need to be involved in planning to ensure their commitment to changes. Any programme incorporating a critical analysis of care would have to take into consideration the teachers' resistances. Courses should develop an understanding and analysis of the issues involved, so that staff come to see the changes as useful and appropriate (Acker 1988). Staff investment in the caring system has to be critically appraised and replaced with developments that would enhance their status by emphasizing occupational care over and above familial care. It would be necessary for staff to undergo anti-sexist and anti-racist training and to be able to put it into practice. In addition staff might pursue a post-graduate degree by independent study (in which a programme could be designed to provide the basics) to explore issues in greater detail. As these suggestions are asking for fundamental changes in attitudes and practice, full support from the college with accompanying support groups for all the staff would be necessary. The role of the staff will become clearer when the suggestions for curricular changes are outlined.

Curricular changes

Ideally, the students would pursue a range of GCSEs (A-levels if they feel able). From follow up research, after one year, two years and five years, all the students expressed regret at not having taken their O-levels seriously. Experience of the labour market has taught them that hard academic currency counts. Although they had been told on entry to the courses that employers would accept their community care certificates (CGLI) and PCSC qualifications (CCETSW), they had experienced a general unwillingness on the part of employers to do so. The emphasis in GCSE on coursework and project-based work, however, could make the pursuit of the academic ticket less painful. If students could be integrated into the GCSE/general education department this would open out further contacts and perceptions of alternative possible futures. Subjects such as needlework, domestic science and creative arts, which involve repetition of knowledge that students already possess, could be replaced with a critical core comprised of social work practice, social administration and social policy.[3]

Social work practice would deal directly with occupational settings; it would also involve the establishment of tutorial groups making links between placement experience and theoretical analysis. Part of this critical core should involve an examination of the following:

- the construction of 'social problems' in relation to class, race and gender;
- the construction of 'needs' and 'dependency' in relation to class, race and gender;
- poverty in relation to class, race and gender and resistance to pathologizing of these groups;
- the power mechanisms and regulatory devices involved in 'care' and how these regulative devices are related to distinct practices (Walkerdine 1985);
- how 'rights' are prioritized in social work practice[4] – the institutionalization of sexism within social work practice;[5]
- the history, role and power relations involved in counselling;
- how caring can be determined by market prerogatives;
- the role of trade unions both in the history of social work practice and in the contemporary situation.

Social policy would provide the students with the critical tools and methodology for analysing many of the contradictions inherent in the present courses. It would involve analysis of the following:

- the social construction of the 'family' as a unitary object (Riley 1983) and the way in which social policies contribute to this construction;
- the historical construction of family ideologies in relation to strategies of 'normalizing' and 'moralizing';
- the movement from overt to covert regulation and the consequent development of self-surveillance;
- the links between femininity, care and the 'family';

- the popularization of theories of care (Bowlby 1965), family therapy, child development and psychoanalysis (Riley 1983; Unwin 1985; Steedman 1985);
- the way in which social policies are underpinned by socio-biology;
- urban planning as an example of how structural problems can be deflected on to individualistic explanations;
- the notion of 'community' and the social policies of 'community care'.

The achievement of these aims would require a change of course text but there are several appropriate alternatives available.

National and local careers advice and help with applications and interviews should be integrated into the course. On a more general level, assertiveness training would be essential in order, not only to develop students' confidence but also to provide strategies for overcoming the daily humiliations of sexism. At least one initial week of basic literacy, essay writing and project structuring skills would increase students' confidence and ability. They need to be treated as mature and competent, as attempts to infantilize them are strongly contested (Skeggs 1989).

In the short term, then, the courses would empower students. They would stop the process of subject positioning whereby the students identify themselves with familial care and enable them to obtain a real job, as a consequence of which they could choose to be economically independent, choose to care, choose to take on family responsibilities. The new courses would enable them to contest the exploitive nature of private and voluntary care.

It is accepted that it would be difficult to stop the students taking on the extra physical and mental burdens of family care (i.e. community care) unless the necessary material and cultural supports were available. If they did, however, their experience of a critical course should enable them to dissipate some of the familial responsibility and guilt that they are likely to encounter. It should also make them less likely to internalize blame for structural problems. Moreover, if they have confidence in themselves as capable people, they are less likely to rely on familial care as a means for generating responsibility.

It is realized that structural and cultural changes in economy, family household structure and femininity are necessary to provide long-term changes. For it is likely that students will go on making a cost–benefit analysis of their investments and 'choose' economic and cultural security. The dilemma lies between advocating changes which may prove to be only ameliorative, or in condoning the current reproduction of these young women as unpaid caring domestic labourers.

Finally, on an optimistic note, the impact of feminism and critical analysis should not be underestimated, even if it not often realized in practical outcomes. Students of sociology, anti-racism, anti-sexism or other critical studies usually reach a point of no return, whereby their critical methodology enables them to see through the layers. This does not necessitate any improvement in their material conditions and it often means that they have to learn to live with and negotiate even greater contradictions. It is, however, a means of empowering, from which students can gain some sense of self-worth without having to rely on the ideological prop of the 'family'. Such an achievement, it is argued, would be sufficient justification for the sweeping changes that have been outlined above.

I would like to express my enormous gratitude to Erica Stratta for her unequivocal support and without whom this chapter could not have been written.

Notes

1 Helterline (1980) and Steedman (1985) have shown how the establishment of nursery and primary schooling within this period similarly distinguished between 'good' and 'bad' mothers on the basis of social class.
2 Costs, which Boudon (1974) argues are associated with the values of a particular group, organized in 'decision fields' which come to structure the choices that the students make (Moore 1983).
3 Developments in new BTEC caring courses suggest that some of these changes are being incorporated into their plans.
4 For example Maynard (1986) showed how 33 per cent of cases from regular social work involved wife abuse which Pahl (1986) argues is the result of the prioritization of 'family' over women's rights.
5 Hanmer and Statham (1988) provide an ideal textbook.

References

Abrams, P. (1977). 'Community care: some research problems and priorities', *Policy and Politics*, 6, 2, 125-51.
Acker, S. (1988). 'Teachers, gender and resistance', *British Journal of Sociology of Education*, 9, 3, 307-22.
Anyon, J. (1983). 'Intersections of gender and class: accommodation and resistance by working-class and affluent females to contradictory sex-role ideologies' in S. Walker and L. Barton (eds), *Gender, Class and Education*, Lewes, Falmer, 19-39.
Arnot, M. (1981). 'Culture and political economy: dual perspectives in the sociology of women's education' *Educational Analysis*, 3, 1, 77-116.
Barrett, M. and McIntosh, M. (1982). *The Anti-social Family*, London, Verso.
Bates, I. et al. (eds) (1984). *Schooling For The Dole: The New Vocationalism*, London, Macmillan.
Beechey, V. (1987). *Unequal Work*, London, Verso.
Beresford, P. (1983). *Patch in Perspective: Decentralising and Democratising Social Services*, London, Battersea Community Action.
Berger, J. and Luckmann, T. (1971). *The Social Construction of Reality*, Harmondsworth, Penguin.
Bland, L. (1981). ' "It's only human nature": sociobiology and sex differences', *Schooling and Culture*, 10, 6-16.
Blunden, G. (1982). *Women's Place in NAFE: The Early Development of Three Colleges in South West England*, Unpublished PhD thesis, University of Bristol.
Boudon, R. (1974). *Education, Opportunity and Social Inequality*, London, John Willey.
Bowlby, J. (1965). *Child Care and the Growth of Love*, Harmondsworth, Penguin.
Brenner, J. and Ramas, M. (1984). 'Rethinking women's oppression', *New Left Review*, 144, 33-72.
Browne, K. (1981). 'Schooling, capitalism and the mental/manual division of labour', *Sociological Review*, 29, 3, 445-73.
Campbell, B. (1983). 'Sex: a family affair', in L. Segal (ed.), *What is to be done about the family?* Harmondsworth, Penguin, 157-68.
Campbell, B. (1988). *Unofficial Secrets, Child Sex Abuse: the Cleveland Case*, London, Virago.
Clarke, J. and Willis, P. (1984). Introduction to I. Bates et al. (eds), *Schooling for the Dole*, London, Macmillan.
Clarke, K. (1985). 'Public and private children: infant education in the 1820s and 1830s', in C. Steedman, C. Urwin, and V. Walkerdine (eds), *Language, Gender and Childhood*, London, Routledge and Kegan Paul, 74-88.

Cockburn, C. (1983). *Brothers: Male Dominance and Technological Change*, London, Pluto.
Cohen, P. (1982). 'School for the dole', *New Socialist*, January/February, 43-7.
Cohen, P. (1984). 'Against the new vocationalism', in I. Bates *et al.* (eds), *Schooling for the Dole*, London, Macmillan, 104-70.
Cook, J. (1988). 'Fictional fathers', in S. Radstone (ed.) *Sweet Dreams: Sexuality, Gender and Popular Fiction*, London, Lawrence and Wishart.
Cousins, J. and Coote, A. (1981). *The Family in the Firing Line: A Discussion Document on Family Policy*, Poverty Pamphlet No 51, March, London, NCCL/CPAG.
Coward, R. (1983). *Patriarchal Precedents: Sexuality and Social Relations*, London, Routledge and Kegan Paul.
CSE State Group (1979). *Struggle Over the State: Cuts and Restructuring in Contemporary Britain*, London, CSE Books.
Croft, S. (1986). 'Women, caring and the recasting of need: a feminist reappraisal', *Critical Social Policy*, 16, 23-40.
David, M.E. (1980). *The State, Family and Education*, London, Routledge and Kegan Paul.
David, M.E. (1984). 'Teaching and preaching sexual morality: the new right's antifeminism in Britain and the USA', *Journal of Education*, 6, 63-76.
David, M.E. (1985). 'Motherhood and social policy — a matter for education?', *Critical Social Policy*, 12, 28-44.
David, M.E. (1986). 'Moral and maternal: the family in the right' in R. Levitas (ed.), *The Ideology of the New Right*, Cambridge, Polity Press, 136-67.
David, M.E. (1987). 'The dilemmas of parent education and parental skills for sexual equality', in S. Walker, and L. Barton (eds), *Changing Policies, Changing Teachers: New Directions for Schooling?*, Milton Keynes, Open University Press, 190-210.
Davin, A. (1978). 'Imperialism and motherhood', *History Workshop Journal*, 5.
Donald, J. (1986). 'Beacons of the future: schooling, subjection and subjectification' in V. Beechey and J. Donald, *Subjectivity and Social Relations*, Milton Keynes, Open University Press, 214-50.
Donzelot, J. (1979). *The Policing of Families: Welfare Versus the State*, London, Hutchinson.
Dyhouse, C. (1981). 'Good wives and little mothers: social anxieties and the school girls curriculum 1890-1920'. *Oxford Review of Education*, 3, 2, 41-58.
Eisenstein, Z.R. (1982). 'The sexual politics of the New Right: understanding the "crisis of liberalism" for the 1980s', *Signs: Journal of Women in Culture and Society*, 7, 3, 567-88.
Finch, J. (1984). 'Community care: developing non-sexist alternatives', *Critical Social Policy*, 9, 3, 3, 6-19.
Finch, J. and Groves D. (1983). *A Labour of Love: Women, Work and Caring*, London, Routledge and Kegan Paul.
Finn, D. (1984). 'Britain's misspent youth', *Marxism Today*, February, 20-4.
Foucault, M. (1977). *The Archaeology of Knowledge*, London, Tavistock.
Further Education Unit (FEU) (1982). *Who Cares?, A Curriculum Policy For Caring Courses at the Initial Level*, November, London, FEU.
Genovese, E.D. (1972). *Roll, Jordan, Roll: The World the Slaves Made*, New York, Vintage Books.
Genovese, E.D. (1975). *The World the Slaveholders Made*, New York, Vintage Books.
Gleeson, D. (1980). 'Streaming at work and college', *Sociological Review*, November.
Gleeson, D. (ed.) (1983). *Youth Training and the Search For Work*, London, Routledge and Kegan Paul.
Gleeson, D. (1986a). 'Life skills training and the politics of personal effectiveness', *The Sociological Review*, 34, 2, 381-95.
Gleeson, D. (1986b). 'Further education, free enterprise and the curriculum', in S. Walker and L. Barton (eds), *Youth Unemployment and Schooling*, Milton Keynes, Open University Press, 46-67.
Gleeson, D. and Hopkins, M. (1987) 'Further education without tiers: countering tripartism in post-sixteen further education and training', *Critical Social Policy*, 19, 77-90.

Gleeson, D. and Mardle, G. (1980). *FE or Training: A Case Study in the Theory and Practice of Day Release Education*, London, Routledge and Kegan Paul.

Hall, C. (1979). 'The early formation of Victorian domestic ideology', in S. Burman (ed.), *Fit Work For Women*, London, Croom Helm.

Hall, R.E. (1985). *Ask Any Woman: A London Inquiry into Rape and Sexual Assault*, Bristol, Falling Wall Press.

Hanmer, J. and Statham, D. (1988). *Women and Social Work: Towards a Woman Centred Practice*, London, Macmillan.

Hargreaves, A. (1984). 'Experience counts, theory doesn't: how teachers talk about their work', *British Journal of Sociology of Education*, 57, 244–54.

Hatton, E. (1987). 'Determinants of teacher work: some causal complications', *Teaching and Teacher Education*, 3, 55–60.

Hebdige, D. (1979). *Subculture and the Meaning of Style*, London, Methuen.

Helterline, M. (1980). 'The emergence of modern motherhood: motherhood in England 1899–1959', *International Journal of Women's Studies*, 3, 6, 590–614.

Johnson, R. (1970). 'Education and social control in early Victorian England', *Past and Present*, 49, 96–119.

Land, H. (1983). 'Family fables', *New Socialist*, May/June, 20–21.

Lee, R. (1980). *Beyond Coping: Some Approaches to Social Education*, London, FEU.

London Rape Crisis Centre (1984). *Sexual Violence: The Reality for Women*, London, The Women's Press.

McIntosh, M. (1984). 'The family, regulation and the public sphere', in D. Held and S. Hall (eds), *State and Society in Contemporary Britain*, Cambridge, Polity Press, 204–41.

McRobbie, A. (1978). *Jackie: An Ideology of Adolescent Feminity*, Stencilled Paper, Birmingham, CCCS.

McRobbie, A. (1982). 'The politics of feminist research: between talk, text and action', *Feminist Review*, 12, 46–57.

Marks, P. (1976). 'Femininity in the classroom: an account of changing attitudes', in J. Mitchell and A. Oakley, *The Rights and Wrongs of Women*, Harmondsworth, Penguin, 176–99.

Maynard, M. (1986). 'The responses of social workers to domestic violence' in J. Pahl (ed.), *Private Violence, Public Policy*, London, Routledge and Kegan Paul.

Moore, R. (1983). 'Further education: pedagogy and production', in D. Gleeson (ed.), *Youth Training and the Search for Work*, Routledge and Kegan Paul, 14–32.

Mort, F. (1987). *Dangerous Sexualities: Medico-Moral Politics in England Since 1830*, London, Routledge and Kegan Paul.

Pahl, J. (ed.) (1986). *Private Violence and Public Policy: The Needs of Battered Women and the Responses of the Public Services*, London, Routledge and Kegan Paul.

Paterson, F. (1988). 'Schooling the family', *Sociology*, 22, 1, 65–86.

Phillips, J. (1988). *Policing the Family: Social Control in Thatcher's Britain*, London, Junius.

Phillips, A. and Taylor, B. (1980). 'Sex and skill: notes towards a feminist economics', *Feminist Review*, 6, 79–89.

Rees, T. (1983). 'Boys off the street and girls in the home: youth unemployment and state intervention in Northern Ireland', in R. Fiddy (ed.), *In Place of Work*, Lewes, Falmer, 167–83.

Riley, D. (1983). *War in the Nursery: Theories of the Child and the Mother*, London, Virago.

Root, A. (1984). 'Return of the nanny', *New Socialist*, 22, 16–19.

Rose, J. (1985). 'State and language: Peter Pan as written for the child', in C. Steedman, C. Urwin and V. Walkerdine (eds), *Language, Gender and Childhood*, London, Routledge and Kegan Paul, 88–113.

Segal, L. (1983). *What is to be Done About the Family*, Harmondsworth, Penguin.

Skeggs, B.E. (1986). *Young Women and Further Education: A Case Study of Young Women's Experience of Caring Courses in a Local College*, Unpublished PhD thesis, University of Keele.

Skeggs, B.E. (1988). 'Gender reproduction and further education: domestic apprenticeships', *British Journal of Sociology of Education*, 9, 2, 131-49.

Skeggs, B.E. (1989). 'Gendered assessment appraisal and accountability: the contradictions in the construction of female sexuality', in L. Barton, and S. Walker (eds), *The Politics of Educational Control*, Milton Keynes, Open University Press, forthcoming.

Stafford, A. (1981). 'Learning not to labour', *Capital and Class*, 15, Autumn, 55-77.

Stanko, E. (1985). *Intimate Intrusions: Women's Experience of Male Violence*, London, Routledge and Kegan Paul.

Stedman-Jones, G. (1971). *Outcast London. A Study in the Relatonship between Classes in Victorian Society*, Oxford, Clarendon Press.

Steedman, C. (1985). ' "The mother made conscious": the historical development of primary school pedagogy', *History Workshop Journal*, 20, 149-63.

Summers, A. (1979). 'A home from home — women's philanthropic work in the 19th century', in S. Burman (ed.) *Fit Work For Women*, London, Croom Helm, 33-64.

Ungerson, C. (1985). 'Paid and unpaid caring: a problem for women or the state?', in P. Close and R. Collins (eds), *Family and Economy in Modern Society*, London, Macmillan.

Ungerson, C. (1987). *Policy is Personal: Sex, Gender and Informal Care*, London, Tavistock.

Urwin, C. (1985). 'Constructing motherhood: the persuasion of normal development', in C. Steedman, C. Urwin and V. Walkerdine (eds), *Language, Gender and Childhood*, London, Routledge and Kegan Paul, 164-203.

Walker, A. (1982). *Community Care: The Family, the State and Social Policy*, Oxford, Blackwells/Martin Robertson.

Walker, S. and Barton L. (eds) (1983). *Gender, Class and Education*, New York, Falmer.

Walker, S. and Barton, L. (1986). *Youth, Unemployment and Schooling*, Milton Keynes, Open University Press.

Walkerdine, V. (1985). 'On the regulation of speaking and silence: subjectivity, class and gender in contemporary schooling', in C. Steedman, C. Urwin, and V. Walkerdine (eds), *Language, Gender and Childhood*, London, Routledge Kegan Paul, 203-42.

Wallace, C. (1986). 'From girls and boys to women and men: the social reproduction of gender roles in the transition from school to (Un)employment', in S. Walker and L. Barton (eds), *Youth, Unemployment and Schooling*, 92-118.

Wearing, B. (1984). *The Ideology of Motherhood*, Sydney, George Allen and Unwin.

Weeks, J. (1981). *Sex, Politics and Society: The Regulation of Sexuality Since 1800*, Harlow, Longman.

Willis, P. (1977). *Learning to Labour: How Working Class Kids get Working Class Jobs*, Farnborough, Saxon House.

Willis, P. (1983). 'Cultural production and theories of reproduction' in L. Barton, and S. Walker (eds), *Race, Class and Education*, London, Croom Helm, 107-39.

Willis, P. (1986). 'Unemployment: The final inequality', *British Journal of Sociology of Education*, 7, 2, 155-69.

Wilson, E. (1977). *Women and the Welfare State*, London, Tavistock.

Wilson, E. (1982). 'Women, the community and the family', in A. Walker (ed.), *Community Care: The Family, the State and Social Policy*, Oxford, Blackwells/Martin Robertson.

Wolpe, A.M. (1988). *Within School Walls: The role of Discipline, Sexuality and the Curriculum*, London, Routledge.

Chris Shilling

Industry and education: changing the meaning of work-experience

9

During the 1980s in England and Wales there has been a large growth in work experience for students of secondary school age. There are now three government departments involved in the organization and delivery of work experience. The Department of Trade and Industry (DTI) actively encourages employers to provide work placements through its business and education initiative. The Department of Employment (DE) runs programmes through the Training Agency in order to promote a context and framework for the expansion of work experience. These include the Technical and Vocational Education Initiative and education–industry compacts. Finally, the Department of Education and Science (DES) has the role of ensuring the *quality* of work experience for all those involved (DES 1988).[1]

One major reason for this growing state concern with work experience is clear. After over a decade of large-scale youth unemployment, many employers are now having great difficulty in attracting sufficient school leavers. Much of this is due to the declining numbers of 16–19 year olds entering the labour market. The size of this age group fell from 3.7 million in 1982 to below 3.4 million in the early months of 1988. It is expected to start rising again only after reaching a low of under 2.6 million in 1994 (*TES*, 13 September 1988). With an increasing proportion of school leavers expected to progress into higher education, regional youth labour shortages are likely to remain a serious problem for some time to come.[2] In this context, vocational activities such as work experience are important not only as a 'bridge' from school to work (MSC 1984), but because of the opportunities they give employers to attract future workers. As the Director General of the Confederation of British Industry argues:

> No business can ignore [the opportunities provided by work experience], particularly in the light of the sharp reduction in the number of school leavers that is in prospect over the next few years. Effective links with local schools will be an important competitive advantage in the tighter labour market of the early 1990s.
>
> (Banham, 1988)

The implications of this statement are clear. Employers should involve themselves in work experience as it can help in the race to employ a shrinking pool of school leavers. In this way, the government promotion of work experience has similarities to what Pierre (1987) has termed a 'market conforming' policy. The intervention of the DES, DE and DTI is not intended mainly to facilitate the *state provision* of work placements. Rather, it is directed toward using state funds as a way of encouraging the participation of *private firms* in this form of education–industry activity. While the state provides resources which create a *context* in which work experience takes place (e.g. through TVEI), it is left primarily to local industrialists and educators to determine the details of these arrangements. In theory, this policy will encourage the growth of work experience of a type which is sensitive to the local economy. Employers are free to choose the types of work placements they offer schools and are able to organize their involvement in ways which conform to their capacity and needs. Consequently, in areas where youth labour shortages are seen as a problem, the possibility of attracting future workers is likely to be a strong incentive for industry and commerce to support and maintain the work experience links promoted by the government.

The Changing Aims of Work Experience

Both government and employer groupings such as the CBI have invested work experience with the task of forging extensive links between employers, schools and students. The feasibility and desirability of accomplishing this, given the present organization of work and the economy, have been challenged from a variety of perspectives (e.g. Steinberg 1982; Watkins 1987 and 1988). However, this does not mean to say that work experience can be used only to facilitate links with, or constitute a 'bridge' from, school to work.

This chapter will examine briefly the changing 'official' aims of work experience before focusing on a current code of practice which seeks to facilitate its operation as an employer-oriented activity. The aim is not only to criticize existing goals for work experience, but to offer suggestions as to how this activity might be reconstructed into a progressive educational resource. In order for this to be achieved, I shall argue that the promotion of work experience has to move away from a 'market conforming' policy.

Since 1974, the Department of Education and Science has offered general guidance on work experience schemes which cater for school students. Circular 7/74 explains the provisions of the Education (Work Experience) Act 1973, and emphasizes that work 'schemes for pupils of compulsory school age must form part of an educational programme' (DES 1974). The principle underlying any work experience scheme should be to provide young people with an 'insight into the world of work' (DES 1974). The DES approach towards work experience did not remain static, though, but changed in the political climate established around the time of the Great Debate (see CCCS 1981). Reflecting the concerns of government and employers, the DES issued a circular in which local authorities were asked what steps they had taken to 'promote the development of work experience' in relation to the 'needs of an industrial society' (DES 1977). Work experience no longer had to be part of a purely educational programme: it also had to be used as an activity to enhance the economic relevance of education.

The Department of Education and Science had brought about a change in the government view of work experience. This was developed further with the involvement of the Manpower Services Commission in vocational schemes. Instead of being confined to programmes with an *educational* orientation (DES 1974), work experience in the 1980s constitutes an integral part of schemes designed to provide students with the knowledge, skills and attitudes which will form an 'early' and 'permanent bridge between school and work' (MSC 1984).[3]

There are several reasons for the changing aims of work experience. These include economic recession and the view that schools have failed in their responsibility to produce an appropriately trained and socialized workforce (see Finn 1987; Shilling 1989a), government attempts to secure greater control over the curriculum, and the changing mandates of the DES, DE and DTI (see Dale *et al.* 1989; Shilling 1989b). However, the important thing to note for the purposes of this discussion is that the aims of work experience *have* been open to change. These aims are not arrived at purely by technical considerations. They are affected deeply by political considerations which are themselves subject to revision. Indeed, I would argue that the projected shortages of youth labour in the 1990s offers educators the potential for increasing the educative value of vocational schemes containing work experience. Such an alternative is not only possible, it is highly necessary given existing proposals for the operation of work experience as an employer-oriented activity.

Education and the organization of work experience

In response to the changing official objectives of work experience, the government, local authorities, and other organizations have begun increasingly to produce (or update) their own codes of practice. These are designed to facilitate the efficient organization and operation of work experience and ensure that students make the most of the opportunity to participate in a firm's activities. This paper will examine a code of practice which was published in 1988 as the result of a joint initiative by the British Institute of Management (BIM) and the British Educational Management and Administration Society (BEMAS).

The significance of the BIM/BEMAS's *Work experience – a Code for Good Practice* is in terms of its intended *scope*, and the *support* it has received from industrial and education–industry bodies. The code is not aimed at any single scheme or geographical locality. Rather, it is designed as an aid to *all* work experience schemes and outlines the responsibilities not only of schools, but of students, local education authorities and employing organizations. Furthermore, the guidelines were produced in association with a variety of interests. The City and Guilds of London Institute, the Confederation of British Industry, the Trades Union Congress, Project Trident, Industry Matters, the Institute of Directors, the Engineering Employers' Federation, and the Department of Trade and Industry's industry–education unit, were all associated with this code of practice (BIM/BEMAS 1988). As a result of these factors, the contents of the code are likely to receive consideration from a wide variety of educators and industrialists involved in work programmes.

The standards by which a code for work experience practice may be judged will obviously vary depending on the interests of those involved. For example, teachers, students and employers face quite different sets of problems in initiating, participating in, and running, work experience placements. Consequently, individuals are likely to assess a code according to the degree to which it addresses adequately their particular concerns.[4] However, the growing number of studies of work experience schemes point to the importance of two major areas which can be seen as relevant to *all* those involved. These are the *organizational problems* posed by any programme of work experience, and the *educational consequences* of students spending a period of time in a place of work (e.g. Watts 1980, 1983; Eggleston 1982; Cole 1983; Simon 1983; Watkins 1987, 1988; Shilling 1989a). The importance of these two factors will obviously vary according to the aims of work experience at any one time. However, they have both been an official concern of governments since the DES issued guidance on work experience in 1974.

The organizational problems which face those participating in work experience concern the actual functioning of work placements. For work experience to take place, certain basic conditions have to be fulfilled. These involve such tasks as finding sufficient placements for a scheme, matching student interests with those placements offered by firms, ensuring that students attend work experience, and providing sufficient teacher back up to help firms and stimulate their future participation. However, organizational problems go beyond ensuring that work experience simply takes place. To achieve a satisfactory programme also requires that work experience placements are located in firms that meet basic safety criteria. For example, it is necessary to ensure that students receive adequate supervision and are not working with dangerous equipment. As work experience forms a compulsory part of schemes which aim to provide equal opportunites (MSC 1984), minimum criteria also necessitate that students are not discriminated against on the basis of their gender, race or social class. For this to be achieved requires that similar placements are made available to all participating students, and that effective steps are taken to ensure that girls and boys, black and white youth, and working and middle class youth, have the *opportunity* to receive positive tasters of work in non-traditional areas.

The educational consequences of work placements refer to what students *learn* from their time at a place of work. While the variety of life experiences students bring with them to a work placement means that learning outcomes cannot be guaranteed in advance, there should be the opportunity for students to acquire knowledge about the 'world of work' (MSC 1984). This knowledge can be divided into that concerning the acquisition of factual knowledge about the *existing* organization and operation of work, and that which concerns reflective and critical thinking about the possible *future* nature of work in our rapidly changing 'high technology' society (MSC 1984). As various studies have demonstrated, work placements represent a remarkable educational resource which students can use for exploring such factors as the labour process of various jobs, and the social relations of production in work sites. Case studies of work experience have also reported the insightful comments that students can make concerning the degree of control exerted by employers on employees and the oppositional responses which are sometimes forthcoming from these employees (e.g. Watkins 1987; Shilling 1987b). Indeed, part of the great potential of work experience as a learning medium seems to be that students perceive it as relevant to their future lives. However, to make the most of work experience as a resource requires that it forms part of an educational programme which not only encourages critical thinking about the existing nature of work, but which stimulates thinking concerning *alternative ways in which industry might be organized*.[5] The danger otherwise is that while work programmes might 'enable some youth to do work' they may 'not enable many youth to understand about the factors that determine patterns, organisation and conditions of work' (Cole 1981).

Work experience – a code for good practice

In several respects, the BIM/BEMAS's code represents a welcome recognition that in order to function effectively and educationally, work experience programmes require more than the simple participation of schools and firms. The code is organized into five sections; an introduction to work experience, followed by a model of what constitutes good practice for the employing organization, the school, the student, and the local education authority. These models are constructed with the aim of enabling participants to plan and achieve a successful learning experience for students. In other words, the code is concerned with both the *functioning* and the *educational consequences* of work experience.

Good practice for the employing organization

The necessity of securing sufficient numbers of work placements for such schemes as TVEI has tended to focus the attention of policy makers on ways of achieving a sufficient *quantity* of work experience. At times, this has had the unfortunate consequence of relegating the importance of questions concerning the quality of work experience (Shilling 1987a).

One of the strengths of the BIM/BEMAS's guidelines is their recognition that it is not just schools, but participating employers who have responsibilities for the quality of work experience. The guidelines include an important focus on employer responsibilities for the safety of the student, the preparation of students and their experience of social relations within the firm. In terms of safety, the employing organization is asked to:

> Ensure that each student knows to whom they are responsible at any time...
> Ensure adequate insurance arrangements exist...
> Emphasise [to students] the safety regulations.

In relation to the preparation of students, and the nature of the social relations they may encounter during the placement, firms are asked to:

> Provide the student with information about the organisation...
> Invite the student to a preliminary interview...
> Circulate employees with information about the work experience scheme...
> Welcome the student formally and give a brief introduction to the organisation.

If these guidelines are followed, they should reduce those occasions when students are simply left to get on with a task without a satisfactory knowledge of the firm for which they are working, and before having been introduced to their colleagues. As a result, these steps may reduce the complaints made by students on work experience concerning isolation and loneliness (e.g. Shilling 1987b). Furthermore, if the employing organization takes care to ensure that students know to whom they are responsible at any time, this should serve the additional function of providing a figure the student can turn to for advice and help. However, irrespective of the support provided by the employing organization, there will be times when students are not content in a placement, and feel they have made a serious mistake in opting for work experience in a particular firm. Similarly, there may be occasions when unforeseen events mean that individuals within a firm are unable to provide adequate supervision to students on work placements. As a way of coping with such situations, the Code makes the constructive suggestion that an amicable 'let out' clause should be built into schemes, 'enabling an unsuccessful placement to end without detriment to the student, school or the employing organisation' (BIM/BEMAS). This aspect of the guidelines could have been profitably complemented by asking firms to facilitate private meetings between teachers visiting placements and their participating students. Teachers may usually visit students during their work experience, but they do not always meet students in an environment conducive to an open assessment of the placement.

Guidelines concerning the safety, preparation and social relations experienced by students can make a significant contribution to improving the quality of work placements. However, the BIM/BEMAS guidelines for employers are inadequate in that they make no mention of equal opportunities. There are no guidelines which detail the responsibility of ensuring that placements are open equally to female and male, and black and white students. This omission is especially unfortunate given the stated emphasis on equal opportunities that exists in government-sponsored initiatives such as TVEI, which include work experience as a compulsory element (MSC 1984). Furthermore, there is no advice concerning how employers may seek to ensure that students gain equal treatment in a place of work irrespective of their gender, race or social class. For example, nowhere do the guidelines suggest that key figures within the management and union (if there is one) should be given the training, responsibility, and recognition for ensuring that black students are not subjected to racism, or girls and boys to sexism.

Good practice for the Local Education Authority and the school

In the contemporary educational environment, schools and teachers are faced with rapidly increasing responsibilities and workloads. In the case of vocational education, liaison with local colleges of further education and industry are just two of the many growth areas in which schools are involved. The BIM/BEMAS guidelines identify some of the many *additional* activities that are necessary for schools and LEAs to engage in if they are to run an efficient and educational work experience programme. The code invests local authorities with the role of providing and managing the context in which schools run work experience. This involves considering the secondment of business people to assist in the 'operation of work related educational programmes', and supplying the financial means to support schools in their efforts. Local education authorities are also encouraged to:

> Provide in-service education for staff involved in work experience schemes ...
> Provide adequate resources for the proper operation of the scheme ...
> Support travel arrangements of students and staff ...
> Create an advisory network or service for staff involved in work placement schemes ...
> Organise the insurance of students and staff involved in visiting organisations ...
> Maintain an LEA wide register of organisations in work placement schemes.

If LEAs undertook these activities, they would represent a significant commitment to supplying the finance and training necessary to equip schools and teachers with the resources and skills required to liaise with employers, and monitor and evaluate the quality of work placements. In particular, for LEAs to establish a register of organizations in work experience schemes, may help minimize the duplication of effort that presently occurs in schemes where work experience is organized on a *laissez-faire* basis.

In addition to the proposed LEA role, the BIM/BEMAS guidelines identify further areas of action for schools. There is a stress on integrating work experience with the school curriculum; involving both sides of industry in the preparation of work experience; observing student activity on placements; monitoring 'the progress of the placement'; and 'working for permanent links with employing organizations in support of the wider aspects of industry education partnership'. Furthermore, the code is keen to emphasize steps which can be taken after the placement to improve the efficiency of future work experience. It advises schools to:

> Monitor the effectiveness of the scheme with the student ...
> Monitor and discuss with organisations the smooth running of the scheme – improving it where necessary.

The immediate reaction of an educationalist to the above would probably be to question whether LEAs and schools were capable of adopting such a role without a large injection of extra resources. To gain credibility with teachers, the BIM/BEMAS guidelines might have done better to start with a section concerned with 'Good practice for the government' which began 'provide adequate resources for the proper operation of work experience'. However, even if the resource question is placed to one side, there remain major areas of operational and educational concern which have been neglected by the guidelines.

First, there is no mention of a set of standards which should be applied to judge the suitability of firms on work experience programmes. The emphasis of the guidelines is on training teachers to cope with industrial liaison, and on devising ways of involving people from business in the schemes. However, there is no conception that some firms may not, in fact, be a suitable place for students to work. Given the wide variety of reasons firms have for participating in work experience – from student-centred to a concern with the labour they can extract from students during a placement (Shilling 1987a; Watkins 1988) – it seems only reasonable that firms meet basic standards before they are allowed to participate in school–industry relations. If it is accepted that industrial concerns should constitute an important part of the education of young people, then it is only proper to expect that industry should take on board the educational aims of schools involved in education–industry links. Otherwise, there is no reason to suppose that work experience programmes can fulfil the educational aims of stimulating in students thought about the existing or future organization of the workplace. This requires more than simply providing a 'brief outline of the objectives and detail of the scheme suitable for circulation within the employing organisation' (BIM/BEMAS 1988). Rather, it necessitates that educators are able to assess (and reassess) firms for their suitability. This would go some way to ensuring that firms who exploited students, or were simply unable to provide placements of sufficient quality, were excluded from work programmes. It is important to note that excluding a firm from work experience would not necessarily be a condemnation of its motives for participating in school–industry relations. Exclusion may simply reflect a situation whereby firms do not have the resources necessary to provide a high quality work placement.

Second, the guidelines' emphasis on ensuring the efficient operation of work experience is not matched by an equal concern with the *educational consequences* of work placements. Schools are encouraged to integrate work experience into their existing curriculum and provide opportunities for 'debriefing students on the experience and enable them to place the experience in the context of personal and educational development'. This is fine as far as it goes. However, given the code's detail concerning the measures necessary to ensure the efficient functioning of work experience, it seems that more could have been said concerning the educational aims of work experience. As the code merely talks about 'integrating' work experience and 'debriefing' students, it is difficult to see how it can have fulfilled its initial aim of outlining responsibilities necessary for 'planning and achieving a successful and formative student learning experience' (BIM/BEMAS 1988). This omission is even less excusable when it is remembered that education–industry bodies (Industry Matters, Project Trident, and the DTI's industry–education unit) were involved in supporting the code.

Good practice for the student

It could justifiably be said that it is the guideline for students which represent a key to the agenda behind any work experience code of practice. In this case, it is interesting to note that the 'model' student portrayed by *Work experience – a Code for Good Practice* is one viewed largely from the position of management. For example, the code advises students to:

Show initiative and look for leadership opportunities ...
Look for the next task as soon as one is completed ...
Ask about *positive* aspects of trade union or professional association influence [my emphasis].

We can only wonder at the response of a shopfloor union representative faced with a school student enthusiastically searching out leadership opportunities on the shop-floor, while asking workers during the tea-break (as opposed to work-time when they would presumably have been too busy anticipating the next task) to describe the positive (as opposed to negative!) aspects of trade union membership! In this context, it is just as well that the code has some sensible things to say about safety procedures.

If the code displays a partial view of the role of the student during work experience, it contains useful advice on finding out about the organization and looking at its role within the local community. Students are recommended to:

Study the organisation's literature and information package ...
Consider the organisation's role in the local social structure ...
Write a critical report and/or engage in classroom discussion on the experience.

These guidelines constitute positive suggestions as to how students might acquire factual information about the firm, and use critically their experiences as an educational resource. However, they can hardly be said to provide sufficient guidance concerning the critical use of work experience. Given the code's tendency to underplay the educational implications of work experience, then, it would seem profitable to both extend and build on these guidelines.

Conclusion

I have argued that existing research into the organizational and educational implications of work experience, coupled with the government's stated concern with equal opportunities in programmes embodying work experience (e.g. MSC 1984), suggests that existing codes of practice can be assessed against two major criteria. These are the *organizational problems* posed by programmes of work experience, and their *educational consequences* for students. The aims of *Work Experience – a Code for Good Practice* are to provide guidelines which address both of these.

The BIM/BEMAS code provides a number of guidelines that may enhance the operation of work experience. It recognizes the important role that the employing organization, the school, the LEA, and the student have in establishing a safe and viable programme of work experience. For work experience to function efficiently requires the collaboration and cooperation of *all* the participants in this activity. It also requires that LEAs provide the general framework, in terms of in-service training and general liaison with local employers, which can support schools and students involved in work experience. However, the strength of the BIM/BEMAS guidelines is not only in their organizational suggestions. In examining the educational implications of work programmes, they recognize the importance of locating this experience in a wider educational provision which includes the preparation and debriefing of students. To this extent, *Work Experience – a Code for Good Practice* may make a valuable contribution to improving the operation of existing work programmes. However, the code ultimately fails in its aim to provide an organizational and educational outline for students to achieve a 'successful and formative learning experience' (BIM/BEMAS 1988). There are no guidelines concerning equal opportunities and the code devotes only brief comments to the question of how schools and students may use work experience as a resource for examining *critically* the existing workplace. Moreover, the guidelines say nothing about how students may reflect on *alternative* conceptions of work and industrial organization. One explanation for these deficiencies may concern the code's treatment of work experience as a 'market conforming' policy. An obvious problem with promoting work experience as an activity designed to attract employers is that the educational goals of this activity may require minimizing in order to maximize room for industrial objectives.

In concluding this paper, I want to suggest how the positive aspects of the BIM/BEMAS's code might be built on as a possible way of reconstructing work experience in the future. The brief points that follow are not intended to constitute a detailed and comprehensive proposal. However, they represent some basic measures which will possibly stimulate debate about what it is necessary to do for work experience to become part of a progressive educational programme. I have argued that such a programme would need to exhibit four central characteristics: (i) students should have equal access to work placements irrespective of their gender, race or social class; (ii) a recognition of the rights of students to have experience of a work environment free from sexual or racial harassment; (iii) the use of work experience to enable students to acquire a factual and critical knowledge and understanding of the existing organization of work; and (iv) the recognition that work experience can be used as a resource to help students consider *alternative* ways in which work and industry might be organized. The proposals that follow are oriented toward these objectives.

Government resources are required to enable a central body within the LEA to be responsible for the screening of new firms, and the regular reassessment of participating firms, involved in work experience. This body could involve educators (careers officers and teachers) and companies with a proven commitment to the provision of equal opportunities. Monitoring would be concerned with the provision of equal opportunities to students in terms of the placements and work experiences offered by firms. This would not be satisfied by merely employing an individual whose role it was to encourage firms to participate in work experience (as envisaged in the DTI's 'signposters' (DES 1988)). The responses of students would constitute a central part of assessment. They should be made aware of the existence and aims of the monitoring body before they begin a work experience placement, have access to a local contact, and have realized the part they play in the evaluation of the placement. Firms unwilling or unable to achieve and maintain satisfactory standards must be prevented from participating in work experience programmes.

To supplement this assessment, designated teachers within each school would have the training, recognition and responsibility for liaising with companies in which their students are placed. This would require visiting students on placements (already a common practice) and establishing regular relations with local employers and union organizations. These teachers would be members of, or at least maintain contact with, the LEA's quality control body.

Within each participating firm, there should be an 'industrial tutor' with the training, recognition and responsibility for the nature of work experience offered by the company. At its most basic, this role would require that steps were taken to ensure that students were not discriminated against during their placement, or subject to sexual or racial abuse. The tutor would have the obligation of investigating and recording any grievances made by participating students, and reporting these to the central LEA body responsible for monitoring the quality of work placements. However, the role of the tutor would also include that of being an advisor and educator to students. For example, educational sessions could be set aside during the week which were devoted to the organization of the company, and the way in which (changing) labour processes and social relations of production have affected the workforce. Trade union members might usefully assume the role, of industrial tutor.

In order to provide students with a democracy of choice in terms of *economics*, firms organized along cooperative lines should be used as sites for work experience wherever possible. This could be supplemented by giving students a variety of work placements which reflect degrees of hierarchical operation (or, in Burns and Stalker's terminology, placements in organizations characterized by 'mechanistic' or 'organic' systems of management).[6] School courses would build on this variety of student practice and experience by examining other methods (existing and potential) of economic organization that students were not able to encounter during their work experience.

A new category of work placement should be created. As a way of encouraging the discussion of equal opportunities, students should experience domestic labour work placements (especially boys, as girls usually have substantial experience of housework) as part of their work experience programme. For a period of time, they would be responsible for the domestic chores of a household. This would probably have to be their own (a contract could be drawn up between the school and family) and would have to be closely monitored. However, in principle this would provide a material basis for the discussion of issues related to equality of opportunity and access to unwaged (as well as waged) labour. The family is not an undifferentiated unit. Women and men usually have very different experiences of working within the family, and it can be just as much a site of conflict as a firm (Hartmann 1987). Consequently, it is important for young people to critically explore the links between the interdependency of and the different experiences women and men have of waged and unwaged labour. The variety of family forms which exist provides an additional dimension to the educational potential of domestic work placements. For example, the experiences of students from different backgrounds (e.g. foster homes, children's homes, single parent families, two parent families, extended family situations, etc.), if sensitively handled, could be used to critically interrogate notions about what is 'women's' and 'men's' work. The environment of the school is a site in which alternative ways of organizing domestic labour could be explored (e.g. the collective organization of services). For example, if it were carefully managed with the full support and involvement of existing workers, students could participate in projects designed to pilot alternative ways of supplementing the meals/cleaning services provided in school. These could then be related to domestic units.

The experiences of students on work placements should be used as a basis for exploring the mechanisms of power as they exist within the present economy. For this purpose, students could be given group projects which use their own work experience as the basis for investigating opportunity, inequality and exploitation as it exists within and between jobs, firms, sectors of the economy, and nations. Here, school-based courses would be supplementing and building on students' experiences. They could be organized to explore ways in which relations of domination and subordination affect different groups of people in different ways (e.g. by gender, race and social class) and how these might be altered in a progressive direction.

In order to increase the relevance of the school-based components of work programmes, further student experiences of work could be used as a basis for discussion and project work. This could include part-time jobs, and the domestic labour undertaken by students. Students' own experiences of work could be complemented by an examination of work/unemployment experienced by other members of their household. One important factor would be an examination of the gender division of labour that operates in society in terms of both waged and unwaged labour.

Trade unions should be brought into closer contact with school-based vocational schemes in order to provide students with information about their legal rights (and how these have changed in recent years), and to inform them about the economic and wider aims and objectives of the union movement.

In suggesting these preliminary guidelines, I am not neglecting the fact that extra educational resources and substantial curriculum development would be required to enable educationalists and industrialists to carry out fully their roles in relation to work experience. Nor am I neglecting the difficulty of implementing the above in the present economic and political environment. For any real change to occur in the 'meaning' of work experience will clearly require a considerable change in the present political climate. However, it seems to me that focusing too closely on short-term and immediately feasible action, has contributed to the lack of alternative conceptions of what educational innovations could be like. Furthermore, with shortages of young people projected in the 1990s, there presently exists a strong incentive for employers to engage in education–industry activities such as work experience. Educators are in a position to recognize these incentives and to argue that if employers are to have the benefits of educational links, then they should be prepared to meet basic educational criteria. This would require moving away from the organization of work experience as a market conforming policy and towards it becoming an education driven policy. Without the resources provided by education, work experience for school students would not be feasible. Employers participating in work experience depend on schools organizing students, finalizing arrangement and providing teacher support in times of difficulty. There is an interdependency here which is important not to overlook. Schools depend on employers to provide work placements, but employers also depend on schools to fill and support these placements. Work experience promotes an *integration* of public and private resources (see Moore and Pierre 1988). The above suggestions for its reform are offered in the belief that there exists the possibility of building a consensus among progressive educators around the principle that if the concerns of industry are to play an important part in the education of students, then the educational concerns of equal opportunity, choice and alternatives should play an important part in such activities as work experience.

Acknowledgement

This chapter is a revised and extended version of an article which originally appeared as

'Work experience codes of practice: a critique and suggestions for reform', in *Journal of Education Policy*, 4, 4, 1989.

Notes

1 Two-thirds of school students presently engage in work experience in their final year of compulsory schooling. The government is seeking 200,000 more work placements in order to extend work experience to all students (DES 1988).
2 However, there is likely to remain a strong north/south divide in youth labour shortages.
3 The average length of a work-experience placement in England and Wales varies from between one to three weeks.
4 A further criterion by which codes of practice may be judged concerns their intended scope. As the BIM/BEMAS's guidelines aim to facilitate efficient planning and student learning, it is reasonable to evaluate them in these terms.
5 I am using the term 'industry' in its broad sense to include manufacturing, commerce, service and agriculture.
6 Burns and Stalker (1966) identify two ideal types of management systems. The 'mechanic system' embodies such features as the hierarchical structure of control, authority and communication, the translation of rights, obligations and methods into the responsibilities of functional positions, and a tendency for interaction between members of the organization to be vertical (i.e. between superior and subordinate). The 'organic system' embodies a much greater degree of flexibility. Characteristics include a lateral rather than a vertical direction of communication, and the emptying out of significance from the hierarchical command system.

References

Banham, J. (1988). Foreword to *Education at Work: A Guide for Employers*, DES.
British Institute of Management (BIM) and British Educational Management and Administration Society (BEMAS) (1988). *Work Experience – a Code for Good Practice* Rugby, Swift Valley.
Burns, T. and Stalker, G. (1966). *The Management of Innovation*, London, Tavistock.
Centre for Contemporary Cultural Studies (CCCS) (1981). *Unpopular Education*, London, Hutchinson.
Cole, P. (1981). 'Work experience: its relationship to the workplace and to the curriculum', An address to the Second National Work Experience Conference, Adelaide, cited in Cole, P. (1983).
Cole, P. (1983). 'Work-experience programmes in schools: some suggestions for programme reorientation', *Discourse*, 3, 2.
Dale, R. et al. (1989). 'TVEI: a policy hybrid' in A. Hargreaves and D. Reynolds (eds), *Education Policy: Contributions and Critiques*, Lewes, Falmer.
Department of Education and Science (DES) (1974) *Work Experience, Circulars and Administrative Memoranda*, Circular 7/74, London, HMSO.
Department of Education and Science (DES) (1977) *Local Education Authority Arrangements for the School Curriculum, Circulars and Administrative Memoranda*, Circular 14/77, London, HMSO.
Department of Education and Science (DES) (1988). *Education at Work: A Guide for Employers*, DES.
Eggleston, J. (1982). 'Work experience and schooling' in J. Eggleston (ed.), *Work Experience in Secondary Schools*, London, RKP, 3–31.

Finn, D. (1987). *Training Without Jobs*, London, Macmillan.
Hartmann, H. (1987). 'The family as the locus of gender, class and political struggle' in S. Harding (ed.), *Feminism and Methodology*, Milton Keynes, Open University Press.
Manpower Services Commission (MSC) (1984). *TVEI Review*, London, MSC.
Moore, C. and Pierre, J. (1988). 'Partnership or privatisation? the political economy of local economic restructuring', *Policy and Politics*, 16, 3, 169-78.
Pierre, J. (1987). 'Industrial policy and meso-corporatism: the policy and implementation of terminating three shipyards in Sweden', Paper cited in Moore, C. and Pierre (1988).
Shilling, C. (1987a). 'Work experience and schools: factors influencing the participation of industry', *Journal of Education Policy*, 2, 2, 131-47.
Shilling, C. (1987b). 'Work-experience as a contradictory practice', *British Journal of Sociology of Education*, 8, 4, 407-23.
Shilling, C. (1989a). *Schooling for Work in Capitalist Britain*, Lewes, Falmer.
Shilling, C. (1989b). 'The mini-enterprise in schools project: a new stage in education-industry relations?', *Journal of Education Policy*, 4.
Simon, R. (1983). 'But who will let you do it? counter hegemonic possibilities for work education', *Journal of Education*, 165, 3, 235-57.
Steinberg, L. (1982). 'Jumping off the work-experience bandwagon', *Journal of Youth and Adolescence*, 11, 3, 183-205.
Watkins, P. (1987). 'Student participation in the contested work place: the policy dilemmas of in-school work-experience', *Journal of Education Policy*, 2, 1, 27-42.
Watkins, P. (1988). 'Reassessing the work-experience bandwagon: confronting students with employers' hopes and the reality of the workplace', *Discourse*, 9, 1, 81-97.
Watts, A. (1980). *Work Experience Programmes: the Views of British Youth*, Paris, OECD.
Watts, A. (ed.) (1983). *Work Experience and Schools*, London, Heinemann.

Anthony Rosie

10

Making YTS responsive to its clients

A substantial critique of the Youth Training Scheme (YTS) has become available to teachers and others in recent years, e.g. Benn and Fairley (1986); Finn (1987); Gleeson (1983). This critique has included a scepticism over the possibility of YTS provision providing any basis for personal or policy change (Scofield *et al.* 1983). But the need to move to alternative practices that confront and engage with the understandings young people may have of their future lives has also been recognized (Cohen 1984). Coffield (1986) has argued that such work, while valuable, needs to be set within a concern for policy development. The particular forms that such policies might take at both national and regional levels are discussed in Coffield *et al.* (1986). It could be suggested that while both practice and policy are important for a progressive approach to YTS there also needs to be a concern for the direct and personal experiences of any particular student group. Coffield *et al.* (1986) present a richly textured description of life in a particular region which can provide a basis for policy debate.

A YTS course in context

Between 1984 and 1986 I was responsible for running a YTS mode B2 course for school leavers who were likely to find gaining entry to employment particularly difficult. During this period I carried out a fieldwork investigation into the lives of the students on the course. The course was provided by a college of higher education. Recruitment was conducted through the careers service and places were available for up to 25 students per year. The course was divided into two main parts. The first part included the off-the-job training which took place in the college. Here the students chose two courses for two days a week each from the following: catering, computing, office and retail, workshop craft. They also followed a social and life skills (SLS) programme for one day a week. During the first month of the course (July–August) the students sampled all four options before choosing two of them for more detailed study. The other component was the work experience element. Students were placed with an employer for blocks of time interspersed with periods of off-the-job training. The alternation of the two elements meant that students did not have to remain with one employer. Indeed, they were encouraged to take up different placements during the year.

Sandra Lane was the course tutor. She was responsible for the work experience element and also for much of the day to day running of the course when the students were in college. She was assisted by Sue Thompson who taught an SLS group and also helped supervise work placements. There were four tutors for each of the four option courses. In addition, the course leader (myself) taught on the course, assisted with placement supervision, and, with Sue Thompson, organized a residential week. The concerns Sandra, Sue and I shared revolved around the importance we attached to developing opportunities for the student group to speak freely, to enter into discussion of contemporary issues, to develop confidence in themselves, and, in Sandra's words, 'get them to be happy'. Naturally the other tutors shared some of these aims but they, for their part, were approaching the task through their subject content. Sandra and Sue had work experience as their focus but in fact their concerns were more all embracing than this. Their work involved a real concern for student identity. The fieldwork involved an exploration of the lives of young people on this particular YTS course.[1] The intention here is to illustrate ways in which Sandra's and Sue's understanding of aspects of identity provided a basis for a personalized teaching strategy, even in situations where they might have felt their efforts were proving to be unsuccessful.

An overview of the inquiry (Rosie 1988a) described the setting for the project and suggested that two distinct approaches to students could be identified. Tutors who only met the YTS students for off-the-job training in college (i.e. option group tutors) largely adopted what was termed a 'YTS perspective'. This latter model was rooted in the ideology and approach of the official YTS documents (MSC 1981, 1982, 1984). However, it was modified according to local circumstances and was far from being merely a behaviourist skills package. But, on the other hand, tutors who came into contact with students in all aspects of the course (Sandra Lane, Sue Thompson) adopted a holistic approach to student activity. They worked with students to link aspects of work experience to in-college work and to support personal growth. The tutors who saw the students holistically adopted varied approaches which are described below through the concepts of *identity* and *discourse*.

The young people who were observed during the fieldwork had either attended special schools or had sometimes endured unhappy experiences in mainstream schooling. The YTS course they attended had no particularly radical founding principles, although it had always maintained its independence from the MSC in terms of content and approaches to teaching. But it was possible to discern within the course the potential for a reconstruction of aspects of education and training. This was never expressed as a coherent philosophy which meant that the possibility for policy development was limited. This is not a point of criticism. It is a mark of the difficulty of bringing about change.

Identity and discourse

Sandra, Sue and I never discussed a rationale for investigating student identity. However, as part of the fieldwork I questioned both tutors at some length on their perceptions and interpretations of events involving students and tutors. The theoretical framework sketched in below was briefly discussed by the three of us but it has been developed from reflection on the events we participated in.

The interpretation of identity and subjective experience adopted here rests upon a guiding definition provided by Henriques et al. (1984): 'to refer to individuality and self awareness the condition of being a subject but understand in this usage that subjects are dynamic and multiple, always positioned in relation to particular discourses and practices' (p. 3). Identity is therefore not seen as a property of an individual, although it arises from the experiences of particular individuals. The condition of subjective experience is that it arises through an interplay between individuals and sets of discourses. Discourse is taken here to refer to language usage in its broadest sense. Thus discourses involve language and symbolic action which both create and support particular practices.[2] In terms of the present discussion the practices of classifying trainees contribute to a discourse that draws on notions of employability, ability, readiness for work, etc. The often opaque language which many studies of the relationship between subjectivity and discourse employ has possibly inhibited the application of these concepts to settings such as YTS courses.

The observations I made over a period of two years indicated that Sandra and Sue developed a rapport with students that enabled them to explore in detail the lives and daily experiences of the student group. In addition, the collective work Sue and I carried out in SLS sessions, particularly on issues such as the economic and political aspects of unemployment, began to raise among some students an awareness of various discourses against which we were all positioned. An example of this was the discussions we had on the theme of employment. What became clear was not so much that we shared common experiences, since we clearly did not, but that we experienced common aspects of compulsion in different ways. This led into a discussion on the way in which wealth is distributed in contemporary society which showed how far removed we all were from being able to control access to wealth. For a few weeks the different aspects of wealth creation and distribution became a focus and a means of supporting students in their experiences of life without permanent work. These various strands of a discourse supported a notion of self-awareness. This was seen in the way they discussed various constraints within their lives. These were sometimes material in form, e.g. lack of money, homelessness, direct pressure from families. On other occasions they could be less obvious but equally intense, such as when they involved feelings about other people either on the course or in work placements. The constraints themselves assumed a distinctive pattern: forms of freedom or control the student experienced within the home; how job seeking was seen and controlled within the student's family; lack of opportunities to explore personal and sexual relationships.

These features have a part to play in the emergence of young people as adults. They indicate a discourse of control, whether exercised by the student or by others acting on and influencing the students' lives. The usual learning and skills packages used on YTS courses often made reference to self-control. But they rarely explore the effects of control on the lives of young people. The work of Foucault has addressed different modes of control including bodily and technological forms (see Foucault 1977, 1979). Control should not be seen as merely a matter of physical or moral restraint (see note 2). The work of Sandra and Sue had a different starting point from that found in many of the standard YTS social and life skills packages. In order to illustrate the effects they achieved, two 'pictures' of students are given. These trace significant features of student lives on the course so as to show how identity concerns were realized. Of the two students one left before the end of the course.

Two student portraits

Deb was about five foot five inches tall. She had dark hair which was always slightly untidy. Her face and manner gave the impression right from the start that she was more mature and experienced in looking after herself than other students. Her whole appearance belied her 16 years of age. She was usually dressed in black and always wore a range of metal jewellery. A favourite piece was a metal cross: 'Don't know why ... I'm not religious ... I like it'. Deb was first interviewed by Sandra in February 1985 after the careers service had asked us to see her. This was a long time before the start date for the course (July 1985). Deb was very open with Sandra during this initial interview. She had rarely lived at home and so described to Sandra her previous career in institutions. Her parents were separated and she was sent to residential care when she was 4 while her brother stayed at home. Her mother hated her. Deb had sometimes stayed with her father after he moved away to another area but she had not seen him now for nearly two years. Unfortunately Deb's mother had considerable difficulties, including alcoholism and severe depression. Both Sandra and I telephoned her on a number of occasions. Her conversation was full of bitterness and invective against her daughter.

Deb had a record of violence. In one of the children's homes she had lived in she had assaulted a member of staff quite severely. She had also run away from residential care a number of times. She was considered by the staff of the residential special school she now attended to be violent, moody and unpredictable. Sandra learned much of this from the careers service and the residential school Deb currently attended.

Sandra felt that Deb should be encouraged to join the course although she felt it would be difficult to retain her. She thought Deb would start items like work placement but would then give up very quickly. She felt the student was lacking in self-confidence, despite the outward self-assurance she showed. By April Deb was still undecided about whether to join the course or not. She was not certain of what she wanted to do, whether to try and get a job or to 'simply do nothing' as she put it. One thing she knew was that she did not want to return home when she finished at her residential special school in June.

I had heard about Deb from Sandra but first met her when she came in one morning in April 1985 long before our July 1985 start. Deb had been staying at home but had had to leave the previous evening. Her mother had thrown a carving knife at her in a drunken rage so she had trekked into town and had gone to see the social services. They had arranged for her to spend the night at a children's home she had frequented in the past. She in fact hated this particular place and described the staff in strongly worded terms. Now she was on our doorstep. Deb came into my room with a confident manner. With the door open for all to see she affected unconcern and pretended to take no notice of what was being said. When I asked if she minded Sandra coming up to join us she said in an offhand way, 'She's all right'. Sandra came up and immediately adopted a tone of mock heavy humour. 'Well, Miss Lee, and what have you been up to?' It was exactly the right strategy. Deb recognized the banter and entered into the spirit of the occasion. A few minutes later we were desperately trying to sort out accommodation for Deb when she suddenly got up and announced she was going back home for a bit. She said of her mother, 'She'll be all right now'. Before she finally left that day Deb turned and said, 'I'm not coming on this if I don't want to.' Throughout her time on the YTS course there was tension between Deb's insistence on contesting adult forms of control and a desire to draw upon selected adults for support.

On the first day, when the students met as a group, Deb was noticeable for a number of reasons. She was the only woman student to mix easily with one group of male students. On the first day she also asked more questions than anyone else. What was interesting was that most of the questions were about the reasons for doing particular things. Deb was anxious to find out the principles underlying the course. The possibility of being positioned as inferior because she lacked skills and employment was one she criticized right from the start. Most of the option tutors soon saw her as a potential troublemaker. When it came to comparatively trivial matters such as chewing gum in the workshop it was Deb who was singled out even though others were chewing as well. Similarly, when she arrived late to one of the option groups with Jock, her boyfriend, the tutor allowed Jock in to the room but excluded Deb. There was an immediate expectation in the first few weeks that wherever Deb went there would be trouble.

One of the option course tutors said after one week, 'She'll never last'. At this point Deb was seen simply as loud and provocative. However, Sandra and Sue did not accept this view of Deb. Sandra saw her frequently, particularly over the arrangements for the first work experience placement, while Sue was her personal tutor. Deb found most forms of control irksome. She disliked rules such as not chewing gum in a workshop or always having to wear protective clothing in such a setting. But Deb did not set out to cause trouble or to break rules. I watched her frequently in my observations of teaching sessions. On only two occasions did I see her behave in ways that might prompt tutor correction. But she was perceived by most tutors as a difficult student.

Part of the reason for the negative perceptions shown by option tutors lay in Deb's habit of constantly asking questions and never being satisfied with half answers or with being fobbed off. One day in office skills she asked why the class had to do a particular task. The teacher ignored her but when I asked Deb about it afterwards she commented, 'What's the point of it?' What she meant was that tasks such as finger exercises were not of much interest but she was perfectly happy to learn how to type what she called 'real letters'. What Deb objected to was the lack of clarity of the purposes behind the tasks. She frequently asked why the group was doing a particular activity. She found answers such as 'It'll help you when you leave' (a common response) particularly irksome. Deb complained first to Sandra and then to me that she was not going to do any 'of those things' at home (cooking meals for her family, DIY or 'mending things').

Deb discussed with me how she saw her future and she then mentioned some of this to Sandra. Deb was one of two women students I questioned at this stage who made it quite clear they were not going to have a permanent husband/partner or childcare responsibilities. Deb said of herself, 'I'd be a rotten mother anyway'. This led into a conversation about her own family upbringing. Deb would not explain why she did not want a permanent partner. A little later she said of the relationship she currently had, 'It won't last ... his parents, see'. When pressed she explained that Jock's parents would feel she was not good enough for their son.

The observation work I carried out in the first weeks of the course included visits to a number of pubs in the town. It was through these observations that I learned that Deb was on the streets. In fact at that particular time (July 1985) she was only just beginning to be involved in prostitution. I made no mention of this to other tutors but Deb's activities were reasonably well known.

I questioned Sandra and Sue about Deb. They had heard about her exploits. Both felt it was even more important to keep Deb on the course. On the other hand the option tutors who were very much in favour of her exclusion were able to point to Deb's pattern of attendance: she was not fulfilling the laid down criteria for being recognized as a YTS trainee. But Sandra gave a perception that was important:

> It's no good asking her to fill in forms or learn to look after herself. She does all that anyway, poor child. She said of this course that it's the one place she's been to where people have listened to her. It doesn't matter what sort of girl she is. She needs this course. I just don't think we should be asking her to do the same things as the others right now ... She knows herself pretty well. It's more important getting her to come in to College.

We might have expected that Deb would be angry towards tutors who were apparently criticizing her. In fact she showed no overt hostility towards any of the option tutors. She did, however, make clear her preference for the support she received from Sandra and Sue. I asked Deb how she felt about office skills, which after all was the option where she was most disliked by a tutor. She said of the tutor, 'She's moany but I get on with her all right'. When she was asked to elaborate on this I gathered that while Deb did not like some of the restrictions placed on her in the group, such as having to sit still for quite long periods of time, she did find she was given a certain amount of freedom to talk with others. It was this which contrasted so strongly with her previous experience. In the past she had been expected to follow a tightly regimented line. One option tutor did adopt this strategy with Deb and the results were predictable. Deb began to turn up late, she became provocative and then swore at the tutor who insisted she be excluded. When all this was discussed at a tutor team meeting the line taken by the affronted tutors was that some students were being harmed by the presence of students such as Deb. This argument took two forms. First, there was a concern for the possible moral danger that other students might face from Deb. Second, there was a fear that other students were being intimidated by Deb. Exclusion was seen as the only feasible option.

Sandra, Sue and I did not take this view and refused to allow students to be excluded at this point. Deb left of her own accord after the first work experience placement. Sandra had sought to keep Deb on the course and to get her on to work experience. She had hoped that if Deb took to this she could become more settled. Deb wanted to have a work placement in a cafe and this was fairly easy to arrange. However, the cafe Sandra found was not the sort of place Deb wanted. Deb had mentioned a cafe that in fact would not take on YTS students. The cafe Sandra chose was busier, catered for office workers, and waitresses were not expected to interact with customers. By way of contrast the cafe Deb had mentioned catered largely for either building site workers or similar, involved a good deal of staff customer banter, and closed much earlier in the afternoon! It was used by a close knit community of workers and was known for its informal position within the local job network. Thus the placement Deb received was at variance with her hopes. Nevertheless, Sandra felt that with encouragement Deb could manage a successful work experience.

Both Sandra and Sue visited her frequently on work experience. At first Deb turned up on time and was attentive. But she soon found the work tedious and disliked the compulsory politeness she was expected to show towards customers. She began to stay away from work. At the same time she and a friend gravitated towards prostitution.

I had interviewed Deb as part of the data collection but, as indicated above, I had learned about her activities through other students. Deb took the decision to come and see me after I found her one morning sitting on some steps instead of being in work experience. On that occasion she looked unkempt, had matted hair and was very tired. She did not want to talk about work so we talked about where she was staying. From this starting point Deb told me the story of her life. She confirmed all the details I had learned from elsewhere. Deb spoke of herself in very disparaging terms, particularly when she compared herself with her brother: 'I'm thick, I am ... got shit for brains'. Deb had no money from any source since she was not receiving her trainee allowance because of her absence from work. I asked her how she managed and she began to tell me about how she went round certain pubs with Jane and was 'doing it'. My face must have registered some reaction because she flared up with, 'Don't like it then! Too bad. I've got to live haven't I?' The defences were up. Deb had admitted a side of her life in which she took no pride, only a feeling of shame at this point. She then said, 'You'd find out anyway'. She seemed oblivious to the fact that so many people knew about it by this time. Deb made it clear that she was not to be watched: 'I'd die, if you did that'.

I never observed Deb directly but I carried out sufficient observation to establish the presence of a network such as she described. Deb came back to talk to me about her life and she did not confide in Sandra although she did talk to Sue. I next spoke to her some months later when she came back from London. She said of her life then. 'I want to drop dead and be in a coffin. What's the point of living. Nothing to live for anyway.'

It is easy to say that the YTS course did nothing for Deb or that she was unsuitable for it. The point is there was little other provision for her. She stayed for only a few months but that was the longest voluntary stay she had made anywhere in her life. She herself praised the way Sandra and Sue listened to her:

> She's all right [Sue]. She listens and she doesn't treat me like dirt. — did. She [Sue] don't ask me stupid questions.
>
> (September 1985)

By 'stupid questions' Deb meant questions that assumed she knew little of how to make a living. She was particularly contemptuous towards SLS and other sessions which looked at mortgages, financial management. As far as Deb was concerned these questions were 'divvy' and not on her personal agenda. She was not alone in this and another student, Paula, can provide some insight into what an alternative agenda might look like.

Paula was about five foot four inches in height. She was slim and her face was distinctive. Sue Thompson described her as having the looks of a model and Sandra referred to her as a 'dark eyed beauty'. She was reserved with most adults on the course and tutors often felt she was laughing behind their backs. Paula came to the college course from a local comprehensive school having gained a number of CSE passes and also a pass at Level One in RSA typing. The college was allowed to recruit her because the careers service accepted the course intake would otherwise be unbalanced. Sandra interviewed Paula and felt she would be well received by option group tutors. She also felt Paula would enjoy work experience.

However, option tutors soon had one or two concerns about Paula. She was felt to be working to less than her full capacity in office skills. My field notes at the time noted she appeared bored and uninterested. Yet Susan Renshaw, the office skills tutor, was disappointed when Paula decided not to choose office skills as a permanent option in the main in college blocks. She chose catering instead. Similarly Roger Kemp, the computer studies tutor, noted that Paula had chosen workshop craft instead of his option and that Paula had probably influenced some of the other students to follow her example.

Paula spent a long time with Sandra discussing her first work experience placement. Sandra told me about the discussion. Apparently Paula was interested in computing and office work for her placement but did not want to follow these courses in college. She felt she had enough skills already in these areas to be able to hold down a job but what she lacked was experience. She was very particular about the sort of company she worked in. It had to be fairly small and one where she would get to know people and be 'treated right'. Paula decided that the focus of influence for her would lie with Sandra and Sue rather than the option tutors. Thus she had little time for a discourse of control through the practices of skill training in college. In fact Paula came to feel that the skills she acquired during the year had more to do with self-understanding.

Paula had family concerns. Her father had not been happy about her coming on a YTS course because it was 'slave labour'. It was her mother who had felt it was a reasonable idea. Paula was interested in the course because she had heard about it from former students who had attended the same secondary school as herself. Paula's brother, Dave, had gone straight into an apprenticeship which was a relief to the family. Paula felt that she was not ready to go straight into work. Her father was a skilled worker at an engineering firm and her mother worked as a cleaner in a large office. Paula described most of her family concerns to Sandra rather than to me although later she and I were to talk more freely. Her fears, as I learned about them, were rooted in the restrictions she felt she was experiencing at home. It was not simply a matter of having to be in early at night or having her friends vetted by her parents; she felt her parents were reasonable in their rules. The problem was that she felt her father expected her to marry young and start a family. In other words her father did not take the idea of his daughter having a work career very seriously. He certainly wanted her to move to work but expected her to work for a short time before marrying and starting a family. Her mother was more understanding but Paula explained her feelings to Sandra: 'I think they're always looking to see what I'm doing because they want me to get married. Dad's always going on about me being married'.

This knowledge only became clear after a few months. But it shows how forms of control can be implicit. As I got to know Paula it became possible to visit her parents and interview them informally. Her perceptions were well founded. Her father had clear ideas on the place of a woman in the home and was a bit worried about his daughter's desire for independent living. At the same time he spoke of her needs: 'She's got to have her head ... try things out before she settles down'.

Paula began to go out with Terry in the third week of the course and this was commented on. Terry was seen as a difficult student as indeed he was (see Rosie 1988b), and it was felt Paula was wasting herself with him. One tutor said of the friendship 'You can't tell her what to do of course but she'll regret it'. Terry had a long criminal record. He was very much the leader of a group of male students. Like Deb he was seen as a troublemaker and as someone who should be excluded from the course. Option tutors felt that Deb and Terry were beyond the capacity of the course team as a whole.

The option tutors felt there was a clearly defined target group for whom the course should be catering. This particularly included those who would find it difficult to gain employment because they lacked confidence, the ability to relate to adults and also certain practical skills. Paula was perfectly competent at typing and so had decided not to follow this particular option course. She was keen to take catering and workshop craft and this was supported by her parents. Her mother and father wanted to see her settle down and marry before she was 20. This meant that college work that supported domestic activity was encouraged. Paula's perception was rather different. She wanted to leave home and live independently in a flat. She had no intention of marrying before she had developed a career at work.

Paula started going out with Terry but the relationship was very much on her terms. They usually walked round a park near Sandra's home. Paula insisted on being in by a certain time and had no intention of going anywhere with Terry other than where she chose. She saw it as a college-based friendship. When the first work experience started Paula was less keen to maintain the friendship on a regular basis. Terry in his turn admitted to me that Paula was unlike any other person he had been out with. The friendship came to an end when Paula found she could not accept Terry's regular drinking. She was also worried because other students were calling her a 'slag' for going around with him. Paula ceased going out with Terry when he left the course after three months but made it quite clear from then on that she was not going to go out with anyone else on the course. This provoked questions such as 'Who does she think she is?' Paula in her turn became aggressive towards other students, particularly male students. She described one as a 'prat' and another as 'a waste of space'.

Gradually Paula began to talk to me about her feelings towards the workplace. On her first work placement she was in a small company doing secretarial work. She did not like it particularly because she was not allowed to do very much. The supervisor took the view that if this was a student's first placement then there was little the student would be capable of doing. In fact Paula could do a lot more than she was allowed to do. This problem improved with the remaining two placements.

Paula had quite a large circle of friends. She knew people outside college who had entered work successfully. For instance, one friend had left secretarial work to take on the book-keeping for her bother-in-law's small firm. Paula saw this sort of activity as attractive and, more importantly, saw work experience as a means of achieving it. Paula made negative comments on some aspects of the college course but this was largely because they were not fulfilling her needs: 'Typing's so boring. It's the same stuff every time'.

Paula felt she could not attain the level of experience she needed from typing or computing. This was not because the tutors would not help her. They certainly would have done. The real problem was that she would have to be given extra work or alternative projects on her own. Another student with high qualifications was happy about accepting this strategy. Paula was unhappy because it would have set her apart from other students. She wanted to be in a group where she was no different from other people and where she could work at the same pace as everyone else. This had guided her final choice of catering and workshop craft for her options.

It was on her second work experience in an office that Paula began to go out with a man in the firm who was in his early 20s. The friendship did not last much beyond the work experience but it signalled a change for Paula. This was the first time she had been out with someone who was older than herself. From now on both she and two other students began to look for older male friends from workplaces. A similar situation happened on her final work experience in a small company. This time her boyfriend did not come from that particular firm but was someone she met through a mutual acquaintance. But this time her friendship upset other students who she had been friendly with in the past. She found she could not talk to them and for a few months after the end of the course there was a considerable rift between herself and other students she normally mixed with.

Paula talked about her boyfriends with Sue. This is not in itself so remarkable. After all, many teachers have built up supportive friendships for pupils. What was distinctive was the way Paula discussed it first with Sue in terms of her personal future. A desire to break free from parental control and ultimately from the control of peers was marked. But this reached a distinct point when Sue and I began a series of sessions under the social and life skills component in January 1986. Sue had from the start taken a particular interest in creating a forum for women students to meet and voice their experiences. But between January and March 1986 we offered an opportunity for any student to come to us instead of their personal tutor for the SLS work. We had made it clear we would be talking about issues such as unemployment, the position of women in work and in the home. In other words we were providing a forum for personal and social identity issues for students.

Most students preferred to remain with their SLS tutors. They felt they needed the more directly perceivable skills such as exercises on personal management, telephone practice and a range of confidence boosting exercises. Their need in these areas was quite clear. A small group came to us most weeks (usually three women and one male student). They went to their regular tutors for about half an hour and then came out and spent an hour with us with their tutors' permission. Paula was one of this group. Her comments in various sessions were revealing. I heard Paula describe her mother's life as one of early marriage and subsequent loss of opportunity. She made it clear she wanted a different future for herself. This was at the directly personal level. In terms of experiences in the workplace Paula became aware of herself as a woman in a place of employment. This included an awareness of how men regarded her and she was determined not to accept exploitative practices. It was through her growing awareness that we had at one point to visit the firm to say that attitudes towards Paula were not acceptable. The issue was handled carefully and tactfully by Sandra. Paula continued in the work placement and then gained permanent employment there. She was to stay in this employ for nearly a year before moving to a bigger company.

Several points became noticeable here. Paula in conversation with me compared herself to her friend who had started in work and had then moved into a family business as book-keeper. She said that her friend had wanted the trappings of position: the personal desk, the typewriter and the possibility of moving upwards. That prospect had not materialized so she had used her skills and resources to good effect within her family network. Paula did not have this opportunity at the time so she felt she had to move out and away from her family:

> My Dad doesn't believe I'll stick it but I will. It's not that he doesn't want me to have a good job, I know he does. But really he's never seen me working in an office. No one else in our family has and I don't see why I shouldn't.

Paula's determination and indeed her ultimate success could be read as an example of how much YTS can offer young school leavers. This should be regarded with some caution. First, Paula achieved what she wanted without reference to the official off-the-job training. She avoided options that would have prepared her directly for office work. But, more importantly, she described her own growing awareness of how she realized what she wanted to achieve. It was quite clear that she saw the work Sue did with her as crucial:

> I really enjoyed the sessions. At first it was just nice to talk ... I found I had things in common with Sue. Now I couldn't believe that. But then I found, I think we all did, that there were things we could do. You know we could say things to other students and to you. We knew you and Sue wouldn't allow them to get away with things. You know, I never even thought about it before. But I can see my Mum and what she's done so much better now.

There is a confidence to this that was simply absent when Paula started the course. The question of confidence building for all students on the course was clearly very important; but both our case studies here suggest that the work of two tutors contributed in different ways to a form of work that was exciting and challenging.

Conclusion

Deb and Paula led very different lives yet both drew on the resources of Sandra and Sue. As indicated in Rosie (1988a, p. 160) a number of students were more likely to draw on the option tutors for support as they prepared for their futures. It is not a matter of saying there was a marked divergence or indeed that one form of support was more productive than another. What is clear is that some students could not accommodate themselves to the officially sanctioned YTS approach and therefore made demands that could not be met within this framework. The example of Paula shows that it was not a matter of Sandra and Sue merely working with students that had no other resource to draw upon. Paula would not have stayed on the course without the support she received.

The approach that has been described here drew at various points on substantial criticisms of YTS training that both Sue and I made. It was not a matter of providing a counselling service, although that was undoubtedly a valuable part of the work. It was the social and political commitment that enabled some tutors to develop approaches that lay outside the official guidelines. However, as has been clear from the two portraits it is not possible to identify a set of useful skills and simply incorporate them into a youth project. The success achieved here by Sandra and Sue derived from a number of distinctive features. First, they had a detailed knowledge of the local economy and the range of placement provision. This was supplemented by a knowledge of substantial parts of the local community. There is a need for detailed community knowledge within any youth training project.

Second, there was no attempt to see student lives as limited by external factors such as home conditions or personal limitations. These features are important. But they were not seen as determining. Perhaps the clearest expression of this lay in the fact that the attempt to discuss social and political issues such as unemployment and home experiences gave some students confidence to create their own needs and demands. As is clear, only a small number of students responded to this part of the course. The very nature of youth training means that such a project is marginalized. But there is much to be gained by working through students' personal experiences and the alternatives they perceive in their lives.

Notes

1. The tutors have been given pseudonyms. The students chose their own names. Some of their choices were amended slightly to prevent identification.
2. The importance of language and non-verbal activity as a carrier and creator of distinct practices cannot be over-estimated. The official MSC literature frequently stressed that young people were 'not yet ready' for certain aspects of adult life. This is part of a discourse of preparation in which forms of control play a significant part. The technologies of control implicit in the MSC documentation (1982, 1984) stress behavioural control through language and activities. The work of tutors on the course inevitably involved a concern with different forms of control over the lives of students. Students themselves became aware of this process. For some, including Paula who is described in some detail, an awareness of forms of control led to a search for strategies to assert her independence. The notion of strategy and discourse employed here draws on Foucault (1974, 1979).

References

Benn, C. and Fairley, J. (eds) (1986). *Challenging the MSC*, London, Pluto.
Coffield, F. (1986). 'From theoretical critique to alternative policy' in A. Hartnett and M. Naish (eds), *Education and Society Today*, Lewes, Falmer, 109–20.

Coffield, F., Borrill, C. and Marshall, S. (1986). *Growing up at the Margins*, Milton Keynes, Open University Press.
Cohen, P. (1984). 'Against the new vocationalism' in I. Bates et al., *Schooling for the Dole? The New Vocationalism*, Basingstoke, Macmillan, 104-69.
Finn, D. (1987). *Training without Jobs*, London, Macmillan.
Foucault, M. (1974). *The Order of Things*, London, Tavistock.
Foucault, M. (1977). *Discipline and Punish*, London, Allen Lane.
Foucault, M. (1979). *The History of Sexuality*, Harmondsworth, Penguin.
Gleeson, D. (ed.) (1983). *Youth Training And The Search for Work*, London, Routledge and Kegan Paul.
Henriques, J., Holloway, W., Urwin, C., Venn, C., Walkerdine, V. (1984). *Changing the Subject: Psychology, Social Regulation and Subjectivity*, London, Methuen.
Manpower Services Commission (MSC) (1981). *New Training Initiative: A Consultative Document*, Moorsfoot, Sheffield.
Manpower Services Commission (MSC) (1982). *Youth Task Group Report*, London, HMSO.
Manpower Services Commission (MSC) (1984). *YTS84(A): Guide to the Revised Scheme Design and Content*, Sheffield, MSC.
Rosie, A.J. (1988a). 'An ethnographic study of a YTS course' in A. Pollard, J. Purvis and G. Walford (eds), *Education Training and The New Vocationalism*, Milton Keynes, Open University Press, 148-64.
Rosie, A.J. (1988b). 'YTS and residential experience' in J. Evans (ed.), *Sociology, Sport and Control*, Lewes, Falmer.
Scofield, P., Preston, E. and Jacques, E. (1983). *The Tories' Poisoned Apple*, Independent Labour Party.

Section 3

Beyond vocationalism

Introduction

Following on the case studies of schools and further education explored in the previous section, we here take up some of the alternative curricular implications involved. A particular obstacle to initiating the sorts of alternatives envisaged by the authors in Section 2 is the current preoccupation with skills training which, in many cases, reinforces tripartism and reduces knowledge in the curriculum to a set of atomized and fragmented modular tasks. According to both Gleeson's (Chapter 11) and Moore's (Chapter 12) contributions this process inhibits learning and understanding and often confirms 'deficit' models of trainees' abilities. For Gleeson the rise of life skills training as an answer to socially equipping young people to stand on their own feet has been ideological rather than practical in nature. He argues that the major weakness of contemporary government training policy in general is that it neither specifies skills training nor provides an adequate general education for young people. Thus, under present conditions, the young lose out both ways; on the one hand, they do not gain marketable or recognized skills and, on the other, they do not acquire the knowledge and understanding that would allow them critical insight into the social, political or economic workings of society. But for Moore, this poses a deeper question: how then are alternatives to training alternative? Using Bernstein's concepts of elaborating and restricting codes, and classification and framing, his contribution looks at the relationship between the formal and the informal in models of skill. Taking as his starting point the view that skills are socially constructed rather than given by the technical nature of the production process, he argues that models of skill 'frame' social practices associated with work in ways which control how those practices should be understood. They do this by imposing upon them particular definitions of the nature of production and social relations. They automatically define 'out of the frame' skills and competences at a level of 'class-cultural practice'. No recognition is given, for instance, of the skills associated with grapevine recruitment or social network membership. Hence, models of skill selectively represent what is to count as 'relevant' to the world of work. He argues that a crucial aspect of this process is that of misrecognition through which deficit models of trainees are constructed in such a way that their real competences are denied and they are presented as lacking in skills as redefined by the training model. A particularly significant aspect of this is the way in which orthodox skills models translate training into a restricting code, insulating the social practices of production from elaborating and potentially critical knowledge. According to both Moore and Gleeson, an alternative approach will attempt to link these social practices with elaborating knowledge. Hence, the task for an alternative paradigm is to critically reconstruct a concept of 'skill' as such, and not simply to seek different institutional means of delivering the orthodox version of challenging gender and race discrimination in their distribution in the existing labour market.

The curricular implications of both Gleeson's and Moore's papers are taken further by Spours and Young (Chapter 13). Rejecting as socially divisive the separation of the school-based academic curriculum and the 'alternative' presented by the new vocationalism, their contribution argues that a democratic reform of the 14–19 curriculum must treat an understanding of changes in the economy and the organization of work as a central issue across the curriculum for all young people. Such a curriculum would be based on developing a critical relationship between academic subjects and the nature of work in our society, already referred to by Avis and Mac an Ghaill in the previous section. Spours and Young suggest that current economic and technological changes which point to the end of an era of Fordist systems of mass production and services, provide the possible conditions for going beyond the academic/vocational divisions that dominate the 14–19 curricula of most schools and colleges today. They develop their alternative from a critical analysis of current 'vocational' initiatives and a clarification of a broader concept of work as 'productive life'. According to Spours and Young, making such connections involves a broadening of the concept of work to relate to far more than paid employment; it also indicates the crucial role such subjects as geography, history, economics and social studies can play in a reformed curriculum. It is necessary, therefore, to explore a new framework for the curriculum which takes work in all its forms as the basis for the development of knowledge (historical, sociological, scientific and technological) and skills (intellectual, technical, practical and communicative).

Denis Gleeson

Skills training and its alternatives

This contribution looks at the ways in which New Right ideology and thinking finds its expression in vocational education and training, in particular at the controversial rise of 'life skills' training. In so doing the paper seeks to provide alternative arguments which go beyond the narrow confines of government training policy, encompassing a broader and more critical curricular perspective within which pupils, teachers and students may work. The principal argument is that the rise of life skills marks a response to certain political and ideological imperatives and should not be confused with making young people either more personally effective or employable, as official sources claim. Viewed critically, the apparent vocational realism currently associated with the 'new' training paradigm conceals its inherent irrationality, its purpose being to create a vocational public whose eventual employment (or unemployment) bears little relation to the content of their training. Irrespective of the apparent realism employed within skills-based training, often associated with jargonized terms such as 'occupational training families', 'generic skills', 'modular training', 'transferable skills', 'economic awareness' and so forth, many of the skills involved are of a regulative rather than of an occupationally useful nature.

Background

There is, of course, more to the debate than the introduction to this chapter suggests. Following publication of the Black Papers in the late 1960s and early 1970s, the New Right have proffered inflated opinions on all matters associated with standards in education, including the political and moral content of the curriculum. More recently the Hillgate Group and other apologists of the New Right have captured media and public attention about political and sexual bias in the curriculum. History, sociology, geography, social studies and physics teachers have, for example, been criticized for introducing 'leftist' ideas into the curriculum, while others have been attacked for increasing racial conflict, or for promoting homosexual attitudes via multicultural, social and health education programmes. Elsewhere controversy has arisen over government attempts to remove political education from youth training schemes. Yet, despite the moral panic which tabloid revelations have excited about such issues, the Secretary of State, HMI, LEAs and courts have found little positive evidence on which to act. Undeterred by this the Conservative government and its supporters have, nevertheless, proceeded to introduce legislation in both 1986 and 1988 Education Acts designed to curb political and sexual bias in the curriculum. Needless to say what has been overlooked in all this is the way in which implicit assumptions and bias are built into New Right thinking itself. While no one would deny that bias exists, or that it is possible to be totally objective, the New Right have been quick to recognize subjectivity in others, without apparently confronting their own in-built prejudices. In view of the recent opinions expressed by the right-wing Hillgate Group about the dangers of bias and indoctrination elsewhere in mainstream education, this controversial aspect of government intervention in vocational training has, for example, escaped critical attention (Scruton *et al.* 1985). If, as Marsland (1987) has recently pointed out, with reference to sociologists' apparent bias against business, '... criticism should not be so one-sidedly selected', there is little evidence that the New Right has heeded its own advice in the selection of what it considered bias in the curriculum. It is to this neglected aspect of the present debate about vocationalism, with reference to skills training, that this chapter is addressed.

The rise and rise of 'life skills'

In recent years the social and life skills curriculum has emerged to occupy an important place in new training initiatives, particularly those associated with YTS and prevocational courses such as TVEI, CPVE, LAPP, RSA, City and Guilds and BTEC. At one level the attraction of 'life skills' training is that it is relevant and addresses, in ways which traditional liberal and general studies could not, the practical problems likely to affect young people in hard times as adults, parents and employees. At another, ambiguity surrounds the criteria upon which such skills for living are constructed and appraised, not least because of their close behavioural connection with altering young people's attitudes towards authority, industry and society. In this respect the more centalized control of this effective domain has made it increasingly difficult to differentiate between the 'official' and the 'hidden' curriculum, not least because the two have become overlapping in many ways. With reference to the behavioural objectives associated with life skills training, it is argued here that the hidden curriculum has become confused with the official curriculum. Here I am referring to the ways in which the implicit ordering of knowledge (attitudes, deference and demeanour, presentation of self and so forth), traditionally separated off from the formal content of the curriculum, has become written down as apparently valid knowledge warranting transmission and evaluation. Perhaps, not surprisingly, in a short space of time life skills training has become detached from the wider objectives associated with liberal humanist education: the point being that teaching young people *about* society has been replaced by criteria designed to alter their *relationship* with it.

If this image of vocational relevance has filled a void left by the apparent failure of liberal humanistic education (to provide a more realistic understanding of society's industrial and commercial values), it has also drawn closer attention to the ways in which radical conservative political and economic thinking finds its expression in the curriculum. From this viewpoint government training policy does not simply represent a response to youth unemployment (or to make workers or industry more efficient), but is also designed to alter existing relations in the workplace in favour of employers (Fairly and Grahl 1983). In this respect training for 'personal effectiveness' is seen here to have a closer relationship with private enterprise than might first appear; it also represents an important ideological mechanism through which labour is made ready and available for work. Thus, a central feature of 'life skills' is that, in contrast with conventional social studies, it is not designed to provide a balanced understanding of society, but to train young people in relevant social skills – associated with surviving, communicating, getting on with people, listening, talking and so forth. If, on the surface, such skills would appear relevant and non controversial, they do little more than encourage students to respond rather than to act on their experiences of life.

Skills training and the disadvantaged

Despite the expressed intention of both government and MSC (or Training Agency as it is now called) to extend the quality and quantity of training for all young people (MSC 1982a), there is little doubt that the Youth Training Scheme (YTS) is principally directed towards the 40 per cent of school leavers who leave school with only the minimal level of formal qualifications (Ainley 1985). What remains less than clear is how skills training 'involving basic literacy and numeracy, practical competence in the use of tools, machinery and office operations' (DES 1981), will enable young people 'to make their way in the increasingly competitive world of the 1980s' (MSC 1982). Part of the problem can be explained in terms of the MSC's insistence on creating a range of 'new' experimental 'skills' designed to replace the apprenticeship system and its links with apparently outmoded work practices. As Cockburn (1987) has pointed out, the content of YTS has been developed on guidelines from the Institute of Manpower Studies, whose vocational orientation was favoured by MSC over the more liberal educational principles being pressed by the Further Education Unit (FEU 1979) at the time. Suspicious that educationalists might subvert the content of the new vocationalism, MSC preferred at the time the services of occupational psychologists working in areas of skills acquisition. According to Cockburn (1987), in practice the content of YTS training is neither educational nor vocational so much as empty of meaning.

> The Institute's 'transferable skills' [Hayes et al. 1983] are so basic as to lend themselves to parody: learning to push, learning to pull. Learning to stand up without falling over? Life and social skills, intended by the MSC to be a core element of all YTS schemes, are widely regarded as a patronising slur on young people's personal qualities. Under this theme they are invited to improve their appearance, their interview technique and the approach to authority.

Much depends, of course, on the view taken of MSC endeavours in the early 1980s to shift the emphasis away from subject-based teaching towards occupational training which is not specific to one particular occupation. There are those who believe, for example, that the skills approach represents little more than an attempt to run down traditional craft principles in line with government policy on apprenticeship and union control (Moos 1983; Ryan 1984; Fairly and Grahl 1984). Others argue that the curriculum guidelines associated with YTS offer a more flexible approach to training than traditional forms allow, and prepare young people in a wide range of generic work skills (Hayes 1983). In recent years it is this latter view which has enjoyed strong official support, and is premised on the assumption that conventional curriculum arrangements have failed the majority of school leavers (Callaghan 1976). However, it is one thing to draw attention to the inadequacies of the conventional academic curriculum, and the apparent 'failure' generated by it, and quite another to legitimate the new vocationalism in terms of that failure. Since the Great Education Debate (1976-79) the eagerness with which the New Right has attacked the apparent inadequacies of progressive and humanistic education has, somewhat ironically, created the space in which the skills-based approach has been allowed to flourish.

Yet, to date, government and Training Agency have offered no tangible evidence that skills training is what industry needs or requires particularly in a period of skill shortage. Since Jim Callaghan's controversial Ruskin Speech (1976) employers have had little to say about the direction which the new training initiatives should follow. They, perhaps more so than government, recognize that the present range of available jobs in the economy are generally routine and undemanding and that, both now and in the future, these jobs will not require a sophisticated level of further education or training despite the apparent upturn in youth employment prospects in the 1990s (Lee 1983). Consequently, it might be argued that in its present form, the debate about training is meaningless since it is not connected with work (Gleeson 1983); it simply obscures the real issue of unemployment and the way in which training itself has become a substitute for employment (Tipton 1983). The problem with this type of critique is, however, that it rather naively equates the success or failure of YTS, and other such schemes, with whether or not young people obtain jobs. While it may not be unreasonable to expect that training should be connected with work, there is no evidence that government training policy is designed to make workers either more productive or employable. For the moment it would seem important to recognize that as recession and unemployment have altered the structural conditions of further education and training, there has been a need to construct different curricular criteria in order to encourage 'new' forms of social control and vocational 'commitment' among the young (Durkheim 1977). According to Offe (1967), training for 'personal effectiveness' represents part of the search for substitute criteria, wherein such characteristics as 'flexibility', 'loyalty', 'involvement' and so forth, are prized higher than the acquisition of technical knowhow. There can be little doubt that it is within this prevailing climate that life skills curriculum now flourishes, and is closely associated with the perceived inadequacies of 'less able' unemployed youth. The question remains, of course, as to whether such skills represent an alternative departure in curricular thinking, or a restatement of what has already gone on before. It will be argued in the section which follows that skills training represents something more than socialization alone, and increasingly assumes a dimension of political importance.

Life skills as social literacy

So far in this chapter it has been argued that the rise of the so called 'new vocationalism' marks a response to certain ideological imperatives. It is not just that the rules governing vocational training permit only a limited expression of intelligence and restrict young people's autonomy; they also regulate the kind of behaviour that is expected of them in terms of young people's social orientation and readiness to work. According to Moore (1983) the sort of vocational realism currently employed in training conceals its inherent irrationality; its purpose is seen as blocking a coherent social and political understanding of the world of work. Evidence from the Scottish leavers study of attitudes among YTS trainees demonstrates a high degree of instrumentalism, both to the scheme and to their own personal situation (Raffe and Smith 1986). How far the strong emphasis upon private enterprise and self-help via training has had an effect on trainees' attitudes remains to be seen. As Lee and others (1987) have noted, the role of training and the labour market itself in educating people into attitudes of calculative individualism has been relatively neglected. What Lee's study (1987) did find, however, was that

> many of our respondents had been inculcated with individualistic values before they joined YTS but that they nevertheless took its moral lessons to heart in appraising their encounter with the scheme.

To date, the curricular implications of this argument have not been taken up. Perhaps, understandably, the dominant emphasis of critiques of youth training remain focused on the macro-elements of training, that is, on the ways in which it represents a substitute for employment, a mechanism of cheap labour, a means of regulating youth labour markets, and so forth. Yet, despite evidence which indicates that training does generate a pool of low wage earners, it is the ideological argument in favour of how private enterprise ought to function that is important for understanding the essential curricular ingredients of the new vocationalism (Esland and Cathcart 1984). As Bates (1984) and others (Holt *et al.* 1987) have recently argued, it is a mistake to view training policy simply as a response to youth unemployment. Instead, it should be looked at in relation to the government's overall political and economic strategy designed to alter social relations in the workplace and to restructure curricular priorities around a greater appreciation of entrepreneurial values and the market. In this respect the kinds of arguments which favour generic skills training and training for 'personal effectivness' do not find their expression in the actual realities of work practice or labour market. Rather, they exist in idealized conceptions of how industrial relations ought to operate under free market conditions and how people ought to behave. The ideological significance of skills training is that it projects the learner within this fantasy as a flexible entity, capable of being employed or re-employed in a variety of jobs and settings. Despite the collapse of youth labour markets, it is within this idealization of the links between work and education that contemporary training policy is located: its aim being to reduce worker dependence on outmoded skills (which are seen to be too closely related to union control and restrictive practices) and to ensure the adaptability of the worker in the face of changing market forces.

If the spirit of individualism evident in such idealism bears the imprint of radical

Conservative thinking, it should not be confused with attempts to increase the freedom or choice of the individual. Rather, it is the uncertainty which surrounds young people's employment prospects which legitimates the construction of 'skills training' and which allows the state to 'protect' youth from the inimical influence of unemployment. Thus, within the context of life skills training, 'standing on one's own feet' is not concerned with the individual acting on his or her own initiative, or with making choices. As the following curricular guidelines would seem to indicate, the social skills involved are more closely connected with those of coping, surviving and adapting to a given view of the world:

> We would like to see life skills as the all embracing term. Life skills could then be divided into 'Social Skills' and 'Coping' (or Life Management) skills. 'Social Skills' would include more than face to face contact, since people may relate to other via letters, the telephone, and on a group or individual basis. 'Coping skills' would include dealing with everyday apparatus and procedures, such as using a public telephone, filling forms, reading maps, finding accommodation and so forth.
>
> (FEU 1980)

There is, of course, little here that is new. Essentially, life management in this context does little more than evoke the traditional rhetoric of liberal and social studies in the 1950s and early 1960s, which emphasized citizenship, form filling, technical report writing and other such skills. Perhaps, not surprisingly, the same criticisms of that approach apply now as they did then (Gleeson and Whitty 1976). Moreover, recent publications designed to serve this new market reinforce this person-orientated approach wherein skills for living are defined mainly in terms of coping with misfortune, establishing personal relationships, handling interviews and so forth (Pring 1985). The danger here is that by redefining knowledge of work into a set of atomized skills it separates off training from mainstream education and presents society as something which can be successfully overcome via manipulation. According to Moore (1987),

> this philosophy provides a rationale for an extreme delimitation of the political power of the individual, restricting it to that of 'consumer' of work whose purchasing power reflects the value of the skills 'owned' within a free market for labour. The exchange implicit in what this approach offers is that by giving up collective action and abandoning the job controls ('restrictive practices') which workers have won in their attempts to restrict managerial power over the labour process, the individual gains the benefits of mobility in a labour market unrestrained by the 'distortions' of trade union power or professional association, collective bargaining (especially at a level above that of the individual firm) or by customary and traditional practice. Free market economic ideology provides the ground (and the implicit legitimations) of 'the new vocationalism'. It is the ideology of the free market and not the reality of economic life which constitutes its real context and principles. What they construct is not so much the model worker required by British Industry, but the model citizen of Thatcherite Britain.

Within this context 'standing on one's own feet' is not concerned with the individual acting of society, or of him or her struggling against entrapping forces.

Essentially, the life management approach to SLS training emphasizes individual adaption and survival: society as such is not thrown open to question other than in the narrowest of entrepreneurial terms – *you can make it if you try*. Thus, despite the apparent veneer of social relevance in SLS there is little reference to the individual learning about society, or of the student acquiring knowledge and concepts which take him/her beyond the immediate and the parochial.

Under these circumstances youth training represents little more than a particular form of mass vocational literacy that shifts responsibility for the reproduction of workers back on to themselves. Training and unemployment not only enables students to 'stand on their own two feet' (after all, we trained them – didn't we?) but also seeks to handle the perceived workers' reproduction deficiencies, i.e. their lack of individualism. By making workers more responsible for their own destinies in this way no recriminations can be made against employers or the state, since it is the market that is the deciding factor.

While there is, of course, no clear evidence that basic skills training has any direct effect on young people's attitudes, it is perhaps what gets left out of the curriculum that is important: notably the absence of any general and political education. Yet attempts to keep politics out of training have ironically only drawn attention to this neglected area. Peter Morrison's now famous proclamation that 'I am totally convinced that the youth training scheme is all about the world of work, and I don't want it to get a bad name if politics get involved' (*TES* 23 September 1983) increased public suspicion of the MSC's political ambitions, in the early 1980s, for redefining curricular priorities in this area. Despite attempts to play down the censorship of political education in YTS there can be little doubt, as the following communique from the MSC to managing agents makes clear, that politics has little to do with learning about British industry:

> Managing agents should note that their agreement with the Commission requires that the training programme be run in a 'manner acceptable to the Commission'. A key requirement will be that it is not involved in any activity of a political nature or any activity likely to bring the Commission into public controversy or discredit. If this requirement is not met it could result in the immediate closure of a programme.
>
> (MSC 1983)

It would seem from such remarks that the debate about 'teacher accountability' has shifted in a direction unforeseen by the DES in the immediate years following Jim Callaghan's Ruskin College speech (1976). Despite the problem of how to teach trainees about work without reference to the wider structures of society, such directives convey a political message regarding the Training Agency's view of training, and its own standing with employers. Perhaps this explains why the Department of Employment chose to opt for 'guidance and counselling' as a more acceptable means of fostering in young people those skills that will enable them to adopt 'the right role at work' (MSC 1983). Closer inspection of the meaning of this phrase indicates that 'acceptance of authority', 'taking orders' and 'work skills' represent the most significant core elements of the skills involved (MSC 1977; 1982).

That this is all there is to life, or that such limited conceptions eschew political involvement, reflects a particular ideological position presenting training as neutral mechanism necessitated by individual rather than structural constraints. From this position questions regarding how industry is organized and managed, how wealth is accumulated, how wages, skills and allowances are legitimated and sustained, can be conveniently edited out of training as politically extraneous. The political effect, however, is to separate off the study of work from the society that surrounds it, thereby reducing the entire framework of industrial relations to a narrow set of technical propositions. As a consequence, 'learning about British industry' and 'entering the world of work' become little more than euphemisms for learning about one's place. It is within this overall structure that trainees' political horizons are controlled and their broader vision of the issues and possibilities surrounding them severely restricted.

Beyond skills training

It has been the argument of this chapter that the call to extend skills training has, in reality, very little to do with changes in production or with the desire, expressed in official jargon, to produce a 'better equipped, better educated and better motivated labour force' (MSC 1982a). However, it would be misleading to assume that the mismatch between policy objectives and training practice affords teachers and students space in which to renegotiate a more realistic curriculum. As I have argued elsewhere (Gleeson 1987, 1989), non-advanced FE and training is at the crossroads between its voluntaristic tradition and the newer compulsory element that have come to challenge it. Since the emergence of the new vocationalism, the degree of decentralized autonomy in FE has been increasingly brought under control by centralized measures designed to incorporate FE within the wider context of government training policy and the law. Moreover, recent attempts to reshape college and LEA budgets to make them more receptive to the dictates of the 1988 Education Act, NCVQ and TEC initiatives has ensured the central place of government in structuring national priorities in the sphere of FE and training curriculum. In this respect the government's unprecedented manipulation of both non-advanced FE and youth labour markets has elicited strong reaction from teachers and students, involving various types of protest and industrial action.

However, the problem that such teachers and students face in opposition to new training measures is that the main political parties and trade unions have, until recently, accepted the role of the Training Agency as better than nothing, and YTS as a necessary evil. This is perhaps best exemplified in Neil Kinnock's denunciation of a major strike by pupils and trainees over job prospects, in which he condemned participants as a 'bunch of dafties' (Ainley 1985). However, as I have sought to demonstrate in this chapter, it is not simply economic exploitation that young people face in training but also political exploitation – not least in terms of bias and experimentation associated with skills training. Whatever the assumed failure of liberal humanist education to 'come up with the goods' (Callaghan 1976), there exists no strong evidence that the skills so far described in this chapter represent a genuine alternative for the vast majority of school leavers. Despite the views held by successive education ministers that the educational system is preoccupied with academic, at the expense of industrial, values there is little to indicate that the criteria governing the new vocationalism either challenge such entrenched values or seek to integrate mental and manual forms of knowledge in the curriculum (Dale

1986). Indeed, recent evidence suggests that training policy has done little to facilitate a more unified system of post school education, or to broaden the patterns of participation in non-advanced FE and training (DES 1985). Perhaps the major weakness of contemporary training policy is that it neither specifies specific skills training nor provides an adequate general education. Thus, under present conditions, the young lose out both ways; on the one hand, they do not gain marketable or recognized skills and, on the other, they do not acquire the knowledge and understanding, however broadly defined, that would allow them critical insight into the political or economic workings of society. Perhaps not surprisingly the expansion of vocational training has resulted in inferior general education, without the employment prospects of young people altering much one way or the other. One effect of the present paranoia of vocational realism is that it can force young people to settle on vocational training and employment options too early on, in many cases before their fourth year at school. Despite the publicity given to core curriculum and transferable skills training, early specialization in primary and secondary education narrows the options open to young people later on in life. Consequently, without a broadly based general education policy it is most unlikely that students will be able to utilize forms of training that they have not been educated to absorb. The danger is that Britain is fast acquiring the most trained and least educated workforce in the industrialized world, at a time when the general education base of most other nations is broadening rather than narrowing.

There is, at the present time in Britain, an obsession with the terms 'skill' and skill 'ownership'. They have come to represent the practical application of almost all facets of human performance not encapsulated in mainstream subjects or time served training. Syllabuses and course outlines, for example, repeatedly emphasize the importance of students achieving *skill ownership*, which they may apply in a variety of occupational and social settings. Hence, enterprise skills, skills for living, transferable skills, interpersonal skills and so forth, are all given a high profile in the behavioural objectives which support prevocational and training schemes. Such skills are premised on the assumed lack of relevance of the mainstream curriculum which, critics argue, emphasizes theoretical understanding at the expense of practical application. While there may be some truth in this, there is little evidence that the skills-based approach being put forward plugs the skill gap. If anything, it has become tacked on rather than integrated within the mainstream curriculum, reinforcing existing distinctions between knowledge, experience and understanding. As Wellington (1987) has argued, 'skills' are not entities in themselves, separated off from the people in whom they reside:

> Skills do not exist in their own right. Employers do not recruit skills. They recruit people. Skills reside in people and are acquired by people.
>
> Skills are not entities which are in short supply. What industries need are people with the abilities to develop new skills, to learn new knowledge, to acquire new concepts and theories and to adapt to technological change with enthusiasm and lack of fear. This is the essential meaning of technological literacy as opposed to technological skill ... The job of both education and training is surely to provide people with the ability and enthusiasm to learn, to adapt to change, and to be aware of and at home with new technology.
>
> In addition, the development of critical and creative abilities (not skills)

would seem to be a necessity for innovation. The aims of education should be couched in these terms, rather than in exhausted and overstretched language of skills which is barking up the wrong linguistic tree. Companies don't recruit or employ skills – they employ people.

All the indications are that employers, educationists and others do not recognize the relevance of contemporary skills training, which is not seen to embody the general indicators of competence required to gain access to the job market (Holt 1987). It is perhaps time to recognize that experimentation with generic skills training has been a failure, and that the sacrifice of general education for a gain in vocationalism has not been worth the trade off (Jackson 1981). The perfunctory time accorded to either learning technical knowhow or acquiring general knowledge suggests that students are getting neither education nor training.

The irony, as Willis (1984) has pointed out, is that working class youth, who know much about work and are prepared to put up with its most boring and exploited forms, should have basic work skills pushed down their throats from a very early age. Moreover, the fact that so few workers eventually end up in trades for which they were trained suggests that training without general education has, anyway, little vocational relevance. The likelihood is that a broadly based education, which combines learning about work alongside the study of society, including options drawn from the arts, sciences, humanities, social sciences and community, will in the long run have more public support and perhaps possess greater vocational relevance. At the moment, the greatest weakness of the new vocationalism is its failure to capture the enthusiasm and inspire the imagination of young people. Its dull utilitarianism and endless messages about the virtues of enterprise and entrepreneurialism reinforce the suspicious isolation in which young people are viewed in society. Essentially, the message of the new vocationalism is that young people cannot be trusted to identify with, or learn the skills necessary, to reproduce contemporary 'enterprise culture'. Almost to reinforce this message those areas of knowledge associated with art, music, literature, political education and criticism, which might turn the heads of young people, have been edited out in favour of an overtly materialist curriculum.

This is not to advocate piecemeal injections of art, liberal studies or political education, which in the 1960s and 1970s were driven like a wedge into the vocational curriculum to offset the worst effects of overspecialization and alienation. What is called for at the present time is a curriculum that integrates arts, sciences and humanities with practical vocational skills, and which seeks to break down existing tripartite divisions. Bringing education back in will not be an easy task, not least because the terms and conditions of conventional liberal humanist education have changed. As Tipton (1983) has argued, if educationists and teachers feel understandably squeamish about becoming involved in 'narrow' training, then the solution is to reconstitute the debate surrounding the relationship between education, training and work. Perhaps the major starting point here is to define vocational education and training more broadly, to emphasize youth's active involvement in rather than separation from mainstream society. As one commentator has noted, it is not dole schools or work experience that the young unemployed require now but 'schools and' (in a well known phrase) 'really useful education and rewarding, unexploitative work' (Horne 1983).

Conclusion

Part of the argument of this chapter has been that the 'alternatives' so far considered cannot be viewed in a political vacuum. They involve a radically different way of making sense of the relations between work, education and training, and represent a rejection of the political assumptions about human nature that inform Conservative training policy. Instead, the active role of the student learning within and outside the workplace is stressed, accentuating the social and political processes involved in linking vocational education and training with productive labour. At the moment the lack of relationship between training and productive labour has led to policies based on the containment of youth, involving discipline and employer-led considerations above all else. In the absence of work, government training policy has been aggressively marketed as the only available alternative open to young people. Yet, as we have seen, many young people reject training without work on the grounds that it is second rate and second best, while others accept it because they have little other choice.

At the present time provision for the majority of school leavers remains patchy and meets the needs of neither individual nor society. In recession government and employers have abandoned any long-term education and training plans, preferring to regulate youth unemployment via special measures and categorical funding. In the circumstances, the folly of allowing employers to dictate training policy will undoubtedly have far reaching effects, not least in reducing skill levels and educational standards throughout the workforce. Ultimately, responsibility for this rests with government, employers and the Training Agency who have failed to establish a coherent policy of education, training and work, and who have sought to control rather than mobilize the labour force via vocational training. In this respect the TA has done little to extend or to improve the quality of further education or training, and has reinforced inequalities by experimenting with skills training with little regard for the education of the whole person.

Yet, despite this apparently depressing scenario, there remains some room for manoeuvre in implementing change at the local level. The paradox of training reflects the simultaneous emergence of two potentially conflicting developments (Harland 1987). On the one hand, it reflects strong central control of a kind which has permitted the detailed intervention of government and employer influence right down to the classroom level. On the other, YTS, TVEI and a variety of other prevocational courses support local initiatives which, in many cases, are highly experimental and creative. Thus, if at one level the ratchet of central control has tightened, at another, the local level, 'progressive' approaches associated with active learning and equal opportunities, integrated approaches, cross-curricular development and so forth, have forced a rethink about the processes through which young people are educated and trained (Pring 1985). If, in the short term, much of what passes for vocational education and training leaves much to be desired, at least the issues involved are now openly on the agenda. No longer can it be said that further education and training is a backwater of the education system with relevance for only a minority of school leavers. By placing vocational education and training initiatives at the centre of the stage government policy has drawn public attention to hitherto ignored issues, in particular the failure of government itself. For this reason alone it is unlikely that the debate regarding the future direction of further education and training will remain the same. Moreover, there is, as McCulloch (1987) has argued, nothing intrinsically narrow, right wing or conservative about technical and vocational knowledge – it remains very much what society makes of it. Historically, the debate about the aims of vocational education and training is recurring (Reeder 1981), and reflects wider social and political struggle over the nature of British society itself. Thus, despite the divisions and distinctions made apparent by training policy, it is equally important to recognize that, in quite unintended ways, there is now greater awareness of what should be on the training agenda and what is worth pursuing. It is a contribution to this aspect of the recurring debate that this chapter is addressed.

Acknowledgement

A modified version of this chapter first appeared in Dale (1986) and Gleeson (1989), and in its present form is substantially revised and updated.

References

Ainley, P. (1985). 'More carrots for the school room dafties', *New Statesman*, 5 July.
Bates, I. *et al.* (1984). *Schooling for the Dole*, London, Macmillan.
Callaghan, J. (1976). *Ruskin College Speech*, The Times Educational Supplement, 22 October.
Cockburn, C. (1987). *Two Track Training*, London, Macmillan.
Dale, R. (ed.) (1986). *Education, Training and Employment; Towards a New Vocationalism*, Oxford, Pergamon.
Department of Education and Science (1981). *A New Training Initiative: A Programme for Action*, London, HMSO.
DES (1985). *Education and Training for Young People*, White Paper, HMSO.
Durkheim, E. (1977). *The Evolution of Educational Thoughts*, London, Routledge and Kegan Paul.
Esland, G. and Cathcart, H. (1984). 'The compliant creative worker', paper presented at the SSRC/CEDEFOP 'Conference on the Transition between School and Work', Berlin.
Fairly, J. and Grahl, J. (1983). Conservative Training Policy and the Alternatives', *Socialist Economic Review*, Autumn.
Further Education Unit (FEU) (1980). *Developing Social and Life Skills*, London, FEU.
Gleeson, D. (1983). *Youth Training and the Search for Work*, London, Routledge and Kegan Paul.
Gleeson, D. (1983). 'FE tripartism and the labour market' in Gleeson, *Youth Training and the Search for Work*, London, Routledge and Kegan Paul.
Gleeson, D. (1986). *Privatisation of Industry and the Nationalisation of Youth*, in R. Dale (ed.), *Education, Training and Employment: Towards a New Vocationalism*, Oxford, Pergamon.
Gleeson, D. (ed.) (1987). *TVEI and Secondary Education: A Critical Appraisal*, Milton Keynes, Open University Press.
Gleeson, D. (1989). *The Paradox of Training: Making Progress out of a Crisis*, Milton Keynes, Open University Press.
Gleeson, D. and Whitty, G. (1976). *Developments in Social Studies Teaching*, London, Open Books.
Harland, J. (1987). 'The TVEI experience: issues of control, response and the professional role of teachers,' in D. Gleeson (ed.), *TVEI and Secondary Education: A Critical Appraisal*, Milton Keynes, Open University Press.
Hayes, C. (1983). *Training for Skill Ownership: Learning to Take it with You*, Institute of Manpower Studies, University of Sussex.

Holt, M. (1987). *Skills and Vocationalism: The Easy Answer*, Milton Keynes, Open University Press.
Horne, J. (1983). 'Youth unemployment programmes: a historical account of the development of "dole colleges" ', in D. Gleeson (ed.), *Youth Training and the Search for Work*, London, Routledge and Kegan Paul.
Jackson, P. (1981). 'Secondary schooling for the poor', *Daedalus*, Fall.
Lee, D. (1983). 'Social policy and institutional autonomy in further education,' in D. Gleeson, *Youth Training and the Search for Work*, Routledge and Kegan Paul.
Lee, D. et al. (1987). 'Youth training, life chances and orientations to work: a case study of the YTS', in P. Brown and D.N. Ashton (eds), *Education, Unemployment and Labour Markets*, London, Falmer Press.
McCulloch, G. (1987). 'History and policy: the politics of the TVEI,' in D. Gleeson (ed.), *TVEI and Secondary Education: A Critical Appraisal*, Milton Keynes, Open University Press.
Manpower Services Commission (MSC) (1977). *Instructional Guide to Social and Life Skills*, London, MSC.
Manpower Services Commission (MSC) (1982a). *A New Training Initiative: Task Group Report*, London, MSC.
Manpower Services Commission (MSC) (1982b). *Guidelines on Content and Standards in YTS*, London, MSC.
Manpower Services Commission (MSC) (1983). *A Handbook for Managing Agents in YTS*, London, MSC.
Manpower Services Commission (MSC) (1984). *Notes of Guidance, Occupational Training Families*, London, MSC.
Marsland, D. (1987). *Bias Against Business: Anti Capitalist Inclinations in Modern Sociology*, London, The Educational Research Trust.
Moore, R. (1983). 'Further education, pedagogy and production', in D. Gleeson, *Youth Training and the Search for Work*, London, Routledge and Kegan Paul.
Moos, M. (1983). 'The training myth', in D. Gleeson, *Youth Training and the Search for Work*, London, Routledge and Kegan Paul.
Offe, C. (1967). *Industry and Inequality*, London, Edward Arnold.
Pring, R. (1985). 'In defence of TVEI', *Forum*, 27, 3.
Raffe, D. and Smith, P. (1986). *Young People's Attitudes to the YTS: The First Two Years*, Edinburgh Centre for Educational Sociology, University of Edinburgh.
Reeder, D. (1981). 'A recurring debate: education and industry', in R. Dale et al. *Education and the State. Vol. 1 Schooling and the National Interest*, London, Falmer Press.
Ryan, P. (1984). 'The New Training Initiative after two years', *Lloyds Bank Review*, 152.
Scruton, R., Ellis-Jones, A. and O'Keefe, D. (1985). *Education and Indoctrination*, London, Educational Research Centre.
Seale, C. (1983). *FEU and MSC: two curricular philosophies and their implications for YTS*, Garnett College of HE, London.
Tipton, B. (1983). 'The quality of training and the design of work', in D. Gleeson, *Youth Training and the Search for Work*, London, Routledge and Kegan Paul.
Wellington, J. (1987). 'Stretching the point', *TES*, 25 December.
Willis, P. (1984). 'Conclusion: theory and practice', in I. Bates et al. *Schooling for the Dole*, London, Macmillan.

Rob Moore

Knowledge, practice and the construction of skill

My purpose in this chapter is to examine the ways in which the concept of 'skill' is constructed in various types of 'educational' discourse.[1] The term 'educational' is being used here in the very broadest sense to refer to bodies of knowledge and practice transmitted through formal means. 'Formal', in this case, refers to socially sanctioned and legitimated institutional processes and contexts. Hence the reference is to institutional contexts which have acquired the authority to define what it is that needs to be learned, how it should be learned and what should count as a demonstration that it has been learned. The purpose is to focus upon alternative approaches to training. The relationship between the formal and the informal will be seen as particularly significant. It will be argued that models of skill transmission are, in the first place, social constructs (as opposed, say, to being simply derived from the technical characteristics of production) and, in the second, that what they construct is a particular classification between formal and informal social practices. I will argue that alternatives to existing models of skills transmission need themselves to be constructed on the basis of an understanding of what it is that the existing models consign to the realm of the informal.

The current debate

The point of developing a critical perspective towards education and training is to define the ground for alternative models and interventions – to attempt to redefine the current agenda of the reform debate. The reconstruction of education around a skills training model is principally associated with the rise of the MSC. In what follows I will focus upon this tendency, which can be termed 'technicist'.[2] It is characterized by a combination of occupationalism with a behaviouristic model of 'skill'. Technicism has particularly significant implications for how educational knowledge comes to be constructed.

Much of the current debate about the New Right's educational reforms has concentrated on the tensions between the 'neo-conservatives' and the 'neo-liberals', especially in terms of the former's support of a strong state and the latter's apparently antithetical commitment to the 'free' market.[3] Both these elements of the New Right, however, are committed to a traditional, liberal–humanist version of education. The neo-conservatives want it enforced by the central state in order to keep the teaching profession and LEAs under control (the National Curriculum), whereas the neo-liberals operate with an implicit presumption that this type of curriculum is what any reasonable person would demand, and, hence, the market can safely take care of things once parents have sufficient 'power' (as consumers rather than as citizens). Dale, however, has also focused attention on a group he calls the 'industrial trainers' (Dale 1989). My 'technicist' group corresponds to this category.[4] They have already had a significant impact upon the educational system through the influence of the MSC, and many of the current instruments through which the new forms of control over education are being enforced (e.g. contract bidding) were first developed by MSC.

The critics of the post-war social democratic reforms in education do not constitute a unified group with a common analysis and programme. Neo-conservatives such as Roger Scruton and Anthony Flew tend to attribute 'the problems' to progressive education and to comprehensivization. They stress the notion of a social decline attributed to progressive permissiveness. Technicists, however, stress economic decline. They go beyond the neo-conservatives and neo-liberals by extending their critique to traditional as well as to progressive liberal education. In this form, it is liberal education as such which has been the problem, especially in its promotion of an elite culture which has been hostile to modernism and in particular to industry, commerce and the practical application of knowledge. For this analysis, it is the condition of the social elite rather than of the mass which is most problematical. In this respect, this approach can be seen as much more radical than the neo-conservative view.

Behind this is a more general view of the nature of 'the problem' which the reform of education and training should be addressing. Essentially, it can be suggested that in the second half of the 1970s a major shift occurred in which 'the problem' of training the workforce ceased to be seen primarily in terms of the failure of industry to create an adequate system of training to the failure of education to adequately prepare young people for working life. This was in keeping with the more general ideological shift towards free market, supply-side analysis. Both training and education are being geared more closely to 'the needs of industry' through an integration between the training and educational systems and their credentials (e.g. under the auspices of the National Council for Vocational Qualifications).

Obviously these things depend upon a particular set of interrelated specifications of problems and solutions and assumptions about the character of central processes in terms of 'the needs of industry', etc. In that 'skills' are grounded in and derived from the production process, the definition of the skills that industry needs implies a particular view of the character of the production process. In this way, constructs of 'skill' imply specific constructs of production as such, e.g. in terms of its technical and social relations. Such constructs are intrinsically ideological.[5] It is on the basis of such understandings that we can explore the sense in which an alternative approach to 'skill' would actually be alternative.

The construction of skills

In the broadest sense, the construction of educational knowledge involves the classification of a particular set of all possible available content as 'educational knowledge' – all that which is fit to teach. I am not concerned here either with the broader epistemological debate about any special prior status which might be attributed to educational knowledge (e.g. as forms of knowledge) or in detail with the social and political processes through which particular classifications and their social forms come to be established and enforced. For present purposes I want to suggest that we can usefully consider the classification of a certain content as 'educational' as constructing a distinction between the formal and the informal and that a further question can then be posed as to how that which is classified as formal, or legitimately educational, comes to be treated.

Here the distinction is between elaborating and restricting educational transmission codes. I will relate this distinction to that between 'knowledge' and 'skill'. It is probably the case that any content can be treated in either way: as 'knowledge' for some groups and 'skills' for others and that this can change over time. Indeed, a social differentiation of this type is fundamental to many of the status distinctions in our occupational structure, e.g. in distinguishing 'technicians' from 'professionals'.

These distinctions can be illustrated by considering the example of 'the world of work'. If 'the world of work' is accepted as a legitimate content within education (and if so, for which social groups?), the first question we can ask is, whose version of 'the world of work'? Of all the available knowledge which could be placed under this heading, which particular 'bits' are going to be formally acknowledged and translated into a legitimated educational form, e.g. in school texts, etc.? This process automatically entails a principle of exclusion. Further questions can then be posed about the strength of the boundary between the formal (included) and the informal (excluded) and how the boundary is maintained. We can then ask, is this content going to be treated as 'knowledge' within an elaborating educational code (e.g. social education), or as 'skill' within a restricting code (e.g. social and life skills training)? Further questions can then be addressed to the issue of maintaining the boundaries within the educational system between elaborating and restricting transmission codes, their social distribution and the regulation of movement between them.

An important aspect of the exclusion of certain areas of knowledge and social practice from the formal definition of 'educational knowledge' is that these areas are not simply subject to non-recognition within the formal system, but are systematically misrecognized[6] when recontextualized within the field of its discourse. The construction of deficit models of certain categories of pupils is largely a result of such 'misrecognition'. Hence, in this examination of 'alternatives to training', I will consider the following sets of relationships:

- Between the categories of education and production in educational policy and the degree of separation between their principles and contexts. Formally this is the issue of classification (e.g. how far is it the case that 'the world of work' or 'the needs of industry' is seen as a legitimate aspect of education).
- Between knowledge and skill. This is to do with whether the educational process is elaborating (i.e. an educational context constructing knowledge) or restricting

(i.e. training context constructing skills). This is the question of the framing of the pedagogic communication – the mode of control of the transmission process and the realization of what counts as educational knowledge and its legitimate forms of transmission and aquisition.
- Between the formal and the informal. This is to do with the manner in which any type of educational context operates with a principle of exclusion which constructs a distinction between that which counts as knowledge or skill and its legitimate modes of transmission and acquisition (formal) and that which does not (informal). The crucial issue here is the way in which social practices are recontextualized within the field of educational practice and systematically misrecognized in the form of constructs of competence (e.g. how middle class social attributes might come to be treated as evidence of 'brightness', or the frustration of working class pupils forced to 'stay-on' when they are perfectly capable of starting work as evidence of 'immaturity').

The substantive focus is upon social practices associated with 'the world of work' and how they are reconstructed within the variety of contexts within the matrix which the above relationships generate.

Education, training and the world of work

In considering the changing relationship between education and training it is necessary to take into account:

- how far education treats issues relating to work as a legitimate part of its concern (the strength of classification or of the boundary between the two categories);
- the manner in which 'work' is represented within education where it is considered legitimate to do so; and
- how the learning process as such is structured (framing).

It is important to stress that it is not simply the particular view or model of the world of work which is at issue here. It is not a question of accuracy or bias in particular 'versions' of 'work'. Rather, the issue is how different constructs of 'work' come to structure different forms of pedagogic communication in terms of the framing of the content and whether the orientation is elaborating or restricting (education versus training, knowledge versus skill).

Educational knowledge and the world of work (classification)

It is possible to describe three basic positions. In the first, the world of work is not seen as a legitimate part of educational knowledge. This corresponds to the traditional form of liberal–humanist education in this country and is associated with a nineteenth-century elitist, classics model of education built around the notion of 'the gentleman'. This form of education is currently under attack from a perspective associated with the Wiener thesis[7] which attributes Britain's industrial decline to an inappropriate (essentially aristocratic) elite ideology. More generally, it is associated with the criticism from employers that education is actively hostile to industry and commerce and has deflected the most able students away from careers in the industrial and commercial sphere. It is seen as promoting the arts and humanities at the expense of science and technology and encouraging knowledge for its own sake rather than for its practical applications. Moves such as TVEI and support for 'enterprise education' are aimed at countering these effects of liberal–humanism.

In the second view the world of work is seen as a legitimate part of a general educational programme. This approach can be associated with the progressive end of the liberal–humanist spectrum and with the post-Newsom developments in secondary education after ROSLA (1972–73). Here the world of work is included in the curriculum because it is held to be 'relevant' to the needs of non-academic pupils. The literature of this time, however, stresses that the topic should be part of a general educational programme[8] rather than preparation for any particular type of work. This form of liberal humanism can be seen as an extension of the child-centred primary approach into the secondary school. It is concerned with personal development and fulfilment. Although hostile to academic traditionalism, it shares with the elitist version an expressive rather than an instrumentalist view of education. It could also be hostile to industry and commerce.[9] Indeed, a major criticism of this approach in the 1970s was that it encouraged pupils to adopt negative attitudes towards work and was overly preoccupied with topics such as trade union rights. This approach was also seen at the time of the Great Debate as associated with a lowering of academic and social standards, especially in 'the basics', and overburdened with 'fringe subjects' such as social education.

The third view relates education directly to 'the needs of industry' and sees it as serving a prevocational or occupationally specific preparation for working life. It is at this point that 'skill' becomes significant in mediating the changing relationship between education and training. This marks the break with liberal humanism. Education is defined as instrumental in purpose. The teaching process itself is reconstructed on a skills training model and the content of what is to be taught is directly related to what are seen to be the actual requirements of industry. TVEI is a primary example of this approach.[10] The MSC has been particularly influential in its development and in particular with its distinctive features such as occupational skills inventories, profiles and notions such as occupational training families, and generic and transferable skills.

The world of work in the curriculum (representation)

The positions defined above differ in terms of their openness to 'the world of work' as a legitimate part of the content of educational knowledge. Hence the three positions represent different ways of constructing what can count as 'educational knowledge'. It should be noted that this is so in terms of content and official orientation rather than in terms of implicit instrumentalism – obviously in reality the prestige of traditional academic elitist educational has a lot to do with its capacity to provide access to high status employment. At the same time it remains the case that more vocational or occupationalist types of education are still associated with relatively low status work. Indeed, recent research indicates that despite the criticisms levelled against liberal humanism, employers still prefer to recruit its products in preference to more vocationally educated students.[11]

The key issue here is who has the power to construct the model of production, 'the needs of industry', etc., which informs education's representations of working life. The basic contrast is between a vocationalism which is constructed from within an educationalist paradigm and a vocationalism constructed from within an occupationalist paradigm. The former tends to start from the perspective of a general educational programme and relevance to the needs of pupils, whilst the latter tends to start from the perspective of skills required in the local labour market and relevance to the needs of industry.

On this basis a distinction can be made between an educationalist vocationalism and an occupationalist vocationalism. This distinction crucially affects the character of the knowledge which pupils are presented with, essentially in terms of its generality – how far is it knowledge about the world of work or skills for the world of work? Which of these is current depends, essentially, upon the degree of autonomy of the educational system and how far it is controlled by professional educationalists or other groups. This, obviously, is the crucial contested issue today.

There is, however, a further source of representations of 'the world of work': from pupils themselves and, more generally, from their families and the communities of which they are a part (class cultural practices). It is in the relationship between this source of knowledge and those represented in school or in training that the distinction between the formal and the informal arises and this, in my view, is crucial for the development of a critical analysis.

The educational process and the construction of skills (framing)

The category the world of work introduces into the curriculum an area of everyday social practice. This represents weak classification between 'education' and 'production' (see above). There is, then, the issue of how the world of work is represented as a specific content in the curriculum. These representations *re-present* the everyday social practices of working life in a particular ideological form. In this way they recontextualize social practices which are also represented and experienced in other ways within the class cultural practices of working life itself. In this way they represent and transform the meanings which those social practices have within class culture. This process of recontextualization of social practices within educational discourse does a number of things:

- It establishes a further dimension of classification between the formal and the informal (principle of exclusion).
- It does not simply exclude certain areas or types of knowledge and experience, it also systematically transforms the meanings of class cultural social practices, e.g. by establishing certain criteria of relevance and competence (as with social and life skills training). It presents a version of what the world of work is like and what is required to enter it and become a competent member of it. It selects and re-presents class-cultural practices.
- Through these transformations of meaning it systematically misrecognizes the competence of individuals. By establishing certain criteria of relevance and defining what is to count as a recognized or legitimate display of competence (e.g. through behavioural skill objectives, performance indicators, profiles) it re-presents individuals as incompetent by those criteria (e.g. writing CVs, filling in forms, using the telephone, presenting a 'smart' appearance to employers) while

failing to acknowledge the competence they in fact possess (e.g. in being able to utilize personal contacts in 'grapevine' recruitment or meet the social expectations of membership of working communities). The behaviour which then results from the experience of this mismatch between the 'formal' representation of the world of work and the young person's actual knowledge and experience of it (informal) at the level of class cultural practice (e.g. their apathy, scepticism or aggression) is then treated as a confirmation of their 'incompetence' (e.g. 'immaturity') and as indicating that they actually need training. In this way the ideologies of 'skill' and 'training' construct particular types of deficit models of 'trainees'.

- Most crucially the framing of the social practices represented in this way within the 'educational' programme regulate the relationship between those practices or areas of social life and elaborating educational knowledge. The form of pedagogy is the crucial variable. Where the world of work is represented within an educational paradigm, it is (at least potentially) subjected to a critical and questioning perspective which attempts to problematize and generalize and even transform its content. The behavioural objectives, skills training model of pedogogy, however, does the precise opposite. Its purpose is to restrict social practices to sets of behavioural objectives. The only 'critical' issue is an individual's level of performance (which comes to be known as 'competence'). Hence the form of pedagogy regulates access to elaborating knowledge and ultimately to the principles through which knowledge is actually produced as opposed to simply transmitted.

If we take the term 'frame' in its simple, figurative sense, we can see framing within the educational process as the construction of a 'picture' of a particular area of social life (the world of work). This area of social reality is represented (*re-presented*) within the confines of the frame; its elements, dimensions, proportions and relationships 'redrawn' according to certain conventions and rules. The 'picture', however, presents itself as 'real', not as a 'representation'. But we must also see the conventions and rules of its construction as themselves constituting a kind of 'internal frame' limiting the 'picture' from within, as it were. Actually, it is this 'internal frame' which positions the external one.

The relationship between 'elaborating' and 'restricting' has to do with how this 'internal frame' (the principles, rules and conventions of construction) 'draws' the external one. Elaborating codes have the capacity to question or problematized from within the frames which they construct – the 'picture's' relationship to 'reality', or where 'the picture' ends and 'reality' begins. An elaborating educational code not only 'draws a picture', it also provides access (to some) to its internal principles. It allows at least the possibility not only of the picture being redrawn but of the frame as such being repositioned or even dissolved.

Restricting educational transmission codes present their practices as literal representations of 'reality', e.g. what the world of work is really like. By confusing itself with reality it denies the very notion of 'framing'. The 'skills' constructed by the skills training model are presented as identical to the social practices of work, as if they have simply been transported from one place (the shopfloor) to another (the school or training centre) from which the successful 'trainee' can then carry them back as tokens of fitness to enter 'the world of work'. In fact, the MSC's 'bridge' from school to work is no more than a *trompe l'œil*, as much a conceit as the more whimsical features of liberal humanism's secret garden which it has derided.

In summary, we can see the classification and framing of skills transmission as constructing and regulating boundaries between the practices they incorporate and (i) educational knowledge (elaborating codes), (ii) the sites of production, (iii) class cultural practices. The important issue is not simply an empirical one of the accuracy of representations, but of the form of the pedagogy and whether it is elaborating or restricting. What is at issue, here, is not, in fact, the world of work as such, but the possibility whereby elaborating educational knowledge and class cultural practices could be brought together. The skills training model, in the combination of its particular ideological representation of production and its behaviouristic restricting pedagogy, effectively blocks the conjuncture between elaborating knowledge and class cultural practice. We can say that the 'purpose' of the skills transmission model is to regulate the social relationships of educational transmission where they come to incorporate a critical social content such as the world of work, rather than to directly serve the immediate interests of production.

The basis for an 'alternative' approach

The sense of any attempt to produce 'alternative' models of training depends in part upon a critical representation of the currently dominant model. At this point I want to consider the ways in which alternative models might be alternative. For this I will draw in part upon my own experience of such an attempt initiated by the Greater London Council: The Charlton Training Centre, established in south-east London in 1984.

The history of the centre and its particular problems are presented elsewhere by Margaret Grieco and Len Holmes.[12] Grieco and Holmes focus upon the problems which radical initiatives encounter in their relationships to their funding agencies and the way in which that relationship is characterized by a process of 'organisational transformation'.

> Our main argument here is that radical aims and forms of radical organisation are frequently subverted or changed as a consequence of this interaction. This process is aptly characterised by the term organisational transformation. Changes take place in the fundamental organisational structure without any accompanying change in the organisational language, a situation which serves to disguise the extent to which fundamental changes have taken place. Put simply, our thesis is that radical intention and initial organisational form typically give way to radical rhetoric accompanied by a conventional management form ...
>
> (Grieco and Holmes in press)

It is not my intention here to attempt to add in any way to Grieco and Holmes' analysis of this process, but to consider the general principles involved in defining 'alternative' models of training.

The Charlton Training Centre (CTC), and any radical alternative to the dominant model, raises issues about (i) the organizational form of such an institution, (ii) its relationship to the local community/labour market and (iii) its model of skills transmission. These three factors are interrelated and that of 'skill' plays a crucial mediating role.

The CTC was particularly concerned to target the training of women, especially in terms of access to non-traditional employment areas, and ethnic minorities. In both these objectives it can be seen as 'radical'. It also intended to operate on a democratic, cooperative management structure. Grieco and Holmes have analysed the process whereby this radical organizational form was translated back into a conventional structure. I will focus upon the construction of 'skill'.

It can be said that the CTC was an alternative model, in that it attempted to provide training to groups in the most vulnerable and marginalized positions in the labour market, to provide them with skills from which they are often excluded, and to do so within an institution which was based on participatory principles. However, the further question can be raised about precisely what it is that agencies such as the CTC attempt to deliver. Do they share an orthodox definition of 'skill' or do they go on to radically examine what they are delivering as well as to who and how?

The question of how skills are to be represented and defined raises issues of 'ownership'. The MSC itself has supported a particular version of 'skill ownership' associated with the Institute of Manpower Studies document *Training for Skill Ownership*. This view can be seen as having two main features: first, it presents an employer's view of what industry needs (or, more precisely, a particular ideological construct of how those needs should be represented), and secondly it individualizes 'ownership' as no more than a set of transferable skills identified with an individual. The skills become an individual possession – a form of 'capital'. This model can be described as possessive individualism and in this respect is commensurate with the broader market economic paradigm of the New Right.[13] It might also be seen (like the neo-liberals) as incorporating an implicit presumption, namely that most people have a purely instrumental approach to education in terms of employment. On this basis there is a complementarity between 'the needs of industry' for skills and the desire of individuals for occupationally relevant credentials.

A radical version of 'skill', however, would start from a different set of initial precepts. First, it would question the given definition of 'what industry needs', especially with reference to the social relations in production. It would take account of the fact that the form of the production process and the associated technical division of labour represent managerial imperatives which are essentially to do with control and not simply given by the technical nature of the task. It would also take into account social relations to do with workers in their position as workers and in opposition to management (but also including anti-sexist and anti-racist strategies at the shopfloor level). Second, it would need to acknowledge the fact that working people are already skilled. It would need to challenge the deficit models which are an intrinsic feature of currently dominant models of skills training. This involves recognizing that people as individuals possess skills and competencies (i.e. the capacity to acquire new skills) anyway and that these skills are class cultural in character.

It is this last point which should provide the basic starting point for a radical model of skill. To say that 'skills' are class cultural is to acknowledge the fact that it is the working class itself which is the repository of productive skills (labour power). These skills are intrinsically embedded within social forms which facilitate their transmission between workers. It is workers who train other workers, not employers or 'industry'. It is precisely this central, effective, dimension of skill transmission which is officially defined as 'informal' and systematically excluded from orthodox training models. It is for this reason that the construction of the categories formal/informal is important and intrinsically political in character.

As Grieco has shown elsewhere, in her work on social network recruitment,[14] workplace skills cannot be separated from the more general attributes of class membership and kinship. Social membership provides both the means of acquiring jobs and support in the workplace (through 'the network') and the reciprocal expectations and 'social skills' which facilitate membership of shopfloor groups. In this sense family, community, labour market and work are interpenetrating. Rather than being distinct and separate spheres of social life between which individuals pass, they should be seen as situated within a continuous matrix of class cultural practice. It is important to emphasize the contradictory character of the relations within this matrix, especially in terms of class and gender.

Such a view in itself needs to be treated critically in terms of the sexist, racist and traditionalist features of these practices. There is no intention, here, to naively romanticize 'working class culture'. By definition, these practices and processes are discriminatory and exclusive. Indeed, the MSC itself has used precisely such observations to justify the imposition of its own model. Similar propositions can be found in relation to progressive equal opportunity contract compliance. What is being suggested, here, is that an explicit acknowledgement of the class cultural character of skills and a critical theorization of their form should be taken as the starting point for radical models. What models of skill do, in effect, is to frame class cultural practices in such a way as to impose a particular mode of control over this process of cultural transmission. Orthodox models of training essentially appropriate what should be seen as a class possession – the specific concrete forms of labour power.

By the same principle, radical or progressive models of training should have as their intention, the reclamation (and critical transformation) of a class resource. Such an approach requires a radically different model of the labour market as a repository of class skill and competence. This is as much a political objective as control of the means of production themselves – indeed, the two things cannot be separated.

Conclusion

In this chapter I have attempted to outline the principles upon which we can understand the sense in which 'alternative' approaches to training and skills transmission can be seen as alternative. In terms of the earlier, theoretical discussion what this would mean is as follows:

- The boundary between the formal and the informal would be reconstructed in such a way that class cultural and gendered skills and competences and interests would become formally acknowledged as the basis for an alternative paradigm.
- On this basis constructs of competence would be radically reconstituted in a

positive way in contrast to the current deficit models, especially for women, young people and ethnic minorities. For instance, this would involve the recognition of the skills and competences of women acquired in domestic labour and child rearing and which are rendered invisible in human capital theory.[15]
- The social practices (and representations) now included within 'the formal' would be located within an elaborating educational paradigm in which they would be treated critically with the objective of transformation. For example, the competences developed in domestic labour and child rearing would not just be recognized, but taken as the basis for a critical examination of the distribution of such tasks between the sexes and the organization of working and family life.
- This last point raises the crucial issue of the character of an elaborating paradigm of this type.

Hence the basic changes would be in the relationships formal/informal and elaborating/restricting. The frame imposed upon skill transmission by the dominant orthodox models can be characterized as 'possessive individualist' and restricting. The alternative being proposed here can be characterized as class cultural and elaborating. Whereas the former systematically misrecognizes competence through the construction of individual deficit models, the latter would start from an acknowledgement of competence and a recognition of its collective form in class and gendered social practice. This would radically alter the model of the labour market (and notions such as 'skill shortage').

Agencies such as the Charlton Training Centre raise the issue of how alternative organizations should construct the concept of skill as such. The alternative agenda should not be limited simply to the question of how to deliver orthodox 'skills' to non-standard groups in terms of current labour market segmentations. In fact, models of skill automatically draw on models of what the labour market is like and what production is like. The reconstruction of skill entails alternative models of the labour market and production. A critical account of these should be intrinsic to an alternative approach to skill.

In terms of the broader debate about education and training, it can be suggested that the crucial issue is how education handles the relationship between contested areas of social practice, such as 'the world of work', and the critical possibilities of elaborating education transmission codes. The neo-conservative 'solution' is to confine the critical to a conservative cultural form (e.g. as with Leavisite anti-modernism). The technicist 'solution' is to confine the social practices associated with the 'world of work' to a restricting educational transmission code. The point of an alternative paradigm is to construct the direct confrontation between these practices and critical, elaborating knowledge.

Notes

1 This chapter is formally theoretical. However, it draws upon three areas of my practical experience as a teacher and researcher. The first was as a social education teacher in London schools in the 1970s. The second, more recently, was working on YTS schemes in FE and as a TVEI evaluator for the Open University TVEI project under Roger Dale. The third was my involvement with the 'alternative' Charlton Training Centre which was

funded by the GLC. I was involved in a support role to the London Economic Policy Unit (South Bank Polytechnic) which was monitoring the project for the GLC. Its history is reported in detail, in a way extremely relevant to the issues being discussed in this chapter, by Margaret Grieco and Len Holmes (in press). As will be obvious, the theoretical perspective is provided by Bernstein's work, in particular the papers, 'On the classification and framing of educational knowledge, class and pedagogies: visible and invisible' and 'Aspects of the relations between education and production' (in *Class, Codes and Control* Vol 3 (1977)). Obviously, space does not allow me to properly explicate the links between this text and its practical and theoretical base. The use of Bernstein's work is still drawing upon papers which are now quite old. To some extent the formulations in this article reflect implicitly the developments contained in his remarkable recent paper 'On pedagogic discourse' (1988). Applications of his earlier ideas now require reformulation in terms of the recapitulation of his project which this paper represents.
2 I am using the term 'technicist' in order to relate this discussion back to the earlier debates in sociology concerned with 'positivism'. Much of that material seems relevant again to what is happening today at the policy level. See, in particular, Fay (1975) and his discussion of 'policy science', especially in relation to the MSC.
3 See G. Whitty (1990).
4 See R. Moore (1987).
5 *ibid*.
6 The use of the term 'misrecognition' can be problematical in that it can be seen as implying that there is some 'true' or 'objective' view against which the 'misrecognition' is being compared. This is not necessarily the case. Nor is it necessary that denying this inevitably commits one to relativism. However, these issues are beyond the scope of this chapter.
7 See M. Wiener (1981), M. Mathieson and G. Bernbaum (1988), J. Ahier (1988), M. Hickox and R. Moore (1990).
8 See, for instance, DES Circular 7/74.
9 See Mathieson and Bernbaum, op. cit.
10 TVEI well illustrates the contradictory character of these developments and the way in which liberal educators can reclaim spaces within occupationalism.
11 See the work associated with the CNAA's Higher Education and the Labour Market (HELM) project (especially Brennan and McGeevor 1988).
12 See Grieco and Holmes (in press).
13 See Moore, op. cit.
14 See Grieco (1987).
15 See, for instance, Crompton and Jones (1984) and Feldberg and Glenn (1984).

References

Ahier, J. (1988). *Industry, Childhood and the Nation*, Lewes, Falmer.
Bernstein, B. (1977). *Class, Codes and Control*, Vol 3, London, Routledge and Kegan Paul.
Bernstein, (1988). 'On pedagogic discourse'. *CORE*, 12, 1.
Brennan, J. and McGeevor, P. (1988), *Graduates at Work*, London, Jessica Kingsley.
Crompton, R. and Jones, G. (1984). *White Collar Proletariat*, Basingstoke, Macmillan.
Dale, R. (1989). *The State and Education Policy*, Milton Keynes, Open University Press.
Fay, B. (1975). *Social Theory and Political Practice*, London, George Allen and Unwin.
Feldberg, R. and Glenn, E. (1984). 'Male and Female: job versus gender models in the sociology of work' in J. Siltanen and M. Stanworth (eds), *Women and the Public Sphere*, London, Hutchinson.
Grieco, M. (1987). *Keeping it in the Family*, London, Tavistock.
Grieco, M. and Holmes, L. (in press). 'Radical beginnings, conventional ends? Organisational

transformation – a problem in the development of radical organisations' in M. Poole and G. Jenkins (eds), *New Forms of Ownership*, London, Routledge.

Hickox, M. and Moore, R (1990). 'TVEI, vocationalism and the crisis of liberal education' in M. Flude and M. Hammer (eds), *The Education Reform Act, 1988: Its Origins and Implications*, Lewes, Falmer.

Mathieson, M. and Bernbaum, G. (1988) 'The British disease: a British tradition?', *British Journal of Educational Studies*, 26, 2.

Moore, R. (1987). 'Education and the ideology of production', *British Journal of Sociology of Education*, 8, 2.

Wiener, M. (1981) *English Culture and the Decline of the Industrial Spirit 1850–1980*, Cambridge, Cambridge University Press.

Whitty, G. (1990). 'The New Right and the National Curriculum,' in M. Flude and M. Hammer (eds), *The Education Reform Act, 1988: Its Origins and Implications*, Lewes, Falmer.

Ken Spours and Michael Young

Beyond vocationalism: a new perspective on the relationship between work and education

We are aware that the issue of work and education is highly contentious in a number of ways. Not only can it appear that we are following a currently fashionable and politically acceptable course, but it is all too easy to slip into a concept of work that sustains rather than challenges existing divisions, particularly those of gender. For some the whole idea of work as an educational principle, regardless of its definition, speaks to the past rather than to the future. It is our view, and it is implicit in the chapter, that work (or productive life) provided that it is not equated solely with manufacturing or paid employment, is a potentially progressive principle for curricula and their possibilities.

To refer to the issue of work and the curriculum in its broadest sense raises some of the most fundamental educational issues. However, the historical separation of educational research from concrete economic as well as many wider social questions, means that much theoretical development is needed. This chapter is therefore very much only a beginning.

The issue, however, is one of more than philosophical or theoretical interest. The more that we talk to academic subject teachers and to those involved in prevocational courses, the more the problems of student progression and continuity of learning in the 14–19 curriculum are raised. In our work on progression it is argued that the root of the problems, at least in education, is in the division between academic and vocational courses and the way this limits the possibilities for students and the potential of teachers to creatively transform the curriculum. This chapter is our initial attempt to develop a proposal to overcome this division by integrating the experience and understanding of work into the curriculum of all pupils. It sets out a new agenda for academic subject teachers, and gives them 'a crucial but no longer protected role'. Above all, it is an attempt to outline an alternative approach, anticipating the needs of a modernizing society rather than simply responding to the highly polarized perspectives of the New

Vocationalism or the existing liberal curriculum. This is why it is entitled 'Beyond vocationalism'.

Addressed initially to history teachers, the chapter is designed to open discussions with as wide a range of practitioners as possible. If our proposals are to have any practical value, it will be through the curricular initiatives of a whole variety of groups of teachers. We underline our invitation to you to respond to this chapter as part of a discussion of alternatives to a divided curriculum.

The National Curriculum and conflicting tendencies within the late secondary curriculum

Two major criticisms of the secondary curriculum have been articulated by the government in justifying its proposals for educational reform. First, they argue that the curriculum does not have a sufficiently close relationship with industry and commerce and, second, that the unevenness allowed under the present system is itself a major cause of low levels of achievement. These criticisms in themselves are not new or the exclusive property of Conservative governments. However, within the context of the rest of the 1988 Reform Bill, and particularly its plans to enable schools to opt out of LEA control and to support the establishment of privately managed CTCs, their proposals represent a new level of political intervention into the curriculum.

The government's proposals are aimed primarily at the public anxieties about pupil failure. Such anxieties are made sharper by the continuing high rates of unemployment and concern about economic performance and competition with other advanced industrial economies. They are also a commentary on the continued and deepening crisis of the liberal curriculum that has been such a distinctive feature of English secondary schooling since the late nineteenth century. The economic aspect of this 'crisis' is of long standing but has taken on a more acute form in the last two decades. It is now expressed in a highly selective enthusiasm for incorporating ideas from Japan and West Germany reflected by the recent prominence given to Richard Lynn's work on the Japanese curriculum (Lynn 1987) and studies such as the HMI report *Education in the Federal Republic of Germany: Aspects of Curriculum and Assessment*.[1]

Two separate and seemingly contradictory responses have emerged from these criticisms and comparisons. From 1981 onwards, and inheriting tendencies from the previous Labour government, there has been a process of what has been termed the vocationalization of the curriculum. This is exemplified by TVEI, the Joint Unit Foundation Programmes (14–16), CPVE and new first level BTEC awards at 16+. The early phase of vocationalization saw the MSC (now Training Agency) in the ascendancy. The second response dates from the appointment of Mr Baker as Secretary of State for Education and the introduction of proposals for a National Curriculum in the Conservative manifesto for the 1987 general election. There is now a new emphasis upon traditional subject teaching lead by testing at 7, 11, 14 and 16 and is expressed in a reassertion of leadership by the DES.

The rapid growth in prevocational courses – CPVE, 14–16 foundation programmes and the lower level BTEC courses and the very different pressures expected from the National Curriculum guidelines, pose serious dilemmas for teachers, particularly those specializing in the currently unfashionable 'humanities'. The success, at least in terms of pupil motivation and attendance, of the new style courses has encouraged some academic subject teachers, physicists and linguists as well as historians and social scientists, to place less emphasis on developing their subject teaching and to join colleagues in developing the new 'vocational' modules with their emphasis on skill and experience.

Countering this trend are the National Curriculum proposals which are designed to maintain traditional subject teaching. One of the objectives of the proposals is to limit the freedom of classroom teachers to develop their subjects, something that applies particularly to the case of history. Inevitably, they also involve promoting certain subjects and excluding others, of which social studies is the most striking example. This narrowing of the academic curriculum, particularly in the humanities, by centralizing testing is not, however, inconsistent with a particular form of vocationalization. In fact the National Curriculum itself can be seen as a form of vocationalization. Though not related directly to particular jobs it does very much reflect the kind of response given by employers when asked their views about education. With its emphasis upon standards and discipline it is clearly concerned with the kind of model citizen envisaged by many employers. There are parallels with many prevocational courses which stress the attitudes and dispositions associated with 'employability' rather than specific skills. This view undoubtedly resonates with sections of the public and has received widespread bipartisan support from the Opposition in the House of Commons. By professionals, however, it is seen as thoroughly inconsistent with the more innovative forms of vocationalization promoted by TVEI – learning outside formal schooling, activity-based methods, modularization, etc.

These disparate responses to the crisis of the liberal curriculum nevertheless have serious shortcomings. The National Curriculum, in underwriting the separation of school knowledge from society and the economy in increasingly restrictive ways, can only add to the crisis. The vocationalization of the curriculum, designed specifically to encourage the low achiever with its emphasis upon activities and 'real life situations', has become part of new divisions of certification. This is a point that we shall return to.

A third way: towards a vocational model of general education

The VAAL (vocational aspects of academic learning) perspective which we outline in this article is offered both as a basis for challenging the developments we have referred to and as a positive framework for developing a truly comprehensive curriculum from 14+. The proposal for linking academic subjects to working life is not in itself entirely new. However, our emphasis upon a clear and critical relationship between the academic curriculum and changes in the economy, work and technology is a new perspective within the current debates about vocationalization and the National Curriculum. We want to bring out five principles in what we refer to as the VAAL perspectives:

- Instead of starting with academic subjects and vocational programmes, it proposes a critical relationship between academic subjects and the changing nature of the world of work. This is in contrast to a vocationalized experientialism

in which there is no concept of knowledge and to the academic subjects of the National Curriculum ossified by a renewed emphasis upon testing.[2]
- It recognizes the central role of economic and technological understanding in the curriculum for all school students from 14+.
- It is a proposal for a general and vocational education for all pupils and not just under achievers. It is therefore a new basis for a common secondary curriculum.
- It is a perspective which encourages the development and renewal of existing academic subjects and their relationship to pupil experience as well as the development of new specializations.
- It is a perspective that incorporates a concept of the future into its definitions of school knowledge, work and skill.

As a perspective on the relationship between education and work it is distinctive in so far as it is based upon the understanding that fundamental changes are taking place in the economies of Western capitalist nations (often referred to as post-Fordism), which have clear educational implications. Post-Fordism refers to a series of historic changes in the nature of advanced economies since the dominance of the assembly line methods first used in the manufacture of Ford cars in the 1920s. The main trends are the declining role of mass production in society due to new technological developments, the declining role of industry and the growth of service sector, the breaking down of old skill barriers in the workforce and the creation of new divisions (core and peripheral workers) and not least, the new levels of capitalist integration in what has been referred to as the 'global economy'. Such changes call for a new and flexible relationship between education and work; a relationship more profound than the 'occupationalist training perspective' that characterizes the New Vocationalism,[3] or the simple rigours of subject-based testing.

Current changes in economic relations appear to make contradictory demands. They open up new possibilities and present new problems. At one level, there is an increasing recognition, particularly within large technologically-based corporations, of the need for a more educated and flexible workforce.[4] At the same time however, these developments in Western economies are creating new demands for low paid service jobs which require little prior training. These processes of technological and economic modernization, though not inherently divisive, inevitably have that potential. It is imperative, therefore, that one of our educational objectives should be to produce a greater level of understanding of these changes in the organization of work in order that all students/trainees are in a stronger position to participate in economic life and are better informed about its possibilities.

At a more immediate level, the VAAL perspective is critical of the separation of personal from economic objectives in education. Instead of separating 'education for personal development' from 'education for employment' (or training), it sees the tension between the intellectual demands of academic subjects and the practical demands from changes in the nature and distribution of work as needing to be at the centre of curriculum decision making. In this respect two related questions need to be asked:

- How does the positive response to work experience by students who have rejected academic subjects become a new possibility for academic subject teachers?

- How can students make informed vocational choices if this process is part of a rejection of academic subjects and based upon 'common sense'? How can they assess their potential without a systematic understanding of the world of work and economic change?

The personal and the economic cannot be separated because they have become deeply intertwined both in reality and in popular imagination in the 1980s. Compared with previous periods there is a far greater density of messages about economic life and work outside of formal schooling. The economic recession of the late 1970s and early 1980s and restructuring of the economy during the second and third Thatcher governments has sharpened the popular perception of 'life chances' as students see themselves as market-oriented consumers before having any idea of what it is like to be a producer.

The argument for a relationship between academic subjects and work is based upon two premises. Academic subjects represent both an organized form of knowledge and an existing social order. They cannot simply be replaced by the 'real life' of employer culture (vocationalism) or the 'real life' of working class culture (however mediated it may be by TV and the tabloid press). Curricula based on either set of assumptions, as we will see, become stratified and themselves produce new divisions. Academic disciplines can go through a process of either development or atrophy. Our main argument is that a progressive route for their development can be found in a dialogue with productive life. But there is a second reason, and this is to do with the need for systematic study. Academic disciplines have two major assets – bodies of knowledge (what Gramsci refers to as necessary 'baggage') and methods of enquiry. It is both these components in articulation with the real life experience of students that must be the basis for a common curriculum for all.

A third implication of the VAAL perspective is the comment it is making about the relationship between specialists and non-specialists. The forging of new relationships between academic subjects and work will lead to the creation of new forms of specialist knowledge. The VAAL perspective gives a new and crucial, but no longer protected role, to teachers of academic subjects. It no longer sees academic subjects exclusively as routes of access to higher education but as areas of specialization whose practitioners have responsibilities to both non-specialists (e.g. parents and pupils), and other specialists (e.g. other academic subjects and vocational areas) as well as their own professional community (fellow subject teachers) whether in the schools or higher education.

Vocational, vocations and occupationalism

Any claim to define education in vocational terms has to confront the way this term has been used in educational debates and policy. This means recognizing the ways in which demands for 'vocationalization' of education have reasserted themselves again and again whenever there is a new period of crisis in the economy. This tendency is in no way specific to this country. However the way in which, in the nineteenth century, the concept of vocation, defined as something unique to the 'liberal professions', was separated from the idea of 'vocational education' which prepares people for specific and inevitably low level occupations, is distinct.

'Vocational' in this sense is usually linked to 'technical' and is familiar in the Technical and Vocational Education Initiative, the National Council for Vocational Qualifications and the MSC's term Vocational Education and Training. It is always seen in relation to and, despite claims to the contrary, inferior to 'academic' education, and inescapably associated with low status courses catering for a student population that is as unrepresenative in social class terms as the intake into Oxford or Cambridge.

In arguing that a concept of the 'vocational' is integral to any democratic model of education we reject the meanings given to it that we described above, which we would refer to as forms of 'occupationalism'.[5] The term 'occupationalism' can be used in two ways: first it refers to the current emphasis on preparing young people for particular jobs rather than adult life in general. In this sense we would wish to draw a distinction between occupationalism and vocational education. But it is also used in another sense as 'behavioural occupationalism' which serves as an 'ideology of production regulating education rather than an educational ideology servicing production'.[6] This refers to the notions of transferable skills and skill ownership associated with YTS and other prevocational courses.

In arguing that we should go beyond these divisive concepts of 'vocation' and 'vocational' we draw on the Gramscian idea of producers understanding the context of their work and the economic, social and cultural implications of the skills they practise. Instead of a concept of vocation based upon the individualistic and essentially backward looking notion of a 'calling' we define vocation as the commitment to, and understanding of the worthwhileness of work or what work could represent if changes in its organization were to take place. Thus to have a vocation, and for education to be vocational, in our terms, requires 'more than mastery of the technical skill and knowledge required to complete an industrial or professional task competently. It also entails an awareness of moral obligation, an appreciation of the political and economic implications of a job of work and often of the aesthetics of 'production' (Entwhistle 1979). For school students this can be begun through a study of the economy and working life that makes direct links to a more diverse experience of workplaces as sites of learning. This elaborated view of working life demands a more central role in the curriculum not only for technology but also for a historically based economics and sociology.

Another approach to the idea of vocational educaton with which we have some sympathy is what Silver and Brennan describe as 'liberal vocationalism' (Silver and Brennan 1988). This could be described as an attempt to construct an English version of Dewey's belief that all true liberal education was vocational and vice versa. The problem with this approach for us is that it does not face up to the reality that in the terms set by the division of labour in Western capitalist societies, only a small range of occupations offer vocational opportunities in the sense meant by Dewey. This means that vocational in the sense that we are using it is also a critical concept; it involves drawing on the academic disciplines to shed light on the social divisions and changes in the current organization of work. It would build on the schools–industry movement and in particular the important work of Jamieson, Miller and Watts who examine the diverse ways in which work simulations in schools and school–industry links can enhance the curriculum (Jamieson, Miller and Watts 1988). In the final part of their most recent work, they recognize the importance of students understanding the causes of economic change and the relationship between these developments and more active forms of pedagogy.

A central aim of going beyond existing definitions of 'vocation' and 'vocational' in developing a broader form of vocational education is to add a new dimension to the new forms of pedagogy which have succeeded in motivating even some of the most disaffected pupils. In providing a broader perspective however it remains important to continue to address the concerns about future employment that many teachers are familiar with among the many 14 and 15 year olds who have failed to find a sense of purpose in O-level, CSE (and in many cases GCSE) programmes.

Social divisions and the new 'vocationalism'

The VAAL perspective also arises out of a concern that attempts at reform of the 14–19 curriculum are producing new forms of division, even though this was not the intention of those involved in the design or development of the courses. The vocationalization of the curriculum in the form of separate certification (e.g. CPVE, RSA diplomas, and Joint Unit Pre-Vocational Programmes) is seen by many teachers as meeting the needs of under achieving students; but it is also producing new forms of division. In relation to post-16 initiatives Stewart Ranson has termed this 'tertiary tripartism' (Ranson 1984). The issue of new forms of division is highlighted by problems of progression between 14–16 and 16+ because of barriers to access to certain vocational courses, particularly for those without O-levels (or GCSEs). There are also problems of repetition of learning due to the focus on narrow definitions of social and life skills which are found in all such courses for pupils between 14 and 19.[7]

The separation of academic from prevocational courses for pupils as young as 14 means that for students on the latter courses knowledge content has tended to be replaced by learning process as the main educational criterion. In a complex and changing industrial society, in which technologies are playing a role in more and more sectors of life, students on such courses are not having the opportunity to develop an adequate foundation of knowledge of any kind.

Divisions between the academic and vocational are part of the continuation of the division between mental and manual labour and its role in the reproduction of wider social divisions. Although education cannot in itself bring about social changes in the absence of broader economic cultural and political initiatives, it can attempt to produce a more open ended schooling in which mental and manual divisions are not simply reproduced. The question raised by the 'new vocationalist' initiatives is whether the division between the academic/vocational which is so widely deplored can be overcome by new forms of active pedagogy and experience-based curricula alone. It is our view that such a change requires not just new pedagogic strategies but more imaginative attempts to create links between academic knowledge and experience, in effect, to create new specializations within the school curriculum. The VAAL perspective would be that curricular divisions must be challenged by new knowledge, not common sense alone.

Academic subjects and the 'world of work'

Instead of accepting the division between academic and vocational courses, we are proposing that teachers should draw on academic disciplines to interrogate the world of work. What does this mean for academic subject teachers?

Each academic discipline has a changing set of practices and traditions of its own and in its relations to each other. For example, physics has changed with the introduction of new topics such as electronics as well as increasingly becoming part of 'balanced science' rather than a separate subject GCSE. We could envisage that physics teachers might, together with colleagues who teach economics and history, examine the ways in which particular industrial processes were socially shaped, and what possibilities were not taken up.

The application of academic subjects to a study and exploration of work involves developments in the nature of those subjects as well as their relations with each other. Despite the priority given to separateness, academic subjects have always had some relationships with each other though they have been largely restricted to familiar kinds of groupings, e.g. humanities, natural sciences, languages, etc. The VAAL perspective proposes that 'the demands of working life' be treated as a new educational principle. This is not a replacement of one principle with another but the holding of the two in tension. It will involve a number of new and difficult developments for which there is little precedent within existing school subject traditions and often little backing within the school and college timetables. Some examples are:

- The deliberate creation of new relationships between subjects across the academic/vocational divide and not simply between academic subjects.
- The development rather than the dissolution of disciplines and the creation therefore of new forms of specialization to reflect new economic, technological and social developments. This points to a less top down model of the origins of school knowledge than has been typical of most academic subjects. It treats secondary school teachers as specialists in their own right rather than interpreters of knowledge filtered down from the universities.
- The implications of relating work experience of pupils to all subject teaching and not simply careers teaching.

Towards a broader understanding and definition of work

Most resistance on the part of academic subject teachers to making connections to work and the economy reflect the very narrow ways that work has become part of educational policy and practice. There has been a tendency to date to view it almost exclusively in employment or occupational terms. This is not just due to MSC's desire to see a closer integration of occupational preparation and the school curriculum. Such a focus has its support within the organization of schools and the close association of work experience with careers education.

We would argue that insofar as work has moved towards the centre of the curriculum, it has remained as occupational preparation largely geared to those pupils who a decade ago would have left school at 15 for vulnerable unskilled jobs. By remaining cut off from the academic curriculum it has sustained divisions in the curriculum without providing any directions as to how work experience might have a real educational role. As we said earlier, the concept of work cannot escape being about future employment and preparation for it. However, if it is to realize its educational possibilities it must also be seen to be about developments in the economy, technology, labour processes and how these structure employment opportunities and the nature of the work. Of equal importance are the relationships between work as employment, work as leisure and work as domestic labour. Making such connections involves a broadening of the concept of work to relate to far more than paid employment; it also indicates the crucial role such subjects as geography, history, economics and social studies can play in a reformed curriculum. It is necessary therefore to explore a new framework for the curriculum which takes work in all its forms as the basis for the development of knowledge (historical, sociological, scientific and technological) and skills (intellectual, technical, practical and communicative).

Creating new forms of knowledge

In stressing the importance of new relations between academic subjects and between them and the world of work, the VAAL perspective points to new forms of knowledge and the forms that they might take. It aims through its concepts of work and vocation to learn from and go beyond earlier attempts to 'integrate' in both the humanities and sciences. In breaking with existing subject traditions without having any clear principles of their own to define content, such attempts were prone to emphasize only the learning process and all too easily collapse into forms of experientialism.

The challenge is to create new forms of specialization which all students can feel part of in ways that the old academic subjects did not make possible except for a few. Much work needs to be done on the potential of modularization as a more flexible means of representing new combinations of knowledge which reflect new social developments (e.g. food sciences, media studies, biotechnology, urban studies, political economy, etc.) as well as providing a new structure for learner participation. As with any innovation, modularization is not itself a solution; it can all too easily be experienced as a kind of self-service cafeteria curriculum with outcomes as divisive as the separated subjects it replaces.

New forms of integration of subject knowledge with work will involve new relationships between groups of teachers who have traditionally kept apart. Overcoming barriers between academic, vocational and prevocational courses will involve drawing on each group of teachers' strengths and developing new models of collaboration. Most traditions of specialist expertise have rules of exclusion and ways of defining others as inferior. This has made difficult any collaboration between academic subject teachers, vocational teachers (with their specific conceptions of work-related and technical skills) and teachers on prevocational programmes. Each can all too easily see the strengths of the others as weaknesses. The VAAL perspective provides a potential framework for the strength of each to be enhanced in collaboration.

In linking academic subjects to productive life, it offers a more realistic basis for achieving the goals often claimed for the National Curriculum. It will improve the explanatory power of school knowledge, enhance the status of teachers who no longer need to feel subservient to higher education for direction, and expand pupil participation in their own learning. However, it is still very much a set of principles; the detailed working out in specific cases as well as some of the fundamental questions of organization and politics remain.

Questions of development and implementation in the 14–19 curriculum

Throughout this chapter we have stressed the contradictory nature of current curricular developments and the potential space for new approaches that this creates. However, any proposals for ambitious developments in the curriculum are bound to face serious constraints. Most notable are impending National Curriculum guidelines and the approaches of examining and validating bodies. It would also be necessary to take into account school/college organization, current teacher understanding and morale and not least of all, the problem of resources and time. All of these point to the need to evaluate the VAAL perspective, not only from the point of view of its logic but the forms in which it can be translated from a perspective into practical strategies.

In this final section we would therefore like to list a series of issues and questions with regard to the development and implementation of a curriculum strategy based on the VAAL principles that we have outlined in this chapter. We hope that these will provide a basis for an on going discussion.

What are the implications of using 'academic disciplines to interrogate the world of work' for your specialism?

- Are there traditions of curriculum development within your subject upon which we can build or is the perspective a more radical departure?
- What limitations and constraints do you associate with your subject?
- How can we proceed to establish practical exemplars?

The dialogue between academic subjects and work will make new demands of teachers if the relationship between work and education is to be more than a pragmatic response to the needs of the classroom or external certification.

- What do teachers need to know about the world of work in order to develop their disciplines and how important is a collaborative approach with specialists in technical fields?

A critical issue is the form in which the dialogue between academic subjects and work takes place.

- What are the specific forms in which the VAAL perspective could be realized within the curriculum?
- How far should identifiable disciplines be retained and how far should forms of integration be encouraged?
- Does modularization as a means for creating new bases for organizing knowledge and of giving students a real involvement in planning their own learning, provide a possible route?

The relationship between the academic, vocational and prevocational approaches and the issue of progression are increasingly important issues.

- Will our proposals for a broad vocational education in school (14–16) lay the proper foundation for greater specialization post-16?
- If so, what are the implications of the proposals for a 14–19 framework of certification and curriculum and in particular the relationship between 14–16 and 16+ certification?

What are the wider economic developments required for a perspective which explicitly challenges divisions between mental and manual labour, to be more fully realized?

Acknowledgements

The first version of this chapter was written for CLIO, the ILEA history teachers' journal. An amended version was published as a working paper for the Post 16 Education Centre, Institute of Education University of London. The editor and authors are grateful to the Trenthan Books for allowing this article to be reprinted from the *British Journal of Education and Work*, 2, 2. 1988.

Notes

1 A critique of selective forms of comparison in the HMI report on West Germany is a paper by Lynne Chisholm 1987.
2 There is a striking resemblance in the subjects of the proposed National Curriculum and that of the 1904 Board of Education regulations. The only difference is that manual work/housewifery has been replaced by technology and music (see Aldrich 1988).
3 By the 'New Vocationalism' we are here referring to the series of government initiatives in the late secondary and college courses – TVEI, CPVE, YTS, etc.
4 In the current political climate, there are a range of economic forces which recognize that workers who are more educated and trained may require less supervision and this is seen as a key to the further reduction of costs. There is also a new tendency in production (just in time production) which demands a more creative and responsive worker.
5 The concept of the New Vocationalism as behavioural occupationalism is explored by Rob Moore (1988).
6 Rob Moore (1988).
7 A detailed analysis of the process of division and reform of qualifications can be found in Spours (1988).

References

Aldrich, R. (1988). 'The National Curriculum: a historical perspective' in D. Lawton and C. Chitty, *The National Curriculum*, London, Bedford Way, Paper No 33.
Chisholm, L. (1987) '*Vorsprung ex machina*: Aspects of curriculum, assessment in cultural comparison,' *Journal of Education Policy*, 2, 2.
Entwhistle, E. (1979) *Antonio Gramsci: Conservative Schooling for Radical Politics*, London, Routledge and Kegan Paul.
HMI (1986). *Education in the Federal Republic of Germany: Aspects of Curriculum and Assessment*, London, DES/HMSO.

Jamieson, I.M., Miller, A. and Watts, A.G. (1988). *Mirror of Work: Work Simulations in Schools*, Lewes, Falmer.
Lynn, R. (1987) *Educational Achievement in Japan: Lessons for the West*. London, Macmillan.
Moore, R. (1988). 'Education and the ideology of production', *British Journal of Sociology of Education*, 8, 2.
Ranson, S. (1984). 'Towards a new tertiary tripartism' in P. Broadfoot (ed.), *Selection, Certification and Control*, Lewes, Falmer.
Silver, H. and Brennan, J. (1988). *A Liberal Vocationalism*, London, Methuen.
Spours, K. (1988). *The Politics of Progression*, Centre Working Paper No 2, Post 16 Education Centre, Institute of Education, University of London.

Postscript

If, at one level, it would seem inappropriate to draw conclusions about alternatives, at another it is important to bring together the key arguments, strategies and policies outlined in the book. This is all the more pressing in view of the authors' overall argument that the education and training reform of the 1980s are inappropriate to meeting the needs of either individual or society in the 1990s. In seeking to address both these issues, *Training and its Alternatives* has sought to open up for discussion the criteria which underpin real reform and lasting educational change. Of course, the danger inherent in suggesting alternatives is, as Chandler and Wallace point out, that these may be utopian or ignore the realities of the capitalist system as it is. Moreover, it would seem ironic that a book such as this should direct critical attention at the ways in which government, education and training reform has, in various ways, rendered British capitalism less flexible and efficient than it might otherwise have been. Hence the poignancy of Moore's question, how are alternatives to training *alternative*?

If a weakness of this book is that it does not entirely get to grips with this question, its strength is that it does at least acknowledge and tackle the question head on. In various education and academic circles, for example, it has been fashionable to be sceptical and even squeamish about vocational education and training matters. To some it may come as a surprise that the authors in this volume support the integration of vocational realism in the curriculum and are prepared to nail their vision of 'alternatives' to the mast. The point has been made that a coordinated system of vocational education, training and qualifications, providing an alternative career route out of unskilled work for the non-academic school leavers, seems preferable to throwing them into the labour market to sink or swim at the age of 16. According to Wallace (1987) this would help to integrate young people into the employment system and go some way towards mitigating the more extreme alienation of youth from the sort of 'shit jobs' which they are expected to do.

Elsewhere in this volume, Raffe maintains the argument can be taken one step further: that debates about education and training for 16–18 year olds are often premised on the assumption that economic and labour market objectives conflict with social and educational ones. He concludes, however, that the long-term needs of the labour market may be for a more general, longer and less differentiated system of education and training for this age group. Such a view, also endorsed by Finegold and Soskice, has important long-term curricular, institutional and policy implications, not least in encouraging *desired* developments within the education system, rather than leaving such developments to the precarious demands of market forces. According to Finegold and Soskice a more effective solution is to balance the interests of those involved in education and training (educationists, employers and government) in a partnership to achieve change.

What supports their argument is that countries with successful economic systems devote substantial resources to research on education and training and labour market developments. In the UK today, policy making has become highly centralized but based on limited information and research. Successful countries also place great reliance on employers' organizations and unions. In the UK their role in the governance of training has been progressively reduced. Thus, if radical reform is to be successful, it will be important to build up expertise and involvement of the various social partners. There is also evidence (see Roberts *et al.* in this volume) which warns against youth labour market policies in the 1990s being viewed in relation to standards from the past. According to these authors, the chances are that in the future most young people will commence full-time permanent employment at a later stage, following phased transitions involving various combinations of earning, learning and work. It is suggested that it would be sensible to recognize a convergence that is already underway, i.e. part-time employment linked with training and learning is becoming for many young people in the 16+ age group the norm. It is Roberts *et al.*'s view that reconizing as a norm part-time employment until 18 or 19 years of age would harmonize with current trends, and could be a more practical way of closing the job deficit than 'attempting to roll back industrial history and regenerate more full-time employment for young school leavers'.

Yet, if integrating imaginative and critical forms of policy and curricular provision into the sorts of structural parameters so far described is not straightforward, neither is it impossible. As the authors in this volume point out, changing labour market conditions, demographic trends, skill shortages and disenchantment with government training policy, have already led LEAs, employers, schools, colleges and students themselves to search for alternative solutions. In institutional terms McCulloch cautions about mistakes made in the past under similar conditions. He argues that, if we are to make use of the Crowther concept in the new schemes of the late 1980s and the 1990s, we should also be aware of its unresolved difficulties. First, he argues, it would seem necessary to decide whether to opt for separate technical schools – a 'practical route' – or for 'absorption' of existing secondary schools within which to develop an alternative road. Failure to make such a choice may well renew confusion, rivalry and conflicts over resources. At the same time, McCulloch maintains it seems crucial to revise Crowther's original notion to replace its tripartite connotations of 'three types of mind', with recognition of the 'rehabilitation of the practical' for *all* pupils. Equally, it remains unfinished business to clarify the nature of the Crowther concept in curriculum terms, with regard to everyday practices and relationships within the schools. For Spours and

Young the argument for a relationship between academic subjects and work is based upon two premises. Academic subjects represent both an organized form of knowledge and an existing social order. They cannot simply be replaced by the 'real life' of employer culture (vocationalism) or the 'real life' of working class culture (however mediated it may be TV and the tabloid press). The authors argue that curricula based on either set of assumptions become stratified and themselves produce new divisions.

From this position it would, of course, be misleading to assume that 'alternatives' can be simply plucked from the air, or imposed on situations once structural changes are in place. According to Skeggs and Avis, for example, this ignores the forms of student 'resistance' which already exist within the social relations of education, and which in everyday situations influence the work of teachers and students. On this basis alone, definitions of students' competence can be radically reconstituted in positive ways, in contrast to the current deficit models which exist, especially for women, young people and ethnic minorities. For Moore and Skeggs, this would involve the recognition of the skills and competences women have acquired in domestic labour and child rearing, but which are presently rendered either invisible or simply open to 'domestic apprenticeship'. Elsewhere in this volume, Rosie and Shilling's discussion of how to make YTS and work-based learning more responsive to students' needs emphasizes key elements of student experience itself in challenging the 'vicious circle' of deficit which envelops many prevocational and training courses. In seeking to address such issues, the alternative agenda cannot simply be limited to the question of how to deliver skills to specific groups in demand (or not, as the case may be) by the labour market. According to Gleeson and Mac an Ghail a broader concept of education is called for, one which does not automatically or passively respond to the assumed needs of the labour market, but rather anticipates and actively redefines the changing skill priorities of work and the labour market.

In conclusion, this book has not sought to produce alternative solutions in the same way that the new vocationalism itself has promised 'answers' to the problems which beset schooling in the 1980s. Its principal argument has been that vocational education and training provision for the majority of school leavers remains patchy and meets the needs of neither individual, economy nor society. Yet, despite the plethora of reforms and initiatives in the period 1981-88, the situation has changed little, perhaps revealing the folly of allowing government and employers to dictate, at the expense of all else, the terms of national education and training policy. What *Training and its Alternatives* has sought to do is identify key areas of curricular, institutional and policy change which intersect with wider political, demographic, labour market and other trends. In this respect the types of alternative discussed in this book are not utopian concepts, but are more or less already in place and relate to real issues and problems experienced by young people at school, college and in the labour market. Thus, while it has not been the intention here to exaggerate the possibilities of change, the evidence and arguments presented in this book at least provide insight as to where the alternative possibilities may lie. A recurring theme has been that life beyond vocationalism is a necessary first step to reform, a major challenge to us all in the years to come.

Some abbreviations

AHSTS	Association of Heads of Secondary Technical Schools
ATO	Approved training organization
ATS	Adult training strategy
BTEC	Business Technician Education Council
CBI	Confederation of British Industry
CDT	Craft, design and technology
CEE	Certificate of Extended Education
CGLI	City and Guilds of London Institute
CILP	Commercial and Industrial Language Project
CITB	Construction Industry Training Board
CP	Community Programme
CPVE	Certificate of Pre-Vocational Education
CTC	City Technology College
DES	Department of Education and Science
DTI	Department of Trade and Industry
EITB	Engineering Industry Training Board
EMA	Educational maintenance allowance
ESG	Education support grant
ET	Employment Training Programme
FE	Further education
FEU	Further Education Unit

Some abbreviations

GCE	General Certificate of Education
GCSE	General Certificate of Secondary Education
GERBIL	Great Education Reform Bill
GRIST	Grant-related in-service training (replaced by LEATGS)
HE	Higher education
HMI	Her Majesty's Inspectors
IAHM	Incorporated Association of Head Masters
IMS	Institute of Manpower Studies
INSET	In Service Education and Training of Teachers
IT	Information technology
ITB	Industrial Training Board
JCPs	Job Creation Projects
JTS	Job Training Scheme
LAPP	Lower Attaining Pupils Programme
LEA	Local education authority
LEATGS	LEA training grant scheme
LENS	Local employer networks
LMS	Local management of schools
MEG	Midlands Examining Group
MRA	Midland Record of Achievement
MSC	Manpower Services Commission (replaced by Training Commission and now the Training Agency)
NAFE	Non-advanced further education
NAHE	National Association of Humanities Education
NCC	National Curriculum Council
NCVQ	National Council for Vocational Qualifications
NEDO	National Economic Development Council
NFER	National Foundation for Educational Research
NLI	New Learning Initiative
NTI	New Training Initiative
NUS	National Union of Students
NWS	New Workers' Scheme
PICKUP	Professional, industrial and commercial updating
RAC	Regional Advisory Council
RAC	Regional Curriculum Base
RoA	Record of Achievement
RSA	Royal Society of Arts

SBE	Shared business experience
SILO	Schools–industry liaison officer
SLS	Social and life skills
SMA	Science Masters' Association
STS	Secondary technical school
TA	Training Agency
TEC	Technician Education Council
TEC	Training and Enterprise Council
TES	*The Times Educational Supplement*
TOPS	Training Opportunities Scheme
TRIST	TVEI-related in-service training
TSAS	Training Standards Advisory Service
TUC	Trades Union Congress
TVEI	Technical and Vocational Education Initiative
UFC	University Funding Council
UVP	Unified vocational preparation
VET	Vocational and educational training
WEP	Work experience programme
WRNAFE	Work-related non-advanced further education
YOP	Youth Opportunities Scheme
YTS	Youth Training Scheme
YWS	Young Workers' Scheme

Author index

Abbott, P.A., 97, 108
Abrams, P., 141, 153
Acker, S., 150, 153
Aggleton, P., 137
Ahier, J., 211
Ainley, P., 92, 93, 95, 108, 189, 194, 198
Aldrich, R., 223
Althusser, L., 137
Anderson, A., 20, 27, 54
Annett, J., 64, 74
Anyon, J., 144, 153
Arnot, M., 142, 153
Aronowitz, S., 137
Ashton, D. N., 43, 54, 67, 74, 75, 94, 108
Avis, J., 111, 124, 136, 137, 227
Ayerst, D., 8, 16

Banham, J., 157, 169
Barratt, M., 148, 153
Barton, L., 138, 153, 154, 156
Bates, I., 108, 114, 122, 138, 153, 154, 191, 198
Beardsworth, A., 61, 74
Beechey, V., 148, 153, 154
Benn, C., 92, 108, 171, 182
Berbaum, G., 4, 15, 211, 212
Beresford, P., 141, 153
Berger, J., 142, 153
Bernstein, B., 211
Bevan, S., 63, 74
Bland, L., 149, 153
Bloomfield, J., 24, 56
Blunden, G., 139, 140, 153

Borrill, C., 117, 171, 183
Bosworth, G., 13, 17
Boudon, R., 153
Bowlby, J., 150, 153
Bowles, H., 137
Brady, T., 26, 54
Brennan, J., 5, 15, 211, 218
Brenner, J., 148, 153
Brown, K., 104, 108, 139, 153
Brown, P., 54, 75, 94, 108
Brown, S., 75
Bryan, B., 120, 122
Bryman, A., 61, 74
Burger, A., 103, 105, 109
Burgess, R., 100, 108
Burns, T., 169

Callaghan, J., 190, 193, 194, 198
Campbell, B., 149, 153
Carspecken, P., 119, 122
Carthcart, H., 191, 198
Caves, R., 27, 55
Chandler, J., 3, 91
Chapman, P., 37, 54, 63, 74
Chisolm, L., 223
Chitty, C., 136
Clarke, J., 108, 114, 122, 138, 153
Clarke, K., 153
Clegg, H., 28, 54
Clement, B., 37, 54
Cockburn, C., 92, 100, 107, 108, 120, 122, 137, 148, 154, 189, 198
Coffield, F., 117, 122, 171, 182, 183

Cohen, P., 114, 122, 148, 154, 171, 183
Cole, P., 160, 161, 169
Connell, R. W., 137
Cook, J., 140, 154
Coopers and Lybrand Associates, 27, 28, 54
Coote, A., 141, 154
Corney, M., 93, 95, 108
Corrigan, P., 119, 122
Cousins, J., 141, 154
Coward, R., 139, 154
Croft, S., 141, 148, 154
Crompton, T., 211
Crowther, G., 7, 8, 9, 10, 16
Cunningham, J., 117, 122

Dadzie, S., 120, 122
Dale, R., x, xiii, 15, 23, 33, 35, 36, 54, 92, 94, 108, 114, 122, 159, 169, 194, 198, 201, 211
Daly, A., 21, 54
David, M. E., 139, 140, 141, 149, 154
Davies, B., 114, 122
Davies, S., 27, 55
Davin, A., 140, 154
Deakin, B. M., 36, 55, 63, 72, 74
Dench, S., 2, 61, 63, 69, 71, 74, 75, 77, 81, 90
De Ville, H. G., 33, 35, 55
Donald, J., 145, 154
Donovan, Lord, 55
Donzelot, J., 138, 139, 145, 154
Dore, R., 37, 55
Durkheim, E., 190, 198
Dutton, P. A., 74
Dyhouse, C., 140, 154

Eccles, D. (Sir), 6, 7, 10, 16
Eggleston, J., 160, 169
Eisenstein, Z. R., 149, 154
Ellis-Jones, A., 188, 199
Entwhistel, E., 218, 223
Esland, G., 191, 198
Evans, J., 114, 122

Fairley, J., 92, 108, 171, 182
Fairly, J., 189, 190, 198
Fay, B., 211
Feldberg, R., 211
Fenwick, I. G. K., 24, 55
Fiddy, R., 108
Field, D., 94, 108
Finch, J., 141, 148, 149, 154
Finegold, D., 1, 2, 18, 226

Finn, D., 70, 74, 108, 115, 122, 138, 154, 159, 170, 171, 183
Flude, M., 212
Fonda, N., 18, 55
Ford, J., 61, 74
Foucault, M., 138, 139, 154, 174, 182, 183
Freire, P., 137

Gapper, J., 26, 55
Genovese, E. D., 148, 154
George, K. D., 27, 55
Giddens, A., 24, 55
Gilroy, P., 137
Gintis, S., 137
Giroux, H., 137
Gleeson, D., x, xiii, 55, 94, 108, 114, 115, 122, 124, 136, 137, 138, 139, 141, 146, 154, 155, 171, 183, 185, 186, 187, 190, 192, 194, 198, 222
Glenn, E., 211
Godson, I., 4, 15
Golby, M., 114, 122
Gow, D., 21, 35, 36, 55
Grahl, J., 189, 190, 198
Gramsci, A., 122
Grant, M., 115
Green, A., 114, 122
Greenhalgh, C., 25, 55
Gretton, J., 54
Grieco, M., 207, 211
Griffin, C., 122
Groves, D., 141, 148, 154

Hall, C., 140, 155
Hall, P., 23, 27, 55
Hall, R. E., 149, 155
Hall, S., 118, 122
Hamilton, S., 102, 109
Hammer, M., 212
Hanmer, J., 153, 155
Hardey, D., 74
Hargreaves, A., 150, 155
Harland, J., x, xiii, 55, 197, 198
Harrison, A., 54
Harrison, G., 11, 12, 13, 17
Hartman, H., 170
Hartnett, A., 182
Hatton, E., 150, 155
Haughton, G., 92, 109
Hayes, C., 18, 55, 189, 190, 198
Hebdige, D., 155
Heinz, W., 104, 109
Helterline, M., 153, 155

Index

Henriques, J., 171, 183
Heywood, J., 17
Hickox, M., 211, 212
Holloway, W., 171, 183
Holmes, L., 207, 211
Holt, M., 15, 104, 109, 191, 198
Hopkins, M., 139, 154
Horne, J., 196, 199
Hotz-Hart, B., 44, 55
Howell, D. A., 55
Howieson, C., 74
Hutt, R., 63, 74
Hyman, R., 55

Jackson, M., 36, 55
Jackson, P., 196, 199
Jacobi, O., 56
Jacques, E., 171, 183
Jamieson, I., 123, 224
Jarvis, 52
Jenkins, E., 17
Jenkins, G., 212
Jenkins, R., 61, 74
Jennings, R. E., 23, 55
Johnson, R., 115, 137, 139, 155
Jones, G., 211
Jones, I., 36, 55
Jowell, L., 117, 123

Kalleberg, A. I., 61, 75
Kautsky, K., 137
Keep, E., 28, 55
Keil, T., 61, 74
King, K., 74
Knasel, E. G., 67, 69, 74
Koditz, V., 104, 109
Krueger, H., 104, 109

Land, H., 141, 148, 155
Lane, C., 55
Lange, P., 50, 56
Layton, D., 15, 17
Leadbeater, C., 36, 56
Lee, D., 74, 190, 191, 199
Lee, G., 109
Lee, R., 146, 155
LeGrant, J., 96, 109
Lenhardt, G., 130, 137
Lettieri, A., 116, 123
Levitas, R., 154
Locke, M., 24, 56
Luckmann, T., 142, 153

Lybrand Associates, Coopers and, 27, 28, 54
Lynn, R., 19, 56, 214, 224

Mac an Ghaill, M., 111, 113, 115, 120, 123, 137, 187, 227
MacFarlane, N., 25, 56
Maclure, S., 15
Maguire, M. J., 43, 54, 67, 74
Maizels, J., 94, 109
Mardle, G., 141, 155
Marks, P., 139, 155
Marsden, D., 67, 75, 94, 95, 109
Marshall, S., 117, 183
Marsland, D., 199
Masters, K., 74
Mathieson, M., 4, 15, 211, 212
Maurice, M., 26, 56
Mayer, C., 28, 56
Mayhew, K., 27, 56
Maynard, M., 153, 155
Mays, J. B., 120, 123
McArthur, A., 56
McCulloch, G., 1, 4, 15, 16, 17, 24, 56, 198, 199, 226
McGeevor, P., 211
McGregor, A., 56
McIntosh, M., 141, 145, 148, 149, 155
McNeil, L., 114, 123
McRobbie, A., 142, 155
Miller, A., 224
Miller, H., 119, 122
Moon, J., 32, 56
Moore, C., 168, 170
Moore, R., 108, 114, 122, 123, 137, 146, 155, 185, 186, 191, 192, 199, 200, 211, 212, 223, 224, 225
Moos, M., 190, 199
Mort, F., 139, 155
Morton, K., 56
Mullard, C., 137
Myers, A., 25, 56

Naish, M., 182
Nash, V., 17
New, C., 25, 56
Nicholson, B., 56

Offe, C., 190, 199
O'Keefe, D., 188, 199

Page, G., 25, 56
Pahl, J., 153, 155

Parsons, K., 101, 109
Paterson, F., 139, 155
Payne, J., 61, 75
Pearson, R., 56
Peck, J., 92, 109
Perry, P. J. C., 25, 56
Phillips, A., 148, 155
Phillips, J., 149, 155
Pierre, J., 158, 168, 170
Pollard, A., 108, 109, 137
Pollitt, J., 17
Poole, M., 212
Porter, D., 11
Postlethwaite, N., 19, 56
Poulantzes, N., 115, 123
Prais, S. J., 45, 47, 52, 56
Pratten, C. F., 36, 55, 63, 72, 74
Preston, E., 171, 183
Pring, R., 15, 192, 199
Przeworski, A., 137
Purvis, J., 108, 109

Raffe, D., 2, 26, 56, 58, 62, 69, 70, 71, 72, 74, 75, 81, 90, 97, 98, 105, 106, 109, 191, 199, 225, 226
Raggatt, P., 78, 90
Rajan, A., 56
Ramas, M., 148, 153
Randall, C., 65, 75
Ranson, S., 36, 56, 219, 224
Reeder, D., 199
Rees, T., 139, 155
Reich, R., 22, 25, 56
Reid, G. L., 23, 56
Reid, W. A., 104, 109
Richardson, D., 2, 61, 63, 69, 71, 74, 75, 76, 77, 81, 90
Richardson, J., 32, 56
Rickman, P., 74
Riddell, P., 32, 56
Riley, D., 139, 150, 155
Roberts, K., 2, 61, 62, 63, 69, 71, 74, 75, 76, 77, 81, 90
Robinson, R., 96, 109
Root, A., 141, 155
Rose, J., 139, 155
Rosie, A., 112, 171, 181, 183
Russell, A. G., 6, 15
Ryan, P., 62, 75, 94, 95, 109, 190, 199

Salter, B., 23, 56
Scafe, S., 120, 122

Scarbrough, H., 27, 56
Scase, R., 108
Scofield, P., 171, 183
Scruton, R., 188, 199
Seale, C., 199
Segal, L., 149, 153, 155
Seidenspinner, G., 103, 105, 109
Sellier, F., 56
Semper, E., 11, 12, 13, 16, 17
Sheldrake, J., 92, 93, 102, 109
Shilling, C., 112, 121, 123, 157, 159, 160, 161, 162, 163, 170
Shor, I., 137
Shorey, J., 27, 55
Silver, H., 5, 15, 16, 218, 224
Silvestre, J. J., 56
Simon, R., 160, 170
Skeggs, B., 112, 127, 137, 138, 139, 150, 155, 227
Smith, D. I., 109
Smith, P., 191, 199
Sommerhoff, G., 12, 17
Sorensen, A. B., 61, 75
Sorge, A., 37, 57
Soskice, D., 1, 2, 18, 226
Sparrow, J., 64, 74
Spence, M., 61, 62, 75
Spilsbury, M., 37, 54
Spours, K., 186, 213, 223, 224, 227
Stafford, A., 138, 156
Stalker, G., 169
Stanko, E., 149, 156
Statham, D., 153, 155
Stedman-Jones, G., 139, 156
Steedman, C., 150, 153, 156
Steedman, H., 22, 57
Steinberg, L., 158, 170
Stenhouse, L., 10, 16
Streeck, W., 22, 26, 44, 55, 57
Summers, A., 139, 156
Susman, G., 22, 57

Tapper, L., 23, 56
Taylor, B., 148
Taylor, R., 29, 57
Thurow, L., 61, 74, 75
Tipton, B., 26, 27, 57, 196, 199
Tomkins, R., 113, 123
Toose, M., 37, 54, 63, 74
Travis, A., 36, 55
Troyna, B., 109, 120, 123
Turner, L., 23, 57

Index

Ungerson, C., 140, 141, 142, 146, 148, 156
Unwin, C., 150, 156
Urwin, C., 171, 183

Venn, C., 171, 183
Vickerstaff, S. A., 92, 93, 102, 109

Wagner, K., 19, 22, 45, 47, 56, 57
Wake, R., 75
Walford, G., 108, 109
Walker, A., 149, 156
Walker, S., 138, 153, 154, 156
Walkerdine, V., 139, 156, 171, 183
Wallace, C., 3, 91, 97, 104, 105, 108, 109, 145, 156, 225
Walton, R. E., 22, 57
Watkins, P., 158, 160, 161, 163, 170
Watts, A. G., 67, 69, 74, 160, 170, 224

Wearing, B., 148, 156
Weeks, J., 139, 156
Weir, A. D., 73, 75
Wellington, J., 195, 199
Whitty, G., 193, 198, 211, 212
Wiener, M., 23, 24, 57, 211, 212
Wilensky, H., 23, 57
Williams, G., 88, 90
Willis, P., 94, 108, 109, 114, 120, 121, 122, 123, 137, 138, 139, 143, 145, 146, 153, 156, 196, 199
Wilson, E., 141, 149, 146
Wolpe, A. M., 150, 156
Woodall, J., 28, 57
Worswick, G. D., 21, 57
Wrench, J., 100, 109

Young, M. F. D., 136, 186, 212, 227

Subject index

Association of Heads of Secondary Technical Schools, 11, 13, 16

Baker, Kenneth, 36, 214
Basis for Choice, A, 30
Better Schools, x, xiii
Black Committee, 36
Black Papers, 29, 187
British Educational Management and Administration Society (BEMAS), 159, 161, 162, 163, 164, 165, 166, 169
British industry, 192, 194
British Institute of Management (BIM), 159, 161, 162, 163, 165, 166, 169
BTEC, xi, 25, 33, 49, 188, 214

Callaghan, 29, 87, 95, 190, 193, 194
CBI, 28, 34, 157, 159
CCCs, 29, 158, 169
CCETSW, 151
Central Advisory Council for Education, 7, 16
CFEs, 39, 49, 125, 126, 128, 129, 131, 132
CGLI, 151
CITB, 30
City and Guilds, 24, 33, 101, 140, 188
City and Guilds of London Institute, 159
Community Programme, 34
CPVE, x, xi, 32, 76, 79, 86, 94, 113, 115, 125, 188, 214, 219
Crowther Report, 1, 4, 5, 10, 11, 12, 14, 15, 16, 26, 93
CSE, 86, 140, 154, 178, 218

CTCs, xi, 14, 31, 214

DE, 58, 69, 70, 71, 72, 73, 157
DEP, 55, 90, 193
Department of Trade and Industry (DTI), 157, 158, 159, 164, 166
DES, xiii, 23, 30, 33, 34, 35, 37, 48, 55, 58, 90, 136, 157, 158, 159, 160, 166, 169, 189, 195, 198, 214
DeVille Committee's Report, The, 33, 35
DHSS, 141, 149, 150
DOE, 29
Donovan Commission, The, 21

Ealing Grammar School, 12
Edinburgh, The Duke of, 12, 13
Education Act 1944, ix, 24
  1973, 159
  1986, 188
  1988, ix, x, xi, xii, 119, 188, 194, 214
Education Training (ET), 18, 19, 20, 21, 23, 24, 29, 30, 32, 33, 34, 35, 36, 37, 38, 39, 40, 42, 43, 44, 46, 47, 48, 49, 50, 51, 52, 53
EITB, 30
EMA (Education Maintenance Allowance), 36
Employment and Training for the 1990s (White Paper), 96, 100
Engineering Employers' Federation, 159
English Electric Co., 8
ESG, x

Fachhochschule, 103

Index

FE, 24, 25, 26, 32, 34, 36, 111, 112, 125, 127, 132, 135, 138, 139, 141, 146, 148, 149, 150, 194, 197, 210
FHS, 149
Further Education Unit (FEU), 30, 140, 189, 192, 194, 195

Gateway Boys School, 8
GCE, 86, 124, 126, 128, 140
GCSE, 35, 86, 118, 124, 125, 151, 218, 220
GERBIL, 31, 33, 35
Gesamtschule, 102
GONOT, 35
Great Debate (1976-9), ix, 29, 94, 158, 190
Greater London Council, 207, 211
Gymnasium, 102, 103, 104

Hansard, 16
Hauptschule, 102, 104
HE, 26, 27, 36, 37, 40, 41, 43
Higher Education – Meeting the Challenge (White Paper), 36
Hillgate Group, 187, 188
Hives, Lord, 6, 7
HMI, 35, 188, 214
HNC, 129
House of Commons, 10, 16, 215

Incorporated Association of Head Masters (IAHM), 5, 6
Industrial Training Act (1964), 25, 88, 106
Industry Matters, 159, 164
Institute of Directors, 159
ITBs, 2, 25, 29, 31, 88, 95

Job Creation Programme, 77
Job Training Scheme 31, 34, 36
Joint Unit Foundation Programmes, 214, 219

Kinnock, Neil, 194

LAPP, 35, 188
LEA, 24, 33, 35, 39, 162, 163, 165, 166, 167, 188, 194, 201, 214, 226
LMS, x

MacFarlane Report, 25
Marx, Karl, 131, 132
Marxism, 132
MSC, x, xiii, 20, 21, 23, 29, 30, 31, 32, 33, 34, 35, 36, 37, 48, 52, 59, 60, 63, 73, 74, 75, 93, 94, 95, 96, 99, 100, 106, 114, 115, 123, 157, 159, 160, 162, 165, 170, 172, 182, 183, 189, 190, 193, 194, 197, 199, 200, 201, 204, 206, 208, 209, 214, 218, 220
see also Training Agency

NAFE, 33, 138, 139
National Curriculum, 33, 36, 201, 214, 215, 222
National Union of Students, 29
NCC, x, xi
NCVQ, x, xi, 31, 33, 45, 49, 52, 76, 94, 105, 194, 201, 218
NEDO, 20, 21, 25, 70, 74, 75, 76, 90
New Learning Initiative (NLI), 35
New Right, 91, 149, 187, 188, 190, 200, 201, 208
New Training Initiative, ix, x, xi, xii, 30, 31, 32, 59, 95, 198
New Workers Scheme (NWS), 78, 79, 85
Newsom, 100, 204
NNEB, 142
Norwood Report, 1943, 10, 24

OCEA, 35
OECD, 20, 23, 56, 91, 104, 109
OES (Oxford Examination Syndicate), 35

PCSC, 138, 140, 143, 151
Percy Report, 5
PHS, 138, 140, 143
PICKUP, 34
Project Trident, 159, 164

Realschule, 102
ROSLA, 204
RSA, 25, 33, 101, 178, 188, 219
Ruskin College, 29, 94
Ruskin Speech, 87, 190, 193

Science Masters Association (SMA), 5, 6
School Approach to Technology, A, 11, 16
Schools Council, 11, 13, 24
Schools Science and Technology Committee, 13
Scottish Leavers Study, 191
SCOVO, 64, 75
Secondary Technical School, 8
Shell Survey, 104, 105, 109
Skills Monitoring Report, 21
SLS, 171, 172, 173, 174, 178, 180, 192, 193
social security, 121
Standing Conference on Schools' Science and Technology, 13, 17

Technical Education (White Paper), 7
TECs x, xi, 96, 100, 125, 129, 131, 194
Thatcher administration, 2, 19, 30, 32
Thatcher Government, 29, 34
Thatcher Education and Training Policies, 31, 34
Thatcher, Mrs, 25, 33, 36, 37
Thatcherite Britain, 192
trade unions, 28, 167, 168
Training Agency, 34, 73, 95, 157, 189, 190, 193, 194, 214
see also MSC
Training for Employment, 33, 34, 36
Training for Jobs (1984), x, xiii
Training for Skill Ownership, 208
Training Opportunities Scheme (TOPS), 29, 31, 34, 36
TUC, 28, 33, 121, 148, 159
TUC Annual Report 1981, 30
TUC Annual Reports 1983-86, 33, 57
TVEI, x, xi, 14, 31, 32, 33, 35, 36, 49, 73, 76, 86, 94, 113, 114, 157, 158, 161, 162, 188, 197, 204, 210, 214, 215, 218

Unified Vocational Preparation (UVP), 30, 88
University Funding Council (UFC), 34

VAAL, 215, 216, 217, 219, 220, 221, 222
VET, 24, 33

Working Experience Programme (WEP), 77, 88
Working Together, x, xiii

Young, Lord, 32
Young Workers Scheme, 37, 78, 79, 81, 85
Youth Opportunities Programme (YOP), 29, 31, 32, 59, 62, 69, 77, 88
Youth Task Group, 60, 123
Youthaid, 29
YTS, x, xi, 2, 31, 32, 33, 35, 36, 37, 39, 40, 49, 52, 58, 59, 60, 61, 62, 63, 64, 65, 66, 67, 68, 69, 70, 71, 72, 73, 76, 77, 78, 79, 80, 81, 82, 85, 88, 95, 96, 97, 98, 99, 100, 101, 105, 113, 114, 116, 121, 171, 172, 173, 174, 175, 176, 177, 181, 182, 188, 189, 190, 191, 193, 194, 197, 210, 218, 227